Consuming Dance

CONSUMING DANCE

Choreography and Advertising

Colleen T. Dunagan

OXFORD
UNIVERSITY PRESS

Oxford University Press is a department of the University of Oxford. It furthers
the University's objective of excellence in research, scholarship, and education
by publishing worldwide. Oxford is a registered trade mark of Oxford University
Press in the UK and certain other countries.

Published in the United States of America by Oxford University Press
198 Madison Avenue, New York, NY 10016, United States of America.

Library of Congress Cataloging-in-Publication Data
Names: Dunagan, Colleen T., 1971– author.
Title: Consuming dance: choreography and advertising / Colleen T. Dunagan.
Description: New York, NY, United States of America : Oxford University Press, [2018] |
Includes bibliographical references and index.
Identifiers: LCCN 2017050042 | ISBN 9780190491376 (pbk.) |
ISBN 9780190491369 (hardcover) | ISBN 9780190491406 (oxford scholarly online) |
ISBN 9780190491413 (companion website) | ISBN 9780190491383 (Updf) |
ISBN 9780190491390 (Epub)
Subjects: LCSH: Dance in motion pictures, television, etc.—History. |
Television advertising—History.
Classification: LCC GV1779 .D86 2018 | DDC 792.7—dc23
LC record available at https://lccn.loc.gov/2017050042

CONTENTS

ACKNOWLEDGMENTS

I am deeply indebted to California State University, Long Beach, for not only providing me with an academic home but also funding this research project. In particular, I want to thank Cyrus Parker-Jeanette, Andrew Vaca, Sylvia Rodriguez-Scholz, and Gregory R.R. Crosby for their support. The project could not have gone forward without access to a number of archives, and I am grateful to the staff at the Prelinger Archive, J. Fred MacDonald Moving Image Archive, Paley Center for Media, Vanderbilt Television News Archive, UCLA Film and Television Archive, the Jerome Robbins Division at the New York Public Library, and the Hartmann Center for Sales, Advertising and Marketing History at Duke University Libraries.

Several of my colleagues have contributed greatly to my process, providing feedback on early drafts and encouraging my progress. In this regard, I am particularly indebted to Roxane Fenton, Andrea Harris, and Tresa Randall and their participation in our writing group. I also owe a debt of gratitude to Caroline Hanley of TBWA\Chiat\Day, Los Angeles, for agreeing to an interview and her efforts to assist me with securing permissions. Others whose assistance helped facilitate the last stages of this project include: the LA Bloc Talent Agency, TBWA\Chiat\Day New York, Pepsi-Cola Co., and BBDO.

Thank you to my family for being supportive of the writing process, and finally, thank you to the student assistants who helped with various stages of the project: Natalie Wong, Oscar Miranda, and Kaitlin Muse. And last, but not least, thank you to my editor Norm Hirschy at Oxford University Press for seeing the potential in earlier renditions of this research. I am most appreciative of his encouragement and support.

ABOUT THE COMPANION WEBSITE

www.oup.com/us/consumingdance

Oxford University Press has created a password-protected website to accompany *Consuming Dance: Choreography and Advertising*. Material that cannot be made available in the book, namely links to video files of commercials discussed in the text and an extensive, though not exhaustive, table of commercials featuring dance since 1948 is provided here. An asterisk (*) marks entries in the table that require additional confirmation. The reader is encouraged to consult these resources in conjunction with the chapters. Video examples available online are indicated in the text with Oxford's symbol ▶.

Consuming Dance

Introduction

Dance and Advertising

GAP AND JEROME ROBBINS' *WEST SIDE STORY*

Gap's *West Side Story* (*WSS*) campaign premiered during the 2000 Academy Awards, airing across three commercial breaks in the following sequence: "America," "Cool," and "Dance at the Gym."[1] Because I watched the awards that year, I had the opportunity to experience the premiere of the ads and their positioning within the television programming first hand. I recall the spots occurring at the start of the commercial breaks, almost as if they were a musical number presented in the ceremony.

Nominees for Best Music/Soundtrack are typically introduced over the course of the ceremony through live musical numbers that often include dance. Thus, airing the ads during the Academy Awards called to mind the practice of including dance performances in the ceremony and reinforced the allusion to Robbins' award-winning work. Coincidentally, the film musical *West Side Story* (1961) received 10 Academy Awards and earned Jerome Robbins recognition "For his brilliant achievements in the art of choreography on film."[2] Thus, placing the spots at the start of the commercial breaks engaged with programming conventions, blurring the line between network programming and advertisements. Their placement called attention to how dance in commercials alters advertising format, merging disciplinary boundaries and conventions through the moving-body-as-spectacle.

Gap's *WSS* spots enclose the main image content within white strips that run across the top and bottom of the frame, as though they were shot in widescreen format, thus evoking mid-century film aesthetics rather than television.[3] In "America" the instrumental bars from the title song are heard as the

Figure I.1 Gap's colorful capris jeans perform Jerome Robbins' "America" from *West Side Story*. Restaged by Al Johnson. Screen shot.

commercial opens on a medium shot of a female soloist framed by female backup dancers and an all-white set design (see figure I.1 and video I.0 ▶). As the dancers move toward the camera, it retreats and moves back into a wide shot, revealing the whole ensemble and a "paper cut-out" roof top set design that resembles the set of the film's musical number. A mobile camera captures this abbreviated version of the original number, adjusting its angle to reveal the space and establish the dancers' downstage frontal facing. In doing so, the camera—like the set design, dancing, and music—echoes the original number and Jerome Robbins's use of crane shots to capture the city and his choreography.

While the ad does not include the musical's lyric verses, it does incorporate the chorus line of "America!" and various vocal punctuations. The TV spot includes enough of the music and its stylistic markers to make the reference to *West Side Story* unmistakable, and it provides markers of Latinidad to reinforce the reference to the musical's representation of Puerto Ricans in America. To make this connection explicit the ad quotes the film musical's choreography. Gap hired Jerome Robbins' performer Al Johnson to create a redux version of "America" for the television spot.[4] Playing on the musical's narrative, the ad ends by cutting from a climatic moment in the choreography to a shot of an all-white screen with the words "when you're a jean" across the center, which is replaced by a shot of the Gap logo and "gap.com" in its signature dark blue as the last "A-mer-i-ca!" sounds.

Relying on image, music, and text, the ad copy's polysemy alludes to the musical's narrative, while letting consumers know what is for sale by calling attention to the dancers' jeans. "America" spotlights the Gap's line of brightly colored (e.g., yellow, red, royal blue, and turquoise) capri jeans and jean jackets for women, while the men wear classic dark blue Gap jeans and a mix of t-shirts in black and primary colors. Thus, rather than use a mortise (i.e., image of the product) in the commercial, each ad features the product by using it to costume the dancers. Merging the signifying image of the ad with the product mortise and moving all ad copy to the end, Gap creates a series of "not-ads" that appear to create separate spaces within the ad, one for advertising (at the end) and one for spectacle or entertainment.[5] The positioning of the Gap logo has the effect of making the corporation appear to be a sponsor— The Gap, patron of the arts. However, the ad copy also anchors the dance musical number to the product, pointing consumers to the product's personality and telling them what to consume and why. More importantly, though, the ad copy hails consumers by prompting them to identify with the product.[6]

Thus, the transformation of the musical numbers into ads does not eliminate their meaning but rather alters it in service of the product. Each Gap spot is named after the musical number it appropriates. However, in the film musical, the corresponding musical numbers appear in a different sequence ("Dance at the Gym," "America," and "Cool") than the ads do during the Academy Awards. The difference in sequence and the ad's lack of diegetic narrative scenes, alongside their placement within commercial breaks, fundamentally changes the context and relationship—but not the *affect* or many of the cultural codes—of the numbers.

In the film musical, "Dance at the Gym" introduces the central plot dilemma of Tony's love for Maria and the rivalry between his former gang, the Jets, and her brother's, the Sharks. "America" offers a view into the world of the Sharks as Puerto Ricans living in New York City, and "Cool" depicts the Jets trying to get their nerves under control after their rumble with the Sharks. Alternatively, the Gap campaign introduces the bold colors and Latina flair of their new spring capri jean line in "America"; a pastel spring-time version of their more conservative, traditional (i.e., "white") capri khakis in "Cool," and then challenges consumers to choose a side (i.e., style) in the battle of "Dance at the Gym" (see figure I.2 and videos I.1 and I.2 ⊙). Thus, the ads draw on and transform the social identities and conflict of the musical's narrative, as well as the codes and conventions of its choreography, in their creation of commodity-sign and marketing agenda. In other words, they reproduce the film musical numbers with a difference, borrowing the choreography's *affect* and redirecting it.[7]

In addition, the Gap's *WSS* ads draw on performance conventions to create free-standing musical numbers that are distinct "acts" within the seemingly endless stream of mass media.[8] The ads treat consumers as audience members, directing their performance and projecting their energy outward to the viewer in a display of expression and spectacle. Their placement within the Academy Awards ceremony commercial breaks supplements their connection

Figure I.2 Gap's pastel line of khakis performs Jerome Robbins' "Cool." Restaged by Al Johnson. Screen shot.

to performance-based genres in film and television. Employing dancing bodies as spectacle, the ads grab viewers' attention and engage them in decoding and/or enjoying the performance. The reliance on spectacle and the merging of product and performer allows the ads to produce bodies-as-objects, while the hailing of direct address (e.g., ad copy and performance conventions) position viewers as both audience members and potential consumers. The Gap *WSS* campaign demonstrates how commercials featuring dance act as assemblages that articulate to cultural discourses and their codes, pulling the disciplines of dance, film, television, and music into themselves. Gap's "parody" of the musical numbers amplifies advertising's symbiotic relation to other media and the construction of advertising as a site of intersecting flows and territorial mappings.

In the many presentations that I have given, dating back to 1998 and the Gap's initial dancing campaign, the most recurring question posed to me was "Why now?" Why was dance suddenly the hip, new content for advertising? The question arose in response to a sudden increase of dance in television advertising for a disparate range of consumer products, which seemingly sprang to life in the wake of the Gap campaigns. While that question did not speak to my immediate interests in the Gap commercials, over the course of my research and the creation of my personal archive of dance in advertising, I have come to realize that the most productive response is a kind of multi-faceted answer that enters an analysis of the ads through various points of intersection. As a result, my work examines how dance *fuels* advertising.

The inclusion of dance as image content in television advertising, in fact, dates to the very beginning of commercially available television. The history of dance in commercials can quite literally be traced from 1948 to the present day. While its presence is not a consistent one and how dance is articulated into the commercial form varies, the Gap campaign built upon a 50-year history of intersecting cultural practices and discourses. Returning to this history offers the possibility of viewing the formation of dance-in-advertising as part of American popular culture and as an active participant in disciplinary discourses.

DANCE IN ADVERTISING AS DISCURSIVE FORMATION

In his cultural study of rock music, Lawrence Grossberg seeks to formulate an understanding of rock that locates its identity not in the boundaries of rock as a musical genre (i.e., as an analytical formalist account) but rather in rock music as a *formation*, "a historical articulation, an accumulation or organization of practices."[9] Grossberg's discussion of rock as a formation draws on Michel Foucault's concept of a *discursive formation* as the articulation of a series of events and processes that is not a static, atemporal form. In Grossberg's terms, understanding a particular formation requires one to "look elsewhere, to the context, the dispersed but structured field of practices in which the specific articulation was accomplished and across which it is sustained over time and space."[10] In the case of dance in television advertising, understanding why The Gap—or Panasonic or Pepsi or any other number of brands—would embrace dance as a marketing vehicle requires attending not only to the historical and cultural context of their production, but also the development of dance-in-advertising as a formation. I confess that my interest is, perhaps, split, lying partially in my desire to understand dance-in-advertising as a formation in its contemporary context and partially in a desire to map the play of formal properties.

In addition to his concept of rock as a formation, I draw on Grossberg's study of the ways in which popular culture directly affects feeling and everyday life. In studying the emotional effects created by popular culture he concluded that "they are the product of the articulation of two planes: signification . . . and *affect*."[11] For Grossberg, *affect* is a rich concept:

> Affect is . . . an ability to affect and to be affected. It is a prepersonal intensity corresponding to the passage from one experiential state of the body to another and implying an augmentation or diminution in that body's capacity to act. . . . Affect is what gives 'color,' 'tone' or 'texture to the lived [and] identifies the strength of the investment which anchors people in particular experiences, practices, identities, meaning and pleasures, but it also determines how invigorated people feel at any moment of their lives, . . . affect privileges passion and volition over meaning, as if simply willing something to happen were sufficient to bring it about.[12]

His notion of *affect* is neither solely equivalent to emotion, nor completely distinct from it; rather it involves a broader understanding of feeling that includes emotional effects, commitment, and personal agency. How one responds to the Gap commercials discussed above depends upon one's relation to their content, including whether, and how, one invests in the dancing, music, graphics, allusions, clothing, and brand. I argue that the dancing body in television advertising acts as a focus for *affect* and that it accomplishes this function, in part, due to its ability to evoke a particular concept of liveness and thereby generate intimacy effects that facilitate *affect*'s production.[13]

While I draw on Grossberg's analysis of rock music as a formation and as a site for *affect*'s production, I have found myself particularly drawn back to the concepts of *assemblage, body without organs (BwO),* and *planes of consistency* as defined by Gilles Deleuze and Félix Guattari.[14] Approaching commercials as assemblages of articulating lines of territorialization and flight emphasizes the productivity of analyzing commercials from a perspective that highlights the ways they activate practices and discourses more commonly associated with a wide category of terms: art, popular culture, film, television, mass, concert/theatrical dance, social dance, consumerism, economics, ideology, performance, and capitalism—to name a few. The notion of the BwO allows for an articulation of their enactment of discursive codes and conventions in support of their appearance as a collection of singular entities or unified works, while also acknowledging how they simultaneously tap into practices, discourses, and ideologies that lie well beyond their borders and generate an excess of competing meanings and associations. Finally, Deleuze and Guattari's planes of consistency concept offers another angle from which I can view the intensification of this cultural practice in the late twentieth century, one that bears similarity to Grossberg's notion of formations and connects it to Brian Massumi's concept of *affect* as intensity and relationality.

DANCE IN ADVERTISING AND THE SPECTACLE OF CONSUMPTION

These conceptual models resonate with how I address the intersecting discourses and cultural practices activated by dance in advertising. The *affective* power of dance and the appropriation of popular and "high" culture actively deploy a range of ideologies, values, and feelings that often seem contradictory on many levels even as they work to associate the product with a dominant meaning, identity, or value. My analysis works to demonstrate how dance contributes to and sometimes alters the operation of advertising codes and conventions, as well as how an analysis of dance in advertising that does not address these lines of intersections fails to fully acknowledge the power of dance and/or advertising's place in American culture.

In the first half of the twentieth century, film musicals established modern-day myths, promoting cultural values that worked in conjunction with capitalism to facilitate the rise of consumer culture. Musical numbers represented utopic worlds of abundance and positive *affect*, creating a space where paradoxes and binaries were resolved through song and dance (i.e., expression and spectacle). In this way, musicals contributed to the development of what Guy Debord designated the "society of spectacle." In the later twentieth and early twenty-first centuries, commercials employ dance as a vehicle for the amplification of consumption-as-spectacle in ways that simultaneously evacuate and proliferate cultural values and *affect*.

In *La Société du Spectacle* (1967) Guy Debord theorizes spectacle as an all-encompassing worldview governing culture, a shift from a worldview grounded in lived experience and human social interaction to one in which images and representation dominate.[15] He argues that images have become the vehicle through which one encounters and navigates the world and other people, and, thus, they function as a means of constituting and reconstituting social order.[16] According to Debord, the proliferation of images within capitalist consumer culture is the result of the reduction of the world to that of appearance in correspondence with the shift to vision as the dominant sensory mode and governing logic for how Western culture encounters the world.

With vision as the primary source of meaning-making and making-sense-of, meaning and social relations become a matter of appearance. Thus spectacle, with its emphasis on visual display and an excess of images, becomes the governing social force. Debord describes it in the following manner: "Considered in its own terms, the spectacle is affirmation of appearance and affirmation of all human life, namely social life, as mere appearance."[17] Busby Berkeley's practice of producing spectacle through the reduction of female chorines to images and/or objects is reborn in advertising where dancing bodies and products are treated as exchangeable, producing an "affirmation of appearance." This practice is evident in the *WSS* Gap commercials where the union of clothing and dancing bodies produce equivalence and spectacle. However, even more exacting mimicry of his strategies appears in commercials such as the kaleidoscopic images of dancers in Gap's *That's Holiday* campaign (1999)[18] (see videos I.3 and I.4 ▶) and women dressed as food in Burger King's *Whopperettes* campaign (2006) (see videos I.5, I.6, and I.7 ▶).[19]

Debord's theory suggests that the role of dance and the body in twentieth and twenty-first-century American capitalism centers on display and visibility, rather than attention to the lived corporeal experience. While the proliferation of dance in advertising might suggest that dance functions as a form of nostalgia for the body and touch as corporeal experiences, dance in mass media also contributes to the spectacle of the body. Movement that exceeds normative social action—that is, any movement that draws attention to itself as movement—transgresses pedestrian and narrative causality and contributes to the production of spectacle. Thus, through dance's spectacle, the body and its movements function as signifiers of excess, abundance, display, and visibility. More to the point, advertising's appropriation of dance-as-spectacle directs attention to the importance of the consumer body as the site of consumption and the *performance* of self. In other words, advertising produces bodies-as-spectacles whose performance signals agency. This notion is evident within neoliberal consumer culture through the proliferation of venues for displaying the self (i.e., dating sites, snap chats, Facebook, etc.). When products are sold via the dancing-body-as-spectacle, the ads highlight dancing bodies to allow dance to animate and display their product and generate meaning.

In correspondence with Debord's ideas, Jean Baudrillard's studies of capitalist consumer culture offer an account of how spectacle contributes to the operation of the sign. Discussing the difference between simulation and representation, Baudrillard states: "Representation stems from the principle of the equivalence of the sign and of the real . . . Simulation, on the contrary, stems from the utopia of the principle of equivalence . . . from the sign as the reversion and death sentence of every reference. . . . simulation envelops the whole edifice of representation itself as a simulacrum."[20] The loss of the *real*, Baudrillard argues, results from capitalism's consumer culture producing both images and objects that function only as images, so that they have no referent other than themselves as image.[21] He argues that capitalism functions based on the production of an endless succession of signs within a system of (re)production based on concepts of aggregation and pastiche.[22]

In correspondence with Debord, Baudrillard argues that capitalism manufactures and maintains the society of spectacle through its emphasis on appearance, display, and the distribution of images. Mass media's production of an endless stream of signs built upon signs evacuates meaning, unmooring signs from referents. The aggregative nature of spectacle promotes this proliferation and the corresponding emptying out of meaning:

> . . . the event and world [are segmented] into discontinuous, successive, non-contradictory messages—signs which can be juxtaposed and combined with other signs within the abstract dimension of the programme. What we consume, then, is . . . the potential succession of all possible spectacles—and the certainty that the law of succession and the segmenting of the schedules will mean that there is no danger of anything emerging within them that is not one spectacle or one sign among others.[23]

Baudrillard points to how the constant production, assemblage and reassemblage of signs insures the evacuation of meaning by reducing all signs to a sea of exchangeable signifiers. Their exchangeability, their equivalence, reduces their ability to be meaningful and distinct in any tangible way. This proliferation and evacuation makes it possible to write off Burger

King's commodification of female bodies as just one more image, one more spectacle—harmless and insignificant, entertaining and without social consequence. Thus, Baudrillard's theory suggests that cultural ideologies and social values are reduced to appearance and lose political relevance as they become nothing more than surface.

Debord's notion of the reduction of culture to appearance and spectacle coincides with Baudrillard's account of shifts in the political economy of the sign. As a result, consumer culture perpetuates a worldview in which signs are free-floating, no longer moored to a particular referent, and meaning is overpowered by the flow of images. Advertising fundamentally relies on this principle of equivalence to construct product and brand identity even as it simultaneously reduces all culture to spectacle and facilitates the evacuation of the real.[24]

Arguably, dance in advertising contributes to a worldview governed by appearance. The emphasis on performance, through the choreographed body, promotes the notion that by accumulating sign value through the consumption of products one can "wear" social relations rather than *live* them. Correspondingly, spectacle can draw viewers into a vortex of abstraction and design that on its most immediate level appears to be simply about distraction, about a world of visual display in which social meanings are called forth only to be reduced to groundless, transitory truths.

Post-structuralist theories and postmodern cultural shifts that liberate meaning and values from the restrictions of transcendental truths, ethnocentric worldviews, and ideological assumptions delineate the very mechanisms by which advertising and consumer culture prosper. Freed from foundational truths, the appearance of love replaces the state of being in love; the appearance of diversity replaces the lived acceptance of diversity. Ads tap into what Jacques Derrida identifies as the endless deferral of meaning, as they proliferate meaning through contextual ambiguity and readerly associations.[25] Ads embrace the lack of universal, fundamental truths and master narratives. The real is the surface, a simulation.[26] Does this mean the imaginary is real? Perhaps. For example, the cable and satellite television channel AMC (i.e., American Movie Classics) promoted its offerings in 2016 with the tagline, "Life is AMC."

Despite the nihilistic tendencies within Baudrillard's analysis, I both borrow and shift his theory of capitalism's semiotics. While I concur with his assessment of advertising's reliance on spectacle and its emphasis on appearance, I find its proliferation of signs to also create a form of relational aesthetics. Advertising's aggregative nature works in conjunction with dance to temporarily suspend linear logic and narrative structures to allow for "poetic" spaces to emerge within the *events* of consumer encounters with ads.[27] This space functions associatively as well as literally, drawing on metonymy and metaphor, creating the potential for an amplification of meaningful relations between images. While this network of images evacuates stable meanings as foundational truths by putting signs into circulation, creating a plane in which advertising dissolves and (re)constructs signifier/signified relationships, this deferral of meaning opens up a space in which consumers can actualize possible meanings in relation to localized contexts.[28] While there may be no singular truth, there are a great many truths potentially at work in the commodity-sign and its *affective* resonance.

DANCE IN ADVERTISING AND THE MULTIPLICITY OF READING

Spectacle's promotion of surface enables and empowers consumers by proliferating associations and thus multiplying ways of reading ads meaningfully. Key to this idea is how consumption as spectacle emphasizes consumption as a form of performance and performative meaning-making. Advertising uses dance to break down distinctions between life and spectacle, between social relations and simulacra. In doing so, ads use spectacle to teach consumption-as-performance and produce polysemy, creating multiple entry points into the work. Advertisers multiply meanings to increase the likelihood that the *affective* power of the brand will resonate in as many ways for as many people as possible.

Grossberg's analysis of *affect* and popular culture supports my reading of advertising's meaning-making: "the real history of the audience provides the codes" and they "are, as Deleuze and Guattari . . . would have it, point-signs always imbricated in contradictory, complex, and changing rhizomatic contexts."[29] Ultimately, advertising relies on consumers to activate and localize specific meanings, relying on a density of references and intertextuality to produce the potential for varied readings dependent on varying contexts. Thus, in encountering ads consumers perform cultural labor and participate in advertising's efforts to engage products in cultural meaning-making. This aspect of advertising allows people to make use of ads, as with other forms of popular culture, in ways that are potentially resistive, if only temporarily so. While the discursive and structural systems of capitalism remain ubiquitous within US culture, consumers continue to find and make meaning within it.

While I attempt to "read" the ads, to decipher their preferred meanings and how dance intersects with other content to produce those meanings, I recognize that I am always already failing in this effort. Thus, how others read the commercials will vary and may differ from my readings depending on where a given reader resides in relation to discursive structures and sociocultural contexts. Despite this inherent potential for contradiction, I find value in deciphering advertisers' preferred readings, because the process allows me to explore the possibilities at work in the commercial and in doing so to concretize concepts and values. However, this process also amplifies the rhizomatic aspect of advertising and reading, so that the possibilities continue to branch out and multiply as I read. As a result, I am always making choices about which potential meanings and *affective* resonances to highlight based on each chapter's conceptual focus. Furthermore, advertising's tendency to simultaneously present cultural values as both stable and always already unstable/mutable complicates my readings.

However, advertisers design commercials with the intent of producing preferred meanings. While these preferred readings often contain quite specific ideas (e.g., Gap clothing is versatile and allows you to express yourself), ads rely heavily on the production of *affect* and associative meaning (e.g., youthful, outgoing, energetic) to engage consumers. The polysemy and *feeling* of the ad contribute to the product or brand's image (i.e., "personality").

Ultimately, my readings work to demonstrate how the dancing body intensifies the *affective* potential of television commercials. While I tend to read advertising's use of dance and its production of positive *affect*, online consumer responses to ads sometimes reveal dance or its use in ads as producing negative *affect*. At times, I call attention to this possibility in relation to specific commercials. Furthermore, while, occasionally, I address the success or failure of a campaign—in instances where its economic performance is particularly noteworthy—overall, the ads are chosen for the cultural and discursive work that they do rather than their monetary performance or their reception by the advertising industry. While the *affective* power of dance connects the topics and ads covered in each chapter, *affect* does not organize the text as a whole; it lives within rather than on the surface of the writing. However, *affect* inhabits my choices, informing which ads I chose to analyze in depth and how I write about them.

The level of detail in my analysis of the commercials discussed in each chapter varies depending on my goals, and I recognize that my readings are always partial and governed by my own contradictory and rhizomatic perspective. In some ways, my analyses are autobiographical, as they reveal as much about how I articulate the ads into my world as they do the construction of the ads. The readings are never exhaustive, even in moments where I attempt to show how deeply the ads resonate with American cultural history. To better contextualize my readings, at least in terms of the scope of this study, I touch briefly on aspects of my methodology and the archival materials on which I draw.

SCOPE OF RESEARCH

I began this research in 1998 as a side project while completing my dissertation on dance aesthetics. The timing was unfortunate. To finish the dissertation, I had to confine my advertising research to collecting examples of dance in commercials. Since technology had not quite reached the era of all things being accessible via Google or Youtube, I resorted to recording hours of television on VHS tapes. Eventually, digital technology caught up with the project and the hunt for dance in advertising moved to the internet, though often the commercials I tracked down were ones I had initially seen on television.[30] I supplemented these efforts with archival research; however, this process came with its own difficulties. As I discovered, the best television archives are the work of individuals and private corporations. I encountered a kind of disavowal of television as a vital cultural form and a further rejection of advertising as culture, which seems to have resulted in haphazard attempts to archive television commercials, both in online databases and physical archives. To make matters worse, archives of television advertising often only have partial production records. There are two consequences to this dearth. One, finding accurate production information—without the assistance of advertising agencies—has not always been possible; even online advertising archives do not always possess complete or accurate details.[31] Two, locating examples of dance in early television commercials meant watching a lot of commercials.

Currently, at the time of writing, I have collected approximately 840 examples of dance in advertising, including commercials that ran on television, cable, or the internet (which includes viral videos and occasionally longer promotional films). However, my archive is neither exhaustive nor complete. While writing, I have continued to encounter new examples both current and historical. Thus, there will inevitably be commercials that I fail to identify and a lack of complete production information for some ads. My collection is digitized and has been culled from several sources. To provide a comprehensive sense of the range of ads and to begin to construct a record of this cultural history, I have compiled a table of the archive, which is included in full on the companion website. Because I have not always been able to locate complete production details for every commercial, the table contains gaps in its data. Unfortunately, though not unexpectedly, one of the most difficult things to identify has been choreographers and dancers—an issue I return to in the book's conclusion.

Dance has been used to advertise a variety of products. At this time, I have identified the following product types employing dance in advertising: beverages (ranging from alcohol to water and soda), food (ranging from candy to fast food), clothing, electronics (ranging from cellphones to computers to the internet), household products (ranging from furniture and appliances to cleaning products), health care and hygiene (ranging from cosmetics and tampons to antifungals), sports and recreation (ranging from fitness to amusement parks), toys, tourism, financial institutions, cars, cigarettes, and public service announcements. While reforms in advertising mean that ads for cigarettes are limited to examples from early television, there are several fascinating examples of cigarette spots.[32] I include a few within the book, both to provide a historical context for advertising's use of dance and to demonstrate common advertising strategies.

Dance-in-advertising reflects the changing format and content of television broadcasts, film, theater, and advertising practices. Sometimes ads consist of choreographed movement, rather than codified dance vocabulary, which tends to resemble postmodern, conceptual dance in the use of pedestrian action. Some ads blend dance and other visual arts by focusing on the creation of moving visual design (i.e., animation and use of editing to emphasize continuity of action, rhythm, dynamics, and visual style). These different forms of dance intersect in various ways with television advertising conventions, and my choreographic analysis approaches each ad as a whole, so that movement shares the stage with text, sound, and other visual elements. However, a key distinction I call attention to is the difference between ads that clearly present themselves as advertisements and those that disguise their agenda by modeling themselves after other television and film genres. While, historically, advertising conventions have shifted over time, my research shows that these changes often reflect larger cultural shifts, production capabilities, and trends within both film and other genres of television that have preceded or are happening concurrently. The ads I look at closely in the body of the book ran the gamut, but the use of dance often disguises the advertising agenda.

While I sometimes draw on or refer to parallel shifts in conventions or relationships between advertising content and socio-cultural events, I do not offer a comprehensive history or sociological analysis. My work demonstrates many of these shifts and identifies relationships; however, my primary goal is to examine conceptual models at work within and promoted by advertising and its use of dance. The following overview of the book's structure provides a sense of each chapter and how the book functions as a site of intersecting readings of dance in advertising. Each chapter adopts a singular but connected conceptual point of entry into the analysis.

STRUCTURAL OVERVIEW

Chapter One introduces the concept of *affect* and its production through dance in advertising. *Affect* plays a key role in advertising's ability to engage consumers in the production of cultural meaning. To this end, I argue that the marketing value of dance lies in the ability of the dancing body to produce *affect* through kinesthetic empathy and correspondingly to create the appearance of relational meaning and agency. By placing *affect* theory into dialogue with cognitive theories of movement and dance studies, I articulate how and why the moving body in advertising requires its own analysis. In these ads, choreographed movement holds the key to fully understanding the power of advertising, its discursive engagements, and its role in the production of social relations and cultural meaning.

Chapter Two demonstrates how commercials operate as discursive assemblages by employing genre-specific codes and conventions. I adopt Grossberg's concept of cultural formations as a model for analyzing dance in advertising. Through close readings of several commercials created for US companies produced between 1948 and 2012, the chapter offers an historicized reading of the strategic intersections between dance, television, film, and advertising within dance commercials to produce a form of advertising that simultaneously reinforces and destabilizes disciplinary boundaries. Several concepts central to the larger project are introduced here, including *liveness*, advertising positioning strategies, direct address and hailing, montage, and film musical conventions. While my study focuses on an analysis of the history and conventions of dance-in-advertising in the United States during the mid-to-late twentieth and early twenty-first centuries, the study also includes examples of dance in TV spots for US products created for foreign markets.[33]

A fundamental aspect of advertising is its strategic reorganization of cultural images, values, and social relations to create new meanings in the form of commodity-signs. Chapter Three addresses this recontextualization of cultural and social meaning through an intertextual analysis of dance in advertising. I examine how advertising employs dance through quotation, allusion, and parody. Through detailed analyses of several examples, I argue that correspondence and difference produce *affect* and contribute to viewers' pleasure by enabling a proliferation of meanings. While advertising agencies work to promote a coherent and intentional identity for the product, the complex interplay of elements within a given ad often produces an array of possible divergent meanings. Thus, dance commercials offer the opportunity to look closely at advertising's participation in the ongoing construction of meaning in popular culture. Introducing the concept of *nostalgia-without-memory*, I argue that the nature of these appropriations reveals the cultural relevance of dance-in-advertising as sites of production that engage in rewriting cultural histories.

Chapter Four examines how advertising engages dance in the promotion of hegemonic ideological notions of social identity (i.e., categories of race, ethnicity, class, gender, and sexuality), while simultaneously promoting difference and responding to contemporary developments. I look closely at how advertising frequently relies on and reproduces conservative social stereotypes in an effort to direct ads toward their target audience. Correspondingly, advertising's tendency to draw on other cultural forms for content has led to a body of work that reinforces traditional gender roles and heterosexual ideologies. In a similar way, dance in advertising sometimes serves as a tool for reinforcing neoliberal economic and social theory. This chapter examines a range of ads that demonstrate dance-in-advertising's relation to hegemony, while also addressing how it promotes shifts in cultural knowledge and encourages *affective* engagement. Ultimately, I demonstrate how the ads function as spaces of intersecting forces and ideologies that reflect, inform, and respond to popular culture, mass media, and consumerism.

In television advertising, dancing bodies engage in the practice of theory, modeling concepts of subjectivity, authenticity, and performance. Chapter Five examines how dance and choreographic form play a central role in advertising and create a philosophical locus that highlights advertising's concepts of subjectivity and identity. I argue that, in advertising, the *liveness, affect,* and spectacle of the dancing body inform the construction of identity, directing viewers to see movement as a form of human agency. By highlighting the body's ability to assume and discard style, dance-in-advertising promotes consumption-as-performance-of-identity. Ultimately, I argue that dance in advertising models subjectivity and identity as fluid and relational.

In the Conclusion, I introduce an area of research that I have not undertaken but which lingers on the edges, occasionally inserting itself for brief moments as I pursue other lines of flight. Looking at three contemporary examples of dance in advertising, I raise the question of bodily labor in relation to concepts of authorship and political economy within the advertising industry. My hope is that the chapter points to possible future lines of inquiry and encourages alternative approaches to studying how dancing bodies negotiate consumer culture and neoliberal capitalism. In the end, while there is much I do not tackle in this project, my goal has been to acknowledge the role advertising potentially plays in the lives of consumers and how dance participates in this relationship.

CHAPTER 1

Dance-in-Advertising, *Affect*, and Contagious Movement

A handheld video camera follows an out of focus blur. As the camera pans to a wide shot, it reveals the blur to be a female toddler running onto a blue play mat to jump, fall to her bottom, bounce up, and begin to jump in time to the music. The camera moves subtlety as it follows her, and the viewer hears a woman's barely audible, encouraging voice asking if she is okay, saying "good," and gently laughing. Behind the girl, other children play with balloons until they decide to use the table against the far wall as a fort, pulling the table cloth aside to crawl into their hiding place. The location appears to be a daycare playroom and the video, a home movie. As the girl bounces to the music, she alternates between swinging her arms at her side and thrusting them skyward. Unexpectedly, an adult woman walks into the background. She briefly watches the girl and then begins to copy her movement. Shortly after, a second woman joins her and begins to jump in place with loose, weighted arms.

The smiling women and gently laughing camera operator are casual and at ease, seemingly spontaneously engaged in the girl's play. However, as the video progresses, they reveal the girl's dance—what at first appeared to be spontaneous, bouncing energy erupting into continuous random movement—to be set choreography. As the girl shifts from jumping in place, arms hanging at her side, to jumping toward the corners of the room and looking down, the two women dance with her. They jump to the diagonals with high forward curves in their torsos paired with limp weight in the arms and head. The three of them hop onto the right leg as the left lifts from the knee and then turn to their left to jump facing the wall. Now, rotating in place, they continue jumping, completing two turns before casually sitting down on their right leg and hip only to immediately bounce back up and resume jumping in place. As

Figure 1.1 Two men join the dance. Choreography by Thomas Michael Voss. Samsung commercial. Screen shot.

they return to jumping, two adult men join them, matching the girl move for move in everything from "explosive" arm movements to a stumbling fall to the knees (see figure 1.1). A third man joins the group; they bounce-walk toward the "upstage" left corner to sit on the right hip again, look back at the camera over their right shoulder, and shift onto all fours to rise and stand in a wide stance while wildly shaking their heads side to side. The adults, in copying the girl, refine the movement to reveal the dance's vocabulary and style.

Suddenly, the back wall of the room lifts away to reveal a courtyard that gradually fills with other adults, who all join the unison choreography (see figure 1.2). The camera alternates between tilting down to look at the girl and tilting up to reveal the extended background. Each time the camera tilts up to look beyond the girl, it reveals a larger and larger crowd of dancers, which eventually includes performers on a truck bed, construction workers on a window washing rig, and five people in a semi-circle formation suspended in mid-air. What began as a home video of a little girl's dance grows into a flash mob and finally reveals itself as a commercial. The dance finishes. As the little girl stands grinning, the ad copy "Use your influence" appears across the screen, followed by the copy "Samsung Galaxy 580" next to an image of the cell phone.[1]

Initially, the girl's dance is infectious in its enthusiasm and unabashed, unfettered, indulgence in motion. Not only does she revel in her movement, she moves continuously, pausing only briefly to pool her energy and send it out in new directions. Moving easily, her energy bounces around in her body, ricocheting within her as she shapes it, capturing it just enough to create a rough sense of form without creating precise lines. Without worrying about

Figure 1.2 The back wall opens to reveal the public "catching on." Choreography by Thomas Michael Voss. Samsung commercial. Screen shot.

shape and appearance, she transforms the bouncing pulse and upbeat tempo of the music into a dance of playful, rebounding energy. She embodies a joyful drive to move. The movement visiblizes *affect* as an intensity of feeling grounded in the flow of rhythm. Kinesthesia activates the camera operator's kinesthetic empathy, evoking her delighted laughs and encouraging words. Thus, the toddler reveals movement's infectiousness, which is made visible by the larger choreography as it accumulates bodies to illustrate the *affective* power of movement and the viral potential of dance.

This commercial nicely introduces a key theme for this chapter: an answer to the question, "why dance?" in advertising. In this chapter, I locate the answer to this question in the crosshairs of kinesthesia, *affect*, and relational aesthetics. The power of dance to enliven people lies in kinesthesia, its ability to generate *affect*, and *affect* as relational aesthetics. The contagious nature of dance resides in its making tangible, if only briefly, *affect* and with it a capacity to act in relation to oneself, others, and the world. While this chapter delves more deeply into current theories and definitions of *affect*, for now I offer the following explanation: *affect* might essentially be understood to indicate psychological and physical feeling.[2]

The question of "Why dance?" in advertising as a means of generating *affect* points to the body-in-motion as key to answering this question. In advertising the body participates in the creation of spectacle and connotative meaning, producing qualitative forms of experience. As bodies move from pedestrian motion into dance, they shift into a heightened mode of physical performance—an amplification that relies on an increased sense of form, the articulation of corporeal detail, and a surrender to rhythm. Screedance theorist Erin Brannigan describes this transition as entailing a "gestural an-acrusis"—that is, the "moment between one mode of performance and an-other."[3] Dance's "capacity to exceed the demands of utility, mobilizing the excess 'vigor', 'suppleness', and 'articular and muscular possibilities' that we as humans possess" feeds the creation of a poetic space.[4] Brannigan uses Maya Deren's term "vertical film form" to describe this poetic film space.[5] Within this space, dance-as-spectacle participates in the production of *affect* through the creation of excess and connotative meaning.

Furthermore, the dancing-body's creation of meaning through *affect* relies on kinesthesia and movement's relationality to garner and hold the attention of its audience. Recent studies of kinesthesia's role in cogni-tion challenge the mind/body dichotomy and demonstrate the power of movement to connect bodies and inform conceptual schemas. Within the poetic space of excess, dance aligns the body's potential for movement with agency, giving form to our ability to *affect* and be *affected* by the world. Thus, this chapter traces relationships between kinesthetic empathy, *affect*, rela-tional aesthetics, and the viral across examples of dance in advertising to illustrate dance's power.

KINESTHETIC EMPATHY AND DANCING BODIES

Through their enabling of kinesthetic empathy and their role in cognition, kinesthesia and proprioception play a fundamental role in dance's relation-ship to *affect*. Glenna Batson and Margaret Wilson note the tendency for these two terms to veer into one another within scientific discourse; how-ever, drawing on more recent publications, their discussion of the terms clarifies them and demonstrates their relevance to studies of dance and *affect*.[6] Kinesthesia, in one sense, might be seen to contain proprioception, which describes the "localized muscular sensations of the body" wherein neurons located in muscles and joints track relative position and force.[7] Proprioception is a body perceiving itself, a phenomenon that precedes kinesthesia as a form of muscular perception and occurs primarily outside, or on the periphery, of conscious thought or awareness.[8] Batson and Wilson identify contemporary uses of the term kinesthesia to indicate two kinds of perception-sensation and awareness: static spatiality (position) and dynamics (movement through space): "Static position sense refers to sensory information issuing from sta-tionary orientation of the body, and the relationship of its parts; dynamic sense incorporates neuromuscular and mechanical feedback about the rate, amplitude, direction and force of movement."[9] When understood to encom-pass proprioception, kinesthesia refers to one's perception of position, touch, and motion. Thus, kinesthesia provides bodyminds with a relational sense of themselves in the world.

This form of perception and its associated experiential knowledge have been revisited by a number of dance scholars in the early twenty-first century.[10] Furthermore, the latter part of the twentieth century and the early 2000s have seen a growing attention to this phenomenon within scientific studies of cognition due to a shift toward trans/interdisciplinary research; increasing interest in the study of consciousness; developments in complexity theory, dynamic systems theory, ecological psychology, and developmental theories; and discoveries in neuroscience associated with advances in brain-mapping technology.[11] Francisco Varela, Evan Thompson, and Eleanor Rosch's concept of *enaction* has played an important role in new theories of embodied cognition.

Enaction argues for a view of "cognition-as-action" composed of "five interdigitated phenomena: autonomy, embodiment, sense-making, emergence and experience."[12] Varela and colleagues explain *enaction* as an approach to understanding cognition that recognizes that "(1) perception consists in perceptually guided action and (2) cognitive structures emerge from the recurrent sensorimotor patterns that enable action to be perceptually guided."[13] Thus, they identify a correspondence between their theory of *enaction* and the concept of "kinesthetic image schemas" put forth by Mark Johnson and George Lakoff.[14]

Johnson and Lakoff argue that kinesthesia informs the development of categorization and corresponding conceptual models within human cognition. According to Varela and colleagues, their "experientialist approach to cognition" suggests that schemas, or meaningful conceptual structures, arise from "the structured nature of bodily and social experience" and an "innate capacity to imaginatively project from certain well-structured aspects of bodily and interactional experience to abstract conceptual structures."[15] Thus, similarly to this notion of schemas, Varela and colleagues propose that cognition and environment are *enacted* together, at once, in relation to one another. These theories suggest that cognition itself is dependent on kinesthesia and fundamentally relational.

Contemporary neuroscience has advanced research on kinesthesia in a number of areas; however, I only discuss two aspects that are particularly relevant to my study: "body image and body schema as representations of self and action . . . and the mirror neuron system and empathy."[16] Concepts arising from these areas of study are pivotal to understanding the potential power of dance to tap into *affect*. Philosopher of cognitive science, Shaun Gallagher, defines body image as "a system of perceptions, attitudes, and beliefs pertaining to one's own body" and body schema as "a system of sensory-motor capacities that function without awareness or the necessity of perceptual monitoring."[17] In essence, he uses the two terms to distinguish between how a subject thinks about his/her body (attitude toward or mental representations of) and a subject's ability to move (motor capacities, habits, or sensory systems). In doing so, he goes so far as to differentiate between a subject's perception of movement ("conscious monitoring") and his/her "actual accomplishment of movement."[18]

Notably, his theory places most conscious perceptions of one's body in the category of the body image, linking it to learned and emotional understandings of one's body.[19] This distinction, or categorization, seems to relegate conscious perceptions of one's body to mental states, whereas he views the body schema as governing "close to automatic" performances of movement and posture—those aspects of motor coordination that allow one to function in the world without one having to consciously control or be aware of them. Contrary to some theorists of bodily cognition—particularly those working in phenomenology, complexity theory, emergence, *affect*, and/or dance—Gallagher argues that the body schema is not a form of consciousness or cognition, though it can both support and undermine cognition.[20]

Having introduced these concepts, I want to return for a moment to the concept of *enaction*. Batson and Wilson sum up it in the following way: "Enaction is a unified, embodied form of perception and action (Thompson 2007)." Quoting Varela and colleagues, they stress that the term *enaction* allows cognitive theory "'to emphasize the growing conviction that cognition is not the representation of a pregiven world by a pregiven mind but is rather the enactment of a world and mind on the basis of a history of the variety of actions that a being in the world performs'."[21] This concept of enaction enables a relational understanding of kinesthetic empathy and the role of body schema in agency at the level of individuation. However, as noted by philosophers Erin Manning and Brian Massumi—in correspondence with the work of dance theorist Maxine Sheets-Johnstone—the concept of enaction lingers within the mind-body dichotomy.

Manning and Massumi argue that enaction's reliance on the notion of body schema continues to posit bodily movement in terms of logical form and thus still as an embodiment of the mental.[22] In this way they critique the notion of the embodiment of cognition, noting its implicit Cartesianism, and they point to its limitation as understanding embodiment primarily as a form of habitual action (i.e., established sensori-motor sequencings). Instead, they posit thinking-in-movement as movement's "bodying," as embodying itself, as the act of "becoming-body."[23] Movement is an activation of the body, the body enacting itself, enacting its potential. Thinking-in-movement is not merely a matter of habit or the embodiment of mental action. Instead, as Sheets-Johnstone argues, "Corporeal-kinetic forms and relations are conceptual by their very nature."[24] Manning and Massumi paraphrase this idea as, "The body itself, with its rhythmic milieu, *is* a motional-notion: a movement of thought."[25] One might think of kinesthesia as a form of bodily recognition, of bodily movement's recognition of movement in the world. As Manning and Massumi describe it: "The task of the dancer on performance night is to make visible what can only be felt."[26] Their description of the dancer's "task" brings me to the concept of kinesthetic empathy.

Body image is relevant to dance in advertising because it speaks to how our perception of movement and ourselves as movers informs our sense of agency. However, the concept of body schema, while contested for its reductive localization of brain functions, points to how the visual perception of movement potentially triggers a "sympathetic response" at the level of neurons in the brain that form part of the motor system.[27] Studies suggest that mirror neurons form part of a biological mechanism that enables kinesthetic empathy.

Recent scholarship on kinesthetic empathy traces the concept back to the work of German philosopher Theodor Lipps and his theory of "Einfühlung," which he theorized was a "process of 'inner mimesis', where the subject internalized the movement of an observed object or another subject."[28] Dee Reynolds describes his theory as postulating a subject's perception of "virtual movement" in static objects as well (e.g., perceiving a vertical line as sinking or rising), and suggests this notion reveals empathy as kinesthetic and grounded in visual perception of objects based on movement dynamics.[29] However, as Reynolds acknowledges, psychology has tended to tie empathy solely to cognitive and emotional interpersonal understanding—in a sense losing the body. This psychological notion of empathy both informs and is challenged by uses of the term arising within dance studies. In the 1920s–30s, John Martin developed a working notion of kinesthetic empathy in relation to dance. Martin, a dance critic with the *New York Times*, popularized the notion as a vehicle for explaining how spectators might understand the intention of a dance based on associations generated through the movement itself, rather than narrative or production elements.[30]

Revisiting the notion, contemporary dance studies examine the concept of kinesthetic empathy in conjunction with an emphasis on the centrality of movement to one's experience, cognition, and inter-subjectivity, arguing for the role of kinesthetic empathy in the perception of dance and delinking the notion from emotion.[31] Writing about the relation between dance, *affect*, and kinesthetic empathy, Dee Reynolds describes kinesthetic empathy as "a mode of relating to choreographed movement . . . as engagement with kinesthetic intentionality . . . [and as] when perception of another's action is also experienced as one's own movement sensation. . . ."[32] Thus, in watching dance, or other movement, studies suggest that mirror neurons allow us to relate to the kinesthesia of other bodies and, in turn, to experience *affect*.

These concepts of bodily cognition and empathy are central to under-standing how dance in advertising not only *affectively* engages viewers but also participates in their performance of identity and relation to culture. Kinesthetic empathy is sense-perception.[33] When viewing choreography, kinesthetic empathy enables and activates our sense of feeling (broadly speaking) and allows us to *affectively* experience human action in a way that enlivens us and our relation to the world. Dance possesses the capacity to ef-fectively inform understandings of empathy and its relation to *affect*. As Dee Reynolds argues, a key to this capacity is dance's aesthetic being: "Just as affect is a relational process, dance is a movement through and across bodies rather than being an attribute of the dancer's body. . . . Affective empathy does not take as its object a perceived other, such as the dancer, but rather the dance's body, which is neither 'self' nor 'other'. [*Affect*'s] impact on the body intensifies sensation such that the 'dance's body' as object of vision is also felt from within, 'enfolded' through kinesthesia."[34] Here Reynolds draws on an aspect of philosopher Susanne Langer's work that contempo-rary theories of *affect* sometimes reference. Langer's work points to how the vitality and potential for action activated by viewing movement arises out of dance's "virtual power."

In her aesthetic theory, philosopher Susanne Langer attempts to capture the aesthetic effect of each artistic discipline (i.e., medium) in her effort to un-derstand art's productive power. She refers to this aesthetic effect, or produc-tive power, as the "primary illusion" generated by each art medium. In *Feeling and Form*, Langer describes the "primary illusion" in dance as "something created . . . with the first motion, performed or even implied. The motion it-self, as a physical reality and therefore 'material' in the art, must suffer trans-formation."[35] Langer describes this motion in dance as *gesture*, arguing that in dance "actual life gestures" become "virtual gestures":

> Every being that makes natural gestures is a center of vital force, and its ex-pressive movements are seen by others as signals of its will . . . The sponta-neously gestic character of dance motions is illusory, and the vital force they express is illusory; the 'powers' (i.e. centers of vital force) in dance are created beings . . . The primary illusion of dance is a virtual realm of Power—not actual, physically exerted power, but appearances of influence and agency created by virtual gesture.[36]

Dance effectively taps into, or transiently manifests, human potential and possibilities. Correspondingly, Langer links dance's production of "virtual power" to the "consciousness of life, the sense of vital power, even of the power to receive impressions, apprehend the environment, and meet changes"

and to the production of "imagined feeling."[37] In addition, by connecting her notion of "virtual power" back to Rudolf von Laban's dance theory and the concept of "feeling-thought-motion,"[38] Langer's theory suggests a tie to kinesthetic empathy and, thus, functions as a precursor to Massumi and Manning's concept of thinking-in-movement as "bodying."

As recent scientific research into embodied cognition suggests, thought and feeling arise out of the relational experiences of the body-in-the-world in motion. While Langer refers to emotion in her description of virtual gesture and her work in many ways strives to explain the differentiation between everyday expressive gestures and dance as an expressive form, what she inadvertently, perhaps, points to is understanding how dance fleetingly manifests *affect* through its engagement with excess and style. Given this connection, Langer's theory resonates with both contemporary scholarship on *affect* as virtual and theories of spectacle's role in consumer culture's evacuation meaning.

Brian Massumi describes the virtual as "inaccessible to the senses" but capable of being conveyed in that the "virtual that cannot be felt also cannot but be felt, in its effects . . . appearance of the virtual is in the twists and folds of formed content, in the movement from one sample to another."[39] Thus, Massumi points to *affect* as relational and pervasive—a flowing, connective mass apparent in the spaces between. Like Langer, he links imagination, feeling, and thought, weaving them together within the virtual:

> Imagination is the mode of thought most precisely suited to the differentiating vagueness of the virtual . . . Imagination can also be called intuition: a thinking feeling. Not feeling something. Feeling thought . . . Imagination is felt thought, thought only-felt, felt as only thought can be . . . The mutual envelopment of thought and sensation, as they arrive together, pre-what they will have become, just beginning to unfold from the unfelt and unthinkable outside: of process, transformation in itself.[40]

Massumi captures the potentiality of the virtual—its relation to process and its nature as undifferentiated sensation, a potential that unfolds into possibilities, a kind of intensity and excess. Massumi's linking of *affect* and excess reinforces Langer's distinction between everyday functional, expressive movement and the vitality and *affective* power of "virtual gesture." Excess and its overflow—not being contained in any one body but being more a force that moves and exists between bodies and through relations—is what distinguishes *affect* from distinct, quantifiable, and labeled emotions defined by psychology.

As Massumi states, "Bodies and objects, their forms and contents, do not account for all of it. They do not catch the momentum. To look only at bodies and objects is to miss the movement."[41] His analysis of *affect* parallels Langer's analysis of dance aesthetics. The dance, as Langer states it, is not the bodies moving in space, but the dance as motion—"driving this way, drawn that way, gathering here, spreading there—fleeing, resting, rising, and so forth; and all the motion seems to spring from powers beyond the performers."[42] In other words, dance manifests bodies as "transducers."[43] Massumi argues that a "transducer transformatively 'manifests rhythms and flows of energy'"; for example, a "body-transducer transforms gravity from an invisible condition of station, locomotion, and action into a visibility."[44] Playing off Massumi's analysis of Stelarc's work, I suggest his description of the body as transducer aptly captures dance's *affectivity*. Thus, *flow* plays a key role in dance's production of "virtual power" and *affect* as it intensifies movement and its relation to agency.[45]

Dance in advertising brings the virtual to light in fleeting glimpses, through movement's excess—the style, form, flow, and energy created by bodily and cinematic movement. Many commercials use dance to manifest rhythm and the flow of energy in a way that potentializes the space of the ad. Through movement's rhythm and flow, advertising taps into this potential to *affectively* and effectively link products and brands to the lived experience of consumers. This flow of energy connects the ability *to be affected* with the *ability to affect*. Massumi points to how the potential for thought and action arises from *affect* (i.e., sensation): "If as Bergson argued a perception is an incipient action, then reciprocally an action is an incipient perception. Enfolded in the muscular, tactile, and visceral sensations of attention are incipient perceptions."[46] In other words, agency, in a sense, rests in the relationship between sensation, perception, and action. Correspondingly, I argue that in the event of its viewing, dance's *affect* allows consumers to imagine the possible. In addition, recognizing dance's ties to excess and style—its production of spectacle through motion's rhythm and flow—is key to understanding the productive power of dance.

UNITED HEALTHCARE, DIRTY DANCING, AND *AFFECTIVE* RESPONSES

A new but mid-century modern style radio sits on a living room shelf playing "The Time of My Life" (1987).[47] As the lyrics begin, the camera cuts to a shot of a middle-age couple getting ready for dinner. The husband is in the foreground, facing the camera, and on cue with an accent in the music (i.e., a little trill) his eyes look up, and he freezes briefly. His wife laughs lightly and says, "It's our song," before turning to face him as he turns to look at her. He shrugs his shoulders, arms opening outward, as if to say, "hey, you know it." She gently shimmy snakes her arms and head upward in a pale (i.e., shape flow, marking)[48] imitation of Jennifer Grey as Baby performing the final dance number in *Dirty Dancing*.[49] This initial exchange continues to develop as the camera cuts back and forth (i.e., sequence of over-the-shoulder and shot

Figure 1.3 Husband and wife initiate the dance. United Healthcare commercial. Screen shot.

reverse-shots) between the husband and wife as they perform short excerpts of the final number's choreography (see figure 1.3).

He crooks his finger at her, à la Patrick Swayze beckoning Jennifer Grey, as his wife arches her back to circle her upper body. The married couple perform bits of the movie couple's mambo choreography, mirroring each other and alternately isolating each shoulder in time to the music. He poses and draws one hand down the side of his body as he looks at her from under "seductive" eyebrows, reminding viewers of a particularly salient montage moment from the film that reveals both Baby's girlishness and her growing sensuality. Their choreographic dialogue continues a bit longer. Until finally, they turn away from each other, as though shrugging off the bodily nostalgia, but then, she turns back. As her husband looks away to move something on the dinner table, she runs at him and propels herself into the movie's choreographic finale, the lift. He turns back just in time to catch her as she flies at him, lifting her partially overhead as she extends her body, only to have the momentum topple them (see figure 1.4). He diverts her energy, sending her onto the table, which comes crashing down, as he falls backward to the floor.

At this point in the scene, a male voiceover interjects, stating: "There are thousands of ways into the complex healthcare system." A graphic banner descends across the screen that reads: "Official Medical Code E005.9: Activity involving dancing and other rhythmic movements." The voiceover continues, ". . . and United Healthcare has ways to make the system simpler, like virtual doctor visits," as the ad cuts to an image of a laptop and a cursor clicking the Virtual Clinics link on the United Healthcare webpage. The ad cuts again, and now the camera looks over the shoulders of the couple as they sit side by side facing the laptop screen. As they watch, a doctor sits down facing them

Figure 1.4 Tom G. McMahon partners Emily Berry in the iconic lift from Kenny Ortega's choreography for *Dirty Dancing* (1987). United Healthcare commercial. Screen shot.

and says, "What happened here?" The camera cuts to a shot of the couple on the couch, bruised and looking a little worse for wear, as she says, "I came in too hot." The husband looks at her wearily, looks back to the doctor, raises his eyebrows and nods subtly. A final shot of the doctor looking concerned, but perhaps still slightly perplexed, as he nods his head leads to the ad's last image: the copy "UnitedHealthcare UHC.com" against a white backdrop (see video 1.1 ▶).[50]

For me, what makes the sequence so charming is the couple's utter abandon to the nostalgia of the filmic *affect* and their embrace of the choreography despite their age and physicality. However, if I am honest, it is my *affective* relation to *Dirty Dancing* that wins me over. My response to the ad is tied to a recognition of the filmic allusion, my nostalgia, and the *structures of feeling* the film choreography houses for me. The film conveys a series of possibilities or potentialities—some that manifest while others are only suggested—that are metaphorically captured in Baby's successful performance of the final dance: loving completely and having that love be returned; moving beyond social boundaries of class or ethnicity; acquiring a new skill; proving oneself; willing oneself to overcome an obstacle that seems insurmountable at first; and finding the ability to trust someone without reservation. I could go on, but I am less interested in naming every possibility than I am in recognizing the *affective* power that the commercial capitalizes on. The choreography matters because of its *affective* resonance, because of *affect*'s relationality and the ways in which it connects individuals to and within the world. Through *affect* the couple is united in the potentiality of movement (both literal and figurative); they reveal an investment in *becoming*.[51]

The *affect* produced by *Dirty Dancing* is grounded in (both tangible and intangible) movement and the potential for movement. The film's *affect* fuels—or at least it did in the 1980s—belief in a whole range of ideologies (e.g., hard work overcomes obstacles and injustices), desires (e.g., a desire for intimacy), and emotions (e.g., falling in love and finding happiness).[52] While I can identify emotional responses I experience in relation to the film, the *affect* that unites audience members precedes this identification. My ability to label the *virtual* feeling generated comes with my ability to reflect on the film and parse out how its *affective* resonances align with lived experience. However, the undifferentiated feeling of *affect* precedes identifiable emotional responses; it is what allows audience members to be united in their response to the film, even when they differ in life experiences or the ability to articulate what draws them to the movie. Furthermore, there are multiple planes of *affective* relations within the film; I've focused on only one aspect of the film's *affect*—that which is generated by the relations between Johnny, Baby, and the choreography.

In the commercial, this relationality and *affective* resonance is tied to how the ad's image content strategically positions itself to appeal to its target audience, aiming for 40-something-year-olds for whom the film, music, or musical number might carry nostalgia and who also might recognize themselves, on some level, in the humorous encounter between husband and wife. The ad juxtaposes the *affect* generated by *Dirty Dancing* with the *affect*, and humor, of the married couple's dance encounter. The humor arises out of not only the failed lift but also the age and physicality of the dancers and the mundane setting. Neither of them possesses the physiques that Jennifer Grey or Patrick Swayze did in the movie. Instead, they are both more heavyset. The song catches them in the act of cooking and setting the table for dinner, so they are in casual clothes (e.g., jeans, flannel, cargo pants, etc.) and handling everyday objects (e.g., silverware, casserole dishes, etc.) intermittently while dancing. Their facial expressions gesture toward those naturalized in film, while remaining pale imitations of them.

The couple-in-their-home represent a contemporary everyday reality that follows falling in love—a set of relations that the film's love story and dancing do not emphasize. However, the ad's couple draws attention to falling's relationality and *affective* resonance—falling demands a literal release into space, a release into the fall, a resignation. The potential for flight, for movement, and for uniting with another body requires this release—a willingness to embrace the potential to fall.

At the same time, the ad aligns with the film in its production of *affect* through the image of success it portrays, not in the performance of the lift but in the stability of the couple's manifested future. This couple lives in a nice house: two walls of nearly floor to ceiling windows, a groomed backyard, polished concrete floors, an open floor plan, shiny chrome appliances in the kitchen, and sleek reproductions of mid-century modern furniture. The commercial could function quite nicely as a West Elm ad, and the use of mid-century furniture calls to mind *Dirty Dancing*'s narrative, while also aligning the ad with retro-styles popular at the time of ad's release (i.e., the year 2015). Thus, the ad's content captures not only an *affective* relation to the film but also speaks to the viewer's relationship to the passage of time and how time's passing connects us: ageing; the experience of having nostalgia for one's body-in-the-past, feelings of agency; and a recalled past that is reimagined and (re) realized in the present. The ad unites viewers in this feeling of housing time within the body, the way in which both past and present reside within us.

My analysis of the ad resonates with Lawrence Grossberg's description of *affect*'s relation to and ability to fuel agency:

> Empowerment . . . refers to the reciprocal nature of affective investment; that is, because something matters (i.e. one invests energy in it), other investments are made possible. Affective empowerment involves the generation of energy and passion, the construction of possibility . . . affective investment . . . always returns some interest through a variety of empowering relations: by producing further energy . . . [or] by placing people in a position from which they feel they have a certain control over their . . . life, or by reaffirming the feeling that one is still alive and that this matters.[53]

I argue that dance in advertising capitalizes on the empowering nature of *affective* investment by drawing on movement's *affect*—its rhythm, energy, and coordination within and between bodies—and its production of spectacle. While all commercials sell the possible—that is, what one can buy, how one's life might be—in advertising dance employs movement and performance to highlight the "construction of possibility" at the site of the individual consumer by linking *affective* resonance and potentiality to one's ability to consume. Dance in advertising links consumption to agency, to the ability to act, to move, and to embody *affective* investments. Dance highlights relationality—the body-self as a set of relations, one body-self's relation to others—and like music manifests the feeling of lived experience. Dance embodies the virtual (i.e., potential) experienced as *affect*.

Grossberg's articulation of the relationship between *affective* investments and ideology offers a productive perspective on the use of dance in advertising. He recognizes a kind of neutrality in *affect*, claiming that *affect* does not define what matters and what does not. Rather, he argues that "affect always demands that ideology legitimate the fact that"[54] some differences matter more than others and those that do become sites of investment. According to Grossberg, ideology shapes what matters by "articulating the investment to a principle of excessiveness. Because something matters, it must have an excess which explains the investment in it, an excess which ex post facto not only legitimates it but demands the investment."[55] At first glance, this understanding of the relationship between *affect* and ideology reinforces binary thinking that associates excess with feeling in opposition to thinking.

Grossberg's theoretical perspective is particularly relevant here because, historically in Western culture, dance has been linked to excess, feeling, and the body in opposition to moderation, thinking, and the mind. At its most fundamental level, dance is distinguishable from pedestrian, everyday actions by its excess of rhythm, coordination, energy, and movement (both size and quantity). This distinction is evident even in less technically polished displays, such as the "Our Song" spot. Thus, this binary structure tends to discount dance as mere spectacle or display. In addition, culturally, dance's connection to excess leads to dance being linked to and/or allowed to stand in for other forms of excess (such as violence or explicit sexuality) within mass media.

However, Grossberg's concept, in fact, also opens the door to seeing how language and ideas are nothing more than ways of explaining this excess, of articulating why things do or do not matter. Rather than being held in opposition, thinking and feeling merge to structure the world. Thus, Grossberg's theory offers insight into why the spectacle of dance generates *affect* and meaning that captures viewers' attention and promotes consumption.

The effectiveness of dance in advertising suggests that Grossberg's explanation of *affect*'s relation to ideology has merit. Returning momentarily to Langer's concept of "virtual power," dance's excess produces a sense of agency through the body's production of *affect* and relationality. According to Langer, among the arts, dance is singular in its production of "virtual power" but shares with other arts (i.e., visual, theater, music) the ability to manifest vitality effects and relationality. The power of the body not only to feel but also to recreate the experience of that feeling through qualitative action allows dance to convey lived experience in a way that resonates with potentiality. Thus dance, often in conjunction with music, offers advertising a way to enhance the *affective* charge[56] of a commercial's signifying image.

As a concept, *affect* is slippery and theoretical accounts can be contentious; they resist my efforts to engage in applied analysis. For example, Grossberg links *affect* to desire and investment, a move that Massumi identifies as veering toward equating *affect* with the particularlity of emotions. Massumi finds this move problematic because it attempts to give a form and structure to what he claims is unformed and unstructured.[57] Rather, Massumi argues that "affect is seen as prior to or apart from the qualitative (understood in terms of determinate properties), and its opposition with the quantitative, and therefore is not fundamentally a matter of investment."[58] I agree that *affect*, at a fundamental level, is not definable in qualitative and quantitative terms, that its virtuality necessitates that it be unformed and unstructured.

However, my analysis of *affect*'s relationship to dance-in-advertising lies, perhaps, between these two perspectives. I recognize, as Grossberg does, the ways in which *affect* fuels the formation of desires, emotions, and investment.

While I do not see these as equivalent to *affect*, the relevance of *affect* lies, in part, in its relation to these actualities. While labeling and parsing *affect* into distinct, identifiable qualitative or quantitative responses is conceptually problematic, I employ these kinds of distinctions to demonstrate dance's *affective* power and resonance. For example, the following analysis of a Cheerios ad highlights how bodily perception and sensation have been linked to positive *affect* and the pleasure of the body in motion.

CHEERIOS, HEALTHY HEARTS, AND HAPPINESS

A woman wearing flowered exercise leggings, a baggy pink top, and sneakers stands in her kitchen eating Cheerios out of the box. A little girl in sweats, a matching pink top, and sneakers walks in from the dining room and cartwheels past the woman, who appears to be her mother. Mid-cartwheel the camera cuts to a shot of a hallway as a boy rounds a corner and runs down it into the sunlit room beyond; his mother follows him. They are barefoot and wearing sweats or leggings with t-shirts. As they reach the room, the image cuts again. This time the camera captures a living room as a little girl sitting on a skateboard and holding a Cheerios box glides across the floor to stop in the center of the shot and look directly at the camera with an animated performative grin. As she stands up, her mother runs in from the right side of the screen (i.e., stage left). The little girl wears a gray jumpsuit with sneakers, while the mom wears ripped-up jeans, ankle boots, and a baggy, long-sleeved, asymmetrical t-shirt. Suddenly, these average-looking homes become performance spaces as the crescendo in the music breaks and settles into a steady beat.

As the camera cuts between locations, each pair dances together. Each duet's choreography reflects the prevalence of Africanist aesthetic principles within American dance and the popularity of jazz and hip hop.[59] The settings place them in approximately the same economic bracket, neither wealthy nor poor but somewhere in the lower middle class. I read their class this way because while they possess well taken care of homes, the living spaces are practical rather than expensively furnished. Their clothing aligns with then current fashions, but it does not suggest wealth. While setting and clothing position them as typical, average, American mothers who see to the everyday needs of their children, their behavior, particularly their dancing, serves to reveal their relationship to both their children and their own bodies. Throughout most of the ad, the mothers dance in unison with their children, echoing their energy and love of movement.

The only pair to perform directly to the camera is the third one, which helps to further the transformation of the private space of the home into a space of performance. While the first mother/daughter and the mother/son duet are caught on camera performing "improvisational" dance sequences, the second mother/daughter duet performs a choreographed dance that functions as a through-line and framing device, leading the viewer through the commercial. Thus, choreographic logic works in tandem with ad copy to create the preferred/intended meaning.

During a shot of the second mother/daughter duet, the ad copy "Healthy hearts start young" appears across the center of the screen, and in smaller font, nutritional information about soluble fiber content and its potential role in reducing the risk of heart disease appears across the bottom. The ad copy stays for three more shots as the ad cuts to the mother and son, to the first mother and daughter, and back to the mother and son as she teaches him how to pop his hand over his heart in time with music, manifesting the pulse of his heartbeat. The camera then cuts back to the "performing" mother and daughter, allowing the audience to watch a longer section of their dance before "Healthy hearts stay young" appears on screen. The ad plays on the similarity between the two lines of copy, suggesting that good health habits begin in childhood ("start") and enable the vitality of youth to endure into adulthood ("stay"). They also imply that taking care of our hearts (both physiologically and psychologically) allows us to be fully present and involved in our children's lives.

As the copy stays on screen, the ad cuts back to the mother/son duet as they dance. Three more shots follow as the viewer is shown each pair still dancing. The ad cuts to a shot of a yellow screen with "Honey Nut Cheerios" in the center and the product's animated bee logo dancing alongside the words, while the cheerio that dots the "I" bounces along to the music. One final cut takes the viewer back to the "performing" mother/daughter duet as they finish their dance and roll backward onto the ground giggling. The final ad copy ("#BeHeartHealthy") appears at the start of the shot but fades away in time for the viewer to be left with the image of happy parent and child (see video 1.2 ▶).[60]

These happily dancing bodies and their relation to each other produce positive *affect* and good feeling.[61] Cultural theorist Sara Ahmed argues that happiness functions as a promise that "directs us toward certain objects that then circulate as social goods" and that "affect is what sticks, or what sustains or preserves the connection between ideas, values, and objects."[62] Ahmed questions the production and search for happiness in relationship to the philosophical concept of the good life. Happiness seems to stand in for positive *affect* and "good" feelings. Ahmed further suggests that to be *affected* by something is to evaluate that thing and that the expression of this evaluation lies in how bodies turn toward things. Thus, she suggests that the experience of positive *affect* involves intention toward something as being good.[63]

According to Ahmed, objects gain *affective* value through location and timing. Thus, objects become associated with good feeling when their presence coincides with the occurrence of that *affect*. This correspondence is then maintained through habitual behaviors. Furthermore, she argues that social bonds rely on feelings, so that social groups form and are reinforced through their "orientation toward some things as being good, treating some things and not others as the cause of delight."[64] Thus, she points to the power of *affect* to unite people and create relationality.

The Healthy Hearts Cheerios commercial accesses this power through its representation of the dancing mother-child duets. The ad portrays three examples of parents investing in their children, exemplifying the importance and value of teaching healthy habits and developing healthy relationships with them. The dancing becomes an embodiment of their unconditional love and support. The cultural ideals of the nurturing mother, the child as heir, youthfulness, and health form a fundamental part of the good life and facilitate the production of *affect* in viewers. The dancing furthers the production of positive *affect* in its shaping of excess feeling into visible form (i.e., choreography) through rhythm, style, and design. The dancing, in this instance, expresses love of parent for child and the thrill of being alive, particularly in the second duet between mother and daughter, who laugh, smile, and convey joy throughout their dance. By featuring the three duets, the ad seeks to generate *affect* in response to already existing cultural values. The ad then places Cheerios into this context to attach positive *affect* to the product through its association with the feelings experienced when watching the commercial. This ability of *affect* to fuel relationality and spread across bodies is aptly captured in contemporary dance-in-advertising.

MT. DEW KICKSTART AND *AFFECT'S* CONTAGION

A Mt. Dew Kickstart commercial, "Come Alive" (2015),[65] employs a scene typical of the Hollywood representation of men—particularly those in their teens and twenties, perhaps—and their "man caves." The ad plays off stereotypical notions about men's need for an out-of-the-way space devoid of female presence where they can pass the time in "appropriately masculine" ways, such as watching sports, playing games, drinking beer, or conversing in ways women might find inappropriate. The man cave is in some ways a hold-over from the fraternity house and boyhood, because it is a site prone to mismatched furniture, snack food, and clutter—a house-cleaning free zone. There are, of course, variations on this idea as men age and move up within the economic structure. However, the Mt. Dew Kickstart commercial stays grounded in a younger, more middle-class version of the man cave.

The commercial opens with a point of view shot showing a large screen television where a video game is in progress—a minotaur in jean shorts is kicking a white-clothed ninja. After a second of minotaur-kicking-ninja action the ad cuts to a shot of a twenty-something guy on a dingy plaid couch, controller in hand as he plays the game. With a nod of his head in the direction of his friend, he says, "Hey, pass me a Kickstart." The next shot shows his friend grabbing three cans of Kickstart from the side table next him, keeping one and passing the other two. The first guy continues playing as he takes the Kickstarts in one hand and reaches across his body to let a third guy, who is sitting in an armchair next to the couch, take one. A wide shot captures the end of this exchange and a view of the whole room. The stairs leading up to a door and the wide, short windows near the ceiling suggest the room is a basement recreation room, as does the assortment of odds and ends it houses, everything from a dart board to a deer head trophy, to a washer and dryer. As soon as one of the guys pops open a Kickstart, the introductory bars of "Out the Speakers" by A-Trak, Milo & Otis (2015) begins to blare, consuming the image in sound.[66]

Once the beat drops in, the camera begins to cut between shots of each guy as he dances while sitting; the movement consists primarily of isolations that either circle in the horizontal plane or thrust in the sagittal. The family dog looks on from his dog bed. When the deer head on the wall comes to life, tilting its head to the left and saying "Hey!," the three guys rise from the couch as though carried upward by their dancing bodies. For the next 30 seconds, the viewer is bombarded by thrusting hips as various objects in the basement "come alive" and dance with the guys. The dog dances; a dog statute joins him. The contagion spreads: the deer busts out of the wall to get in on the action; the armchair begins to groove; the side table starts freaking with one of them; the male and female stick figures in a crosswalk sign pelvic thrust in unison; a portrait on the wall starts to shimmy her shoulders; the figure on the hockey trophy gallops and "spanks the baby"; a coat rack dances; a deep sea diver figurine in a fish tank pelvic thrusts and later does the running man; and the video game characters shimmy their shoulders in unison (see figure 1.5).

The men's dancing develops; however, it still consists largely of pelvic thrusts and chest isolations intermixed with rolling the movement through their bodies (i.e., a less articulate form of popping), the worm, knee pops from a deep squat, swaying side to side, and generally just gyrating in one way or another. At the end of the first minute, the guys dance their way out of the basement. The next 30 seconds is filled by ad copy, including the mantra, "Go Ahead. Touch Stuff," which is followed by a 15-second shot of the quiet, still basement (see video 1.3 ⓟ). According to an *Adweek* article online, when the ad premiered in digital media formats, consumers had the opportunity to click on various things in the basement in order to see remixes of video content, including clips of the "twerking" dog and the talking deer.[67]

While the ad seems to most clearly promote the idea captured in the product's name, "Kickstart," portraying how people (and objects) come alive with one sip of the "Dew," the choreography and its viral nature seem to suggest more. I find the ad fascinating and contagious—I want to get up and

Figure 1.5 Video game characters dance in "Come Alive." Mt. Dew Kickstart commercial. Choreography by Bijoya Das. Screen shot.

dance, and I want to watch the ad. The ad's content speaks to me about contagiousness (e.g., of dancing, video games, sex, alcohol). In addition, the choreography promotes a sense of agency via movement, tapping into *feeling* and dance's actualization of *affect*. To a degree, I read the feeling produced here as linked to sexuality—what I would argue is a particularly heterosexual, masculinist perspective on sex that has been promoted by rap music videos but which is now much more widespread and tied to representations of both men and women. I see this connection in the references to twerking and freaking in conjunction with the dog imagery and the crosswalk sign's heterosexual contextualization of the pelvic thrust; the version featured here is seen in krumping as well as other social dances. While, on the surface, the dancing captures the viewer's attention with its absurdity (e.g., human quirkiness and inanimate objects coming to life), the spontaneous social dancing also visually represents *aliveness* within the world of the ad. The young men, consumed by dance, abandon their sedentary, relatively solitary activity of playing video games to go in search of excitement—presumably through more social and physical forms of interaction and activity. Given the references to dogs and twerking, I lean toward imagining them going out and "getting some," but the ad is just as likely to be indicating other activities out in the world.

The ad's content raises questions pertaining to the idea of *affect* as both contagion and contingent, depending on one's context, as well as the relationship between participatory culture (i.e., relational aesthetics), advertising, and *affect*. The sense of contagion communicated through *dancing-as-affect* is further promoted in the sequel to the Mt. Dew Kickstart commercial, "Neighborhood" (2015) (see video 1.4 ⓟ).[68] In this second commercial, the same three guys from "Come Alive" take a break in front of a brownstone. Two of the men sit on the steps while the third stands to one side. They wear the same clothes they wore while playing games in the basement, and the camera comes upon them just as they are taking Mt. Dew Kickstarts out of a brown paper bag. Once they pop open the cans, the music quickly swells to fill the space. As the two men sitting down finish their first swig of soda, their shoulders and chests begin to circle, and they look at each other in concerned confusion. When they glance over at their buddy, he is once again overwhelmed by his rapidly thrusting chest as he looks back at them helplessly.

This time, a raccoon, instead of a mounted stag, pops up out of a trashcan and says, "hey," triggering the drop in the beat. The camera immediately cuts back to a medium-wide shot of all three men, who are now standing; the driving pulse that began in their chests consumes them as the movement pops and ripples through their bodies awkwardly. Just as their bodies *really* get going, the camera cuts to another man walking down the street whose chest suddenly begins to thrust on its own. His chest-popping triggers a sequence of quick shots featuring dancing people and things: a cross walk sign with hip-thrusting female and male figures; an old man wearing a t-shirt and robe with a towel wrapped around his waist stands on a balcony with arms raised as he circles his hips and glares at the camera; a couple carrying groceries tosses them aside as their bodies begin to thrust and isolate, and a balloon figure billows to the beat (see figure 1.6).

The camera cuts back to the original trio, still dancing, before once again cutting between shots of the neighborhood. This time every body is fully consumed by dance, thrusting, wiggling, and gyrating madly. New characters are revealed: a female postal worker bobs up and down; a black woman kicks down the door of her brownstone and begins krumping; the car balloon, now

Figure 1.6 Mt. Dew's *affect* infects a couple from the neighborhood. Commercial. Screen shot.

tied to the crosswalk sign, ripples madly; a fireman with a fire hose shooting water steps in place as he pumps his torso, and a woman in a business suit pops up from the splits.[69] Their facial expressions join their bodies in producing *affect*, as their features assume expressions that resemble everything from awe, confusion and wonder to determination, aggression, and a release of their inhibitions.

In this ad, unlike the first, the reaction to the drink seems to spread like a contagion from the three guys to the rest of neighborhood. None of the other people appear to consume Mt. Dew Kickstart, and yet they all break out into similar fits of spontaneous, uncontrollable dancing. Given that the music overwhelms the sonic space of the commercial and the trio's consumption of Dew triggered the song, the ad suggests a linking of the two and thus positions dancing as an *affective* response not only to Mt. Dew Kickstart but also to music.

In his analysis of the rock and roll apparatus within popular culture, Grossberg makes a similar argument about music, *affect*, and the body. He argues that:

> There is an immediate material relation to the music and its movements. This relation, while true of music in general, is foregrounded in rock and roll. At its simplest level, the body vibrates with the sounds and rhythms, and that vibration can be articulated with other practices and events to produce complex effects. The materiality of music gives it its affective power to translate individuals (an ideological construct) into bodies . . . The body becomes the site at which pleasure is restructured and desire potentially redirected.[70]

Grossberg suggest that music, specifically rock-n-roll, transforms individuals into bodies and further that music's *affective* power unites bodies. This representation of music's power also points to how music shapes what viewers see, revealing twenty-first-century America's relationship to sound and its increasing influence on perception. In the ad, the transformative power of music overwhelms the commercial's characters. They quite literally dance in spite of themselves. One might read the Mt. Dew commercials as depictions of music vibrations literally translating individuals into bodies-united-by-their-*affective*-response. Through the spectacle of rhythm's infectiousness,[71] the commercials and their commands to "click them clicky things" threaten, or promise, to infect the consumer via Mt. Dew Kickstart.

INFECTIOUS RHYTHMS AND BODIES OF *AFFECT*

As Grossberg's analysis demonstrates, studies of *affect* occasionally address its contagious nature. For example, Reynolds also connects *affect* to concepts of contagion, comparing it to ideas of emotional contagion in which another's "feelings are transferred to us and we are 'saturated' by them, rather than 'turning toward or submerging ourselves in the foreign experience, which is the attitude characteristic of empathy.'"[72] Reynolds suggests that contagion is distinct from empathy in its focus on the "embodied impact of the emotion," suggesting that *affect*, like emotional contagion, is "highly infectious and does not respect individual boundaries."[73] Reynolds connects this idea to the work of dance critic John Martin and his theory that the contagion of bodily movement plays a part in the perception of dance. Extending his theory, I argue that dance's infectiousness derives, in part, from its association with concepts of liveness and expression, which infuse it with a vitality that is both relational and *affect-ridden*.

Dance, like music, resonates through the bodies of participants and observers, producing *affect* that on reflection one might later describe as a feeling, emotion, or mental state.[74] Thus, just as one might describe the way music feels in terms of mood, emotion, or movement, one might also describe the experience of watching dance. Grossberg stresses *affect's* ability to spread across bodies, breaking down distinctions between individuals and uniting them in "affective alliances"[75] or in a shared investment in "particular experiences, practices, identities, meanings and pleasures."[76] Thus, *affect*, like viral contagion, is communicated within and across bodies.

Correspondingly, the concept of contagion occupies a central place in twenty-first-century culture. Its achievement of this level of "notoriety" seems to owe much to consumer culture and the development of digital technology, which in conjunction with medical discourse and biological crises (such as the AIDS epidemic) have promoted the concept of the viral as a cultural logic. Additionally, digital culture has made the concept of viral media essentially synonymous with mass media and popular culture. In this context, the term "viral" typically refers to images or videos that increase in relevance as they circulate—usually digitally via the internet—gaining a growing audience, who in turn participate in its dissemination.[77]

In her analysis of "viral performance" forms, Miriam Felton-Dansky traces a history of the concept of the "viral" in cultural discourse back to Douglas Rushkoff's work, *Media Virus!* Rushkoff identifies the media virus as an image or idea circulated by mass media in the digital age, but he also connects the concept to earlier twentieth-century avant-garde artistic and theatrical experiments.[78] In turn, Rushkoff's work helped to popularize social scientist Richard Dawkins' term, meme, which he used to describe "a unit of cultural transmission" that replicates through imitation.[79] Rushkoff's expansion of Dawkins' meme essentially incorporates the notion of contagion, or infection, to arrive at the idea of the media virus as an exponentially proliferating meme that spreads through mass media (such as television or the internet) and social groups.[80] With the rise of digital culture, this notion of the media virus has evolved into the concept of the "viral."

While a whole set of strategies have developed around the production of viral media, the basic concept of the viral informs the underlying principles of advertising and consumer culture.[81] For example, advertising jingles functioned as a precursor to viral marketing. Instead of proliferating through distribution across mass media and digital reproductions, jingles used the mnemonic values of music/song to engage consumers in the ad and its distribution.[82] In contemporary advertising, this strategy often piggybacks on popular music, transforming pop songs into jingles or using them as a framing device and thus infecting the song with new intent. Consumers become conduits in the circulation of musical memes; however, movement memes sometimes also achieve this kind of viral distribution and mnemonic resonance. For example, in the 1980s, Toyota's "Oh What a Feeling" campaign launched the movement meme of the celebratory body—arms thrown overhead as the happy consumer jumps with joy. This jump became both ubiquitous and equated with Toyota, the joy of consumption, and feelings of success and absurd happiness. It also functioned as a precursor to the infectious nature of consumption and its effects on the body, as seen in the Mt. Dew ads.

Both Mt. Dew commercials play with this concept of the viral, employing forms of self-reference that fuel the ad's proliferation. The symptoms of the infectious nature of Mt. Dew are visible and corporeal in form and are all-consuming. The body stops all other activity as the force of the contagion takes over. This visibility and corporeality emphasizes tactility and the corporeal nature of consumption and infection. Furthermore, it highlights the paradoxical nature of consumption; to consume is not only to ingest but also to receive, to use up, to purchase, and to destroy. Thus, the Mt. Dew ads comment on consumer culture's pervasiveness and the *affective* nature of consumption by highlighting the productive and destructive powers of contagion. In doing so, the ad ironically comments on the omnipresence and widespread circulation of mass media and popular culture even as it engages in that very system.[83]

As in Ishmael Reed's *Mumbo Jumbo*,[84] symptoms of this *affective* infection take the form of dance, a physical excess that transgresses the boundaries of acceptable behavior (i.e., breaks free from constraints to be the unruly, unbound body) but does so in a manner that enthralls even as it disrupts. Most of the movement vocabulary in Mt. Dew's contagion draws on black social dance, particularly echoing elements of 1980s' freaking, 1990s' clowning, and 2000s' krumping. The lineage of the movement is not surprising given the position of black social dance in US culture and mass media. Thomas F. DeFrantz argues that neoliberal discursive uses of black social dance suggest such a reading: "African American corporealities have been recurrently called upon to generate a danced rhetoric of freedom in terms of an easy, appealing musicality-in-motion apparently endemic to the conditions of black life."[85] Thus, the Mt. Dew commercial engages black social dance as a sign of *affect* and the body's freedom of expression.

Thus, like Toyota's jump for joy, dance in the Mt. Dew ads offers the release of unfettered expression, the body's total consumption by feeling. In doing so, the ad makes *affect* tangible, demonstrating its unquantifiable, qualitative variability as it manifests across bodies in related but highly differentiated ways. At the same time, it demonstrates how *affect* can be roughly categorizable, as demonstrated by psychologist Silvan Tomkins' research on *affect*.[86] For example, the Mt. Dew dancing embodies a sense of force and desire through its emphasis on thrusting. As the dance spreads across bodies, it is generally recognizable but appears experientially specific to each individual. As the movement travels from one body to the next, it visualizes Aristotle's catharsis and Antonin Artaud's destructive theatrical contagion.[87]

RELATIONAL AESTHETICS AND DANCING BODIES

This notion of contagious performance in combination with participatory strategies employed in the Mt. Dew campaign generates a form of relationality. Nicolas Bourriaud first identified the field of relational aesthetics in the visual arts in the late 1990s. He defines relational aesthetics as follows: "Aesthetic theory consisting in judging artworks on the basis of the inter-human relation which they represent, produce or prompt."[88] Bourriaud analyzes relational art, a movement that took root in the 1990s and deals with forms that are essentially relational and create "lasting encounters" that produce (or highlight) "inter-subjectivity."[89] He positions this movement in relation to consumer culture's reduction of human relations to goods and their consumption, identifying relational art as site for modeling ways of living and active social relations that correspond to everyday realities.[90] Relational art activates different kinds of "inter-human relations" in the viewer's encounter with it, bringing awareness to these relations through participation and engagement.[91] Bourriaud posits relational art as a response to the reification of social relations. The art work he discusses places its viewers in specific environments that physically engage and tangibly model worlds of social relations. Thus, relational art seeks to connect individuals and groups.

However, I argue that dance in commercials demonstrates how this emphasis on inter-subjectivity and human relations—what is essentially a creation of relational encounters within the liminal space of the museum—has been taken up by consumer culture and advertising, in part, through the emergence of convergence culture, *affect*, and the spread of participatory aesthetics. Henry Jenkins examines the "relationship between three concepts—media convergence, participatory culture, and collective intelligence" in his text, *Convergence Culture* (2006).[92] Jenkins defines convergence as the "flow of content across multiple media platforms, the cooperation between multiple media industries, and the migratory behavior of media audiences who will go almost anywhere in search of the kinds of entertainment experiences they want."[93] His analysis demonstrates how the interconnectedness of media and the development of digital culture have enabled consumers to engage more directly with neoliberal capitalism and its discourses. Boundaries between popular culture and capitalism seem less clear in the twenty-first century.

According to Jenkins, media circulates across systems, economies, and nations as a result of consumer participation as consumers seek out the information they want and develop their own connections across media content. He defines participatory culture as a cultural model in which both media producers and consumers are "participants who interact with each other according to a new set of rules that none of us fully understands."[94] He acknowledges that participants' power and access varies widely—corporations retain greater power than consumers, and consumer access to media formats is not equal. However, he argues that active participation of consumers in media culture has led to the development of consumption as a collective process (i.e., collective intelligence) that functions as an alternative source of agency.[95]

Here, I return briefly to the Kickstart commercials, both of which end with an invitation to "touch" or interact with the visual text. Each ad ends with the trio of male buddies dancing their way out of the shot and leaving the location (i.e., basement game room, or city block) behind them awash with frantically dancing bodies. In the second ad, their exit leaves the logo, "IT ALL STARTS WITH A KICK," and #KICKSTART centered over the image. A shot of two Kickstart cans accompanied by the ad copy "DEW/JUICE/COCONUT WATER" and a male voiceover stating, "Mt. Dew Kickstart with two new flavors that taste *good*" follows their exit. The commercial then cuts back to the extreme wide shot of the street for the last 20 seconds of the video, during which time the following ad copy appears, one word at a time, in the center of the screen: "GO AHEAD. CLICK THEM CLICKY THINGS."

After a couple of seconds, the ad copy, and its command to the consumer, fades away, leaving unobstructed access to the visual image and the still dancing bodies. Thus, the end of the commercial, as in the case of the first ad, invites viewers to interact with the commercial's content by clicking on objects or characters to see them dance more. This participation requires viewing a digital version of the ad on the company's website to enable the interactive component. In other words, the versions of the commercials posted on Youtube and other sites (e.g., advertising archives, online newspaper and magazine articles, etc.) allow access to the digital video but not the interactive elements.[96]

The interactive aspects of these Mt. Dew commercials demonstrate how advertising continually navigates shifts in culture and technology even as it continues to respond to, promote, and influence popular culture—both physical culture and mass media. I argue that the Mt. Dew Kickstart ads use the advances of digital technology to tap into the relational aesthetics of participatory culture; they provide an example of how advertising navigates convergence culture in ways that integrate new media into already existing strategies.[97] However, though these ads point to important innovations within advertising, they are not without analog predecessors. Consumer culture has always encouraged consumer participation in various ways. Before digital culture this participation was not so immediate, but advertising speaks to consumers directly and needs consumer responses to better gauge its effectiveness. The development of digital technology has amplified the logic of the commodity-sign and consumer culture as corporations and advertisers have sought to capitalize on interactive models that activate social relations in tangible ways.

Thus, the concept of convergence culture speaks not only to increasing levels of consumers' active participation in media but also to increasing levels of active integration of media formats. In other words, technology since the 1990s has continued to find ways for the various forms of media to work symbiotically. Jenkins uses buying a cell phone as an example. He shares his experience of trying to buy a phone that is just a phone (not a camera or game player or way to surf the internet) and the sales staff's amusement at the backwardness of his request. Digital technology allows for increasing integration: flat screen televisions with wireless capabilities, cars that can park themselves, refrigerators that homeowners can monitor through their phones, et cetera.

Integration across formats allows consumers to access the same technologies from a variety of entry points. Applications on the phone also provide new access points to both media and non-media culture: catch a ride with Lyft, order food with Eat24, or watch the latest television show. Similarly, mass media content is increasingly integrated. Books and comic books become movies and games, or show up in advertising, as seen in the first Mt. Dew ad. The arts and popular culture alike become source material for movies, television, and advertising.

Thus far, commercials have remained a part of mass media, appearing on television, cable, radio, the internet, and cell phones. While the internet has led to increased product accessibility and provided new entryways into capitalism, it has also increased consumer participation. For example, self-employed artists and designers can reach a larger audience and sometimes cross the line into the corporate world when consumer responses indicate a sufficient market for their product. Furthermore, consumers now have multiple venues for responding to media culture as well as opportunities to create and share their own media.

Convergence culture has opened the door to a participatory aesthetics that effectually attempts to achieve its own model of relational aesthetics. Consumers actively pursue and produce opportunities to speak back to and manipulate the artifacts of culture and, in doing so, engage in social relations—even if those social relations are mediated. While mediation has replaced and/or modified the nature of "live" social relations to varying degrees, it has also produced new forms of inter-subjectivity and relationality. *Affect* plays an important role in these new forms and in the production of relationality within neoliberal capitalist consumer culture. To close this chapter, I visit one more example where dance helps extend advertising's production of infectiousness, relationality, and *affect*.

T-MOBILE: THE VIRAL NATURE OF THE VIRTUAL, DANCE, AND *AFFECT*

A high-angle shot looks down on the interior of the London Liverpool Street busy main terminal. Commuters enter and exit—some cross the space, heading toward a train or toward the exit, while others stand littered about the terminal floor talking on cell phones or waiting. One man, casually dressed in jeans and a jean jacket, walks pointedly to the center of the space, stops, and turns, planting his legs in a wide stance and facing the camera. He is too far away to see well. The intercom voice announces the next train arriving at Platform 17 only to be immediately followed by the much clearer and louder sound of Lulu's "Shout" (1964) as it reverberates through the hall. The jean-clad man drops into an asymmetrical squat, one leg turned in with his arms extended diagonally out forward low. As the music swells with Lulu's opening "well," he raises his arms, tracing the edge of his kinesphere as they move to the forward high diagonals.[98] When the lyrics start in earnest and the beat kicks in, he transforms the action into an up tempo embodiment of the lyrics, raising and lowering his arms and torso as he drops down toward the floor and then raises his body up to the ceiling ("You make me wanna shout, put my hands up and shout . . .").

Suddenly, the point of view changes, and he is now seen from the perspective of the terminal floor as the camera looks through the mingling commuters to where he dances. The perspective shifts further back and up to reveal that others are joining his dance, performing in unison with him. The unison continues as the music switches to Yazz's "The Only Way is Up" (1988); dancers smoothly transition into the song's choreography as their numbers grow. Music and dance continue to change as more and more members of the crowd reveal themselves to be a part of the dancing mob.

By the time the choreography arrives at the waltz and the dancers form couples to glide across the floor to Johann Strauss's "Blue Danube Waltz" (1867), the mob assumes a rough grid pattern that occupies the center of the terminal. The mob continues to grow in number with each song until it occupies most of the floor space and commuters have retreated to the edges to watch and film the event with their camera phones. While the event's music, except for the waltz, is twentieth-century pop songs and much of the choreography incorporates social dance, the movement—particularly the tempo and the transitions—suggests concert dance training, particularly jazz. The choreography's end reinforces this theatricality, organizing bodies to establish a single front for the final measures of The Contours' "Do You Love Me" (1962).

Just as suddenly as it began, this merger of performance and everyday expression ends; The Contours are cut off, and the dancers disperse, transforming back into everyday commuters. Shots of commuters talking animatedly on their cell phones, presumably about what just happened, follow. At one point, the ad copy "Life's for sharing" appears over the image, and in the next shot, the train station is replaced by an all pink screen and the following ad copy: "Life's for sharing" T-Mobile" and "t-mobile.co.uk/youtube."[99] What began as a snapshot of a London flash mob, seemingly captured on camera by chance, transforms into advertising (see video 1.5 ▶).

In the twenty-first century, the flash mob as social practice, political tool, and advertising strategy was a key cultural phenomenon that emerged to reinforce and highlight the role of *affect* in global capitalism. The power of *affect* and its connection to kinesthetic empathy is, perhaps, nowhere more evident in advertising than in T-Mobile's flash mob. These ads also draw attention to the power of the *real* in mass media forms and the *affective* power of relational and participatory aesthetics in the twenty-first century. T-Mobile's Liverpool Street Station flash mob on January 15, 2009, featured 350 dancers and consisted of three minutes of choreography captured by ten hidden television cameras, though it was ultimately filmed by commuters with their phone cameras as they watched the event unfold. The footage was edited to premiere as a commercial break during *Celebrity Big Brother* (Channel 4 UK) at 9 pm on Friday, January 16, 2009.[100]

While this example falls outside of the US context, the nature of viral videos is such that that the commercial was effectively being viewed online in the US shortly after its premiere. Furthermore, the viral ad helped to reignite, if briefly, the flash mob as a cultural practice and led to several other commercials grounded in the social phenomenon. Scholars from a range of disciplines have analyzed flash mobs, their historical precedents, their relationship to the rise of social networking in digital culture, and their transformation of public spaces.[101] Thomas Marchbank points to myths of their origin, linking them to related cyber concepts such as journalist Howard Rheingold's concept of the smart mob as a leaderless organization and Larry Niven's concept of the flash crowd as a term describing swarms in net traffic (e.g., in response to advertisements, etc.).[102]

Writing in 2004, Marchbank identifies the first flash mobs as occurring in 2003, citing examples in Auckland, Melbourne, and New York City. However, Thea Brejzek and Georgiana Gore cite Bill Wasik's claim to have coined the term and created the first flash mob event in June 2003 in a New York City Macy's.[103] All three authors connect flash mobs to historical precedents such as the Happenings and "yippie" prankster actions of the late 1960s and the Situationists' *dérive* of the 1950s.[104] Each of these forms aligns with some flash mob principles, as defined by Wasik and other organizers. Flash mobs ground themselves in participatory strategies of these earlier forms, transforming public spaces into performative ones and (potentially) disrupting economic and cultural order (i.e., symbolic order) with an apparent injection of spontaneity, play, and controlled anarchy. Overall, critical reception of flash mobs emphasizes their potential for effectively disrupting cultural systems to effect change and/or create community. However, the politics of these events are complex, being contingent on several factors, including who is participating and sponsoring the event, the relationship to bystanders, and ideologies furthered by the choreography.[105]

Flash mobs were thought to embody the viral culture of digital technology, spatially mobilizing a mass of people in subversive and absurdist action.[106] In the spirit of this embodiment, the mobilization occurred via the very digital technology it resembled. Mobs were typically organized via instructions sent through email, text, and Twitter, making T-Mobile's use of the flash mob an apt choice in marketing their product. In addition, they built on previous flash mob events: Liverpool Street and Paddington stations in London were previously sites for mobile clubbing flash mobs in 2006.[107] Despite the flash mob's subversive potential, T-Mobile's strategic use of the flash mob as a marketing tool points to the validity of Marchbank's critique of the form's similarity to neoliberal capitalism's consumer culture.

Marchbank's critique identifies a conundrum in that the agency in flash mobs resides within their very relationship to digital and consumer culture models of relation. On the one hand, he acknowledges that for individual flash mobbers the temporary collective identity of the mob might offer "possibilities for action and belonging" that lie outside of the numbing normality of mass media and consumer culture. As he puts it, these groups emerge from virtual communities "based on a de-centred, grassroots 'tribe'—a social grouping accreting around a shared interest that does not require its members to be 'actually' present for them to gather" and which subsumes individual identity within the collective.[108]

However, as he suggests, this model, while offering the possibility to "reinvigorate social ties" and "devise new molecular assemblages of sociality," also aligns with the machine of neoliberal consumer culture. The collective identity of the flash mob and its dynamics echoes that of consumer identity—where "identity [is] composed by brand (group) allegiance, infinitely susceptible to mutations in product, concretising for the brief instant around a mode, a style, a form, and then dispersing again in the buffeting volatility of the market."[109] As he points out, flash mobs enact consumer culture concepts of identity as defined by "brand (group) allegiance" that coalesces around a product or style for a period of time only to disperse and reform in a new place.

Thus, while he aligns the practice with the effort to instill relationality in twenty-first-century technology and consumer culture, he reveals the limitations of the model. Flash mobs adopt the tactic rather than the strategy, modeling a means of identity and agency based on emergence.[110] Thus, while they offer temporary possibilities for relationality and social assemblage to emerge as embodied forms, their potential has been rerouted to feed into the logic of neoliberal capitalism.

All sociality, I argue, is molecular and molecular assemblages of sociality are always emergent—like other forms of emergence, social formations have tipping points, states of being that are optimum for self-organization. Culture emerges out of these related social assemblages and forms at a "higher" level as social formations work to produce larger structures. The impact of molecular social assemblages, once the system reaches a certain size, resembles the impact consumers have on the capitalist market as they speak back to producers through their consumption and social practices. This idea makes me think back to Grossberg's notion of mattering and how *affective* participation works to fill gaps in belonging and power/potential. Thus, the flash mob choreography of T-mobile employs spectacle and kinesthetic empathy to model *affective contagion*.

T-Mobile capitalizes on the relationship between the flash mob's sense of collective agency (at the molecular level) and participatory culture's production of mattering and relationality. At the level of the flash mob, dance's *affect* is amplified across and between bodies as they come together within a social space in a way that temporarily reorganizes its typical spatial flows to highlight social relations. T-Mobile intensifies advertising's production of *affect* through spectacle and excess, demonstrating how dance allows advertisers to tap into the concept of mass as a vehicle for collective and individual agency. Dance in advertising visually mobilizes *affect* as mass and movement.

CHAPTER 2
Commercials as Discursive Assemblages

By the time television spots began to be a viable advertising practice within the American context (1948–1950), print advertising was well established and had standardized its basic codes and conventions, as well as weathered drastic economic and cultural shifts (Prohibition, WWI, the Great Depression, WWII).[1] Commercials entered the US economy at a moment when the country was moving from scarcity to abundance and consumerism was becoming a driving force. In addition, television advertising entered the American scene during a period in which radio, cinema, and dance were already established forms of entertainment with both their own conventions and a complex shared history of development as American cultural practices.[2] While the debts television owes to radio, cinema, and the performing arts have been acknowledged to some extent within television studies, these intersections, or *lines of articulation*, have yet to be fully explored in terms of how they participate in both the *territorialization* and *flight* of disciplinary boundaries, of their simultaneous delineation and rupture.

An analysis of dance-commercials as *assemblages*, as sites of discursive collage, offers an opportunity to look more closely at the ways in which they articulate with other cultural practices and the conventions, codes, and strategies those employ. In this chapter, I trace these *lines of articulation*, drawing attention to the ways in which these commercials put advertising positioning strategies into play with live performance conventions, television production practices, film musicals' narrative/number syntax, music video codes, and cinematic conventions. These *lines of articulation* generate *affect* and meaning-making through their production of *liveness, spectacle,* and *polysemy.* The structure of my analysis seeks to map *lines of territorialization,* while also drawing attention to *lines of flight*. In other words, I trace these lines across several examples to show how dance-in-advertising articulates a range of codes and conventions.[3] To do this, I follow the body in motion and the choreography of moving images as they enact and invoke conventions, sometimes helping to establish disciplinary territories and at other times working to escape them. My analysis demonstrates how the dancing body in advertising multiples the productive flows of signification by facilitating advertising's increasingly hybrid deployment of discursive structures.

THE ADVERTISING FORM: STRATEGIES AND COMMODITY-SIGNS

A L&M cigarette commercial (1966) demonstrates how standard advertising positioning strategies operate within television commercials (see video 2.0 ▶).[4] This black-and-white television spot opens with a heterosexual, white, adult couple dancing at a quick tempo in a standard ballroom embrace. The tempo, step pattern, and time period suggest a standardized Latin Ballroom form, such as the mambo or cha cha.[5] The setting seems to be a studio space: there are tables in the background, one appears to hold a record player, and the wall behind them has large cut-out stars and a banner announcing a contest. As the couple dances, the music climaxes; in the silence that follows, they pose in an embrace, facing the camera and smiling.

A masculine voice announces, "A couple of years ago at Pete Taylor's Dance Studio, only Jack smoked L&Ms," and the ad cuts to a close-up of his face while he looks downward but toward Kim. The announcer continues, "Now Kim Kelly's come over." As the ad cuts to a close-up of her face, she leans forward to let Jack light her cigarette. Kim nods her head "yes" and takes a drag before the spot cuts to a shot of a table where a L&M pack leans against a trophy. On the left side of the image, print ad copy appears that reads, "Today's best taste in smoking." Simultaneously, the announcer continues, "When you've got today's best taste in smoking," which is followed by a shot of Kim looking toward the camera and smiling as the announcer finishes, "people find out."

This L&M commercial includes dance as part of its visual content while still retaining the overall appearance and structure of standard advertising. The spot offers an early example of the dance-in-advertising *formation* and the transfer of standard print advertising positioning strategies to television. The standard semiotic analyses of print advertising by theorists such as Roland Barthes and Judith Williamson in the 1970s and the transferal of these ideas to television commercial analysis by scholars such as Robert Goldman in the 1990s reveal common positioning strategies that shape advertising discourse.[6] Drawing on their work, I use the L&M cigarette spot to demonstrate advertising's meaning-making strategies.

Semiotic analyses of print advertising address how the ad functions as a complex sign, consisting of images and text, that interacts with the product to produce a new level of meaning, the commodity-sign.[7] In his analysis of print advertising, Goldman defines the commodity-sign in the following manner: "The commodity-as-sign operates when images are allied to particular products and the product images are then deployed as signifiers of particular relations or experiences."[8] Modeled after the sign in semiotics, the commodity-sign consists of a signifying unit and a signified meaning. However, it joins the sign structure found in semiotics with that of the product or commodity-form.[9]

The commodity-form contains three levels of value (use, surplus, and exchange), as described in Jean Baudrillard's expansion of Karl Marx's study of capitalism.[10] The function of the commodity-sign is to create exchange value for the product by eliding the difference between the product and the socio-cultural values, relations, and/or experiences conveyed in the signifying images and text. In equating the product with the signifying images and text, the ad-as-commodity-sign transfers the signified meaning to the product.[11] Consumers then purchase not only the product but also the signified values/meanings produced by advertising. As Baudrillard argues, the creation of the commodity-sign is an extension of the capitalist model of production and sustains capitalist consumer culture by creating need through what is, essentially, an enhancement of the exchange value of a given product (i.e., commodity).[12]

Simply put, advertising operates by linking signs (i.e., images/text and their values/meanings) to products to create commodity-signs. Semiotic analyses of the discursive operations of the commodity-sign reveal the advertising positioning strategies conventionally employed to create this enhanced product exchange value. Early semiotic analyses focused on two central aspects of the advertising form: the sign structure of the ads and the conventions governing how various elements of the ad inter-relate to generate meaning.[13] These studies identified how standard print advertising creates the commodity-sign through four basic conventions: the main photographic signifying image, the mortise (product inset), graphic framing devices, and framing copy. These elements guide one's reading of advertising by using graphic design and ad copy to frame and provide a context for the main photographic image, as well as to link that image to an inset separate image of the product (i.e., the mortise).[14]

In the L&M commercial described above the signifying image is broken up into five basic shots: the couple dancing, his close-up, her close-up, the mortise shot of the cigarette pack that joins the other shots and the ad copy to the product, and her second close-up. Four of these shots, the two-shot and the solo shots,[15] work primarily as the filmic/video version of print advertising's main signifying image. They serve to establish: 1) the function (i.e., use value) of the product, and 2) its social context and meaning (i.e., exchange value). By providing a social context for the product, the images contribute social relationships and cultural values to the commodity-sign.

In this instance, dance serves as a means of marketing the product to a target audience by appealing to consumers who share similar interests and/or identify with the socio-cultural categories they recognize in the couple. For example, at first, the couple appears to be unaware of the camera, reducing the sense of dance-as-performance and encouraging viewers to see it as a social activity. However, the presence of the trophy in the mortise shot alludes to social dance competitions, suggesting this activity would be familiar to television audiences of the time and that their dancing *also* occurs within a performance context.

An expectation of familiarity is supported by the histories of dance and television. As demonstrated by the popularity of the Arthur Murray dance studio franchise and the *Arthur Murray Dance Party*, which aired 1950–1962, ballroom dance would have been a widely recognized social practice among middle-class white adults and television audiences.[16] Understanding social dance in this context also links the ad to the concept of dance-as-performance, which is furthered by the use of the phrase "best taste" and its suggestion of competition.[17] The use of the word "taste" effectively signifies not only the physical sense of taste, but also the aesthetic connotation of refinement and an artistic sense of perception.[18] Thus, the commercial works to join L&M cigarettes to social relationships, the values of heterosexual, middle-class life, and a certain level of cultural sophistication (see figure 2.1).

The shots that comprise the signifying images and the meaning they carry are joined to the product by the fourth shot in the ad, which assumes the function of the mortise. Rather than being an inset of the product as in classic print ads, this mortise consists of a medium two-shot of the L&M cigarette pack and a trophy sitting on a table. While the product appears in its own distinct shot, a parallel to the inset image within print advertising, the shot also appears to capture another view of the space, which emphasizes the product as a part of the signifying image. This shot's mortise function results from its emphasizing the product and the ad copy within the image and its being the only time a distinct product image is shown. As a result, this L&M cigarette spot serves as an early example of a commercial that combines the signifying image and the product image within the same visual space. This strategy works to collapse even further the distance between image and product, thereby collapsing the distance between product and social relations.

While placing the cigarette pack against the trophy links the product to competitive ballroom dancing, the mortise also promotes product recognition by providing a clear image of the packaging and logo. Thus, rather than aggressively asserting the product image or its logo, the ad simply conveys the purpose of the advertisement through the combination of images, voiceover,

Figure 2.1 The L&M Cigarette ad's mortise. Commercial. Screen shot.

ad copy, and mortise shot. Additionally, the voiceover and the visuals that depict the product in use demonstrate not only the product's function but also its role in positive social experiences. As the television commercial format developed, this strategy of uniting the mortise and signifying image recurred and continued to be effectively employed in a variety of formats featuring dance. More importantly, this strategy of embedding the mortise within the signifying image has been particularly effective in ads where the product and the dancing body can be easily united, such as those for clothing.[19]

In addition to showing this blurring of mortise and signifying image, the L&M ad demonstrates some of the ways in which camerawork, editing, music, voiceovers, dancing, and graphic design serve as framing devices that lead the viewer toward the advertiser's intended meaning. While print ads have to rely solely on graphic framing devices, television commercials can deploy sound and motion to unite individual shots with the product. For example, in the L&M ad, the voiceover functions as both framing device and ad copy. It establishes the dance studio setting and further contextualizes the dancing and the relationship of Jack and Kim Kelly. Additionally, the timing of the voiceover works in conjunction with the various shots, so that the announcer identifies Jack (as he is shown in close-up), then Kim Kelly (in a close-up leaning forward as he lights her cigarette), and then the "best taste in smoking" (the shot of the pack resting against the trophy).

This example highlights a primary difference between print and television ads: duration.[20] Since commercials do not occur all at once as print ads do, the element of time alters advertising conventions and how consumers *read* them.[21] Three key ways in which print conventions are modified within the commercial format include: the incorporation of sound (both music and spoken text) as an additional framing device, as a form of ad copy, and as part of the signifying image (content); the use of editing (including montage) to connect a series of images over time; and the merging of the mortise—often, but not always, and to varying degrees—with the signifying image. As in print ads, advertising conventions in commercials promote the transferal of the signified meaning from the signifying images, including sound, to the product named. In other words, advertising conventions function as positioning strategies that seek to guide consumers in the creation of associative links between cultural meanings, products, and marketing points.[22] Thus, the commodity-sign offers consumers access to social meaning and value through the vehicle of the commodity.

The L&M commercial demonstrates the carryover of the basic conventions of print advertising into television commercials. However, I argue that, within the medium of television, advertising conventions have been, and continue to be, merged with those of live performance, television, and film. As I will demonstrate in this chapter, in the case of dance in advertising, advertisers often model commercials after other media forms by integrating advertising positioning strategies with the codes and conventions of concert dance, film musicals, narrative film, music videos, and screendance. In addition, the positioning strategies of advertising bear a resemblance to both the choreographic conventions and devices employed in dance, which seek to frame, contextualize, and guide the viewer's encounter with the work, and to conventions governing shot composition, filming, and editing that contribute to filmic meaning and effect. In the next section, I turn to the live performance convention of direct address and its parallel within advertising.

DANCE-IN-ADVERTISING, DIRECT ADDRESS, AND ALTHUSSER'S HAIL

The ideological and discursive conventions of advertising's positioning strategies, Louis Althusser's concept of *hailing*,[23] and the performance practice of *direct address* intersect within television commercials like the L&M cigarette ad. Within commercials, advertising employs dancing bodies and the relational dynamics of performance as a form of address. Borrowing Althusser's terms, advertising is ideological, striving to transform viewers into consumers by literally *hailing* them, putting into play the signifying image and its sociocultural connotations, and thus, presenting the task of sorting through the puzzle of the ad's visual text. Consequently, by deciphering the commercial, viewers accept their positioning as subjects and consumers in relation to the ad and, implicitly, the larger economic structure of capitalism. Thus, consumers' participation in reading the ad completes the dynamic relationship initiated by the ad's address.

The merging of advertising and performance conventions played a key role in my initial recognition of dance-in-advertising as a distinct formation within mass media. While television commercials have developed both overt and subtle ways of speaking to the viewer, the use of direct address is always present in advertising through at least one of the following strategies: actors directly addressing or performing to the viewer, visual ad copy, voiceovers that use "you," and performance conventions. The *hailing* that occurs within advertising through the pronoun "you" parallels live performance's convention of direct address.

Direct address appears in both live and recorded performance[24] whenever there are distinct roles for performers and audience members (e.g., comedians, talk shows, newscasters, etc.). Direct address, both within commercials and other forms of television content, occurs not only in language but also through staging and bodily comportment. Additionally, however, the knowledge that one is watching a performance creates the appearance, or expectation, of direct address.[25]

While many analyses of advertising point to the use of the pronoun "you" and the use of imperatives and commands as forms of direct address, my analysis of dance in advertising demonstrates the significance of non-verbal forms of direct address. For example, in the L&M commercial, non-verbal direct address occurs when the actors look directly at the camera (and thus at home viewers) but also through the frontal facings of the dancers' bodies. However, direct address is also evident in how the dance is framed and the body "performs."

In the opening shot of the L&M ad, once the couple stops dancing, they swivel their upper bodies to face the camera and smile as though posing for a picture. In this moment, they acknowledge the camera and thus the viewer, creating the impression that perhaps the dancing that came before was, in fact, intended for an audience. When the spot is almost over, a medium shot of Kim reveals her turning to look directly at the camera as she smiles and tilts her head in agreement with the voiceover. She has discovered that L&M cigarettes have the best taste, and the viewer can make this same discovery by joining in her consumption. In this commercial, when the actors face the camera and assume an outward focus, they support the direct address of the ad copy's pronouns and syntax. In addition, the performance of stylized action invites *being seen* and reinforces the hailing of the viewer (see figure 2.2).

In other words, the act of dancing and the ways in which dance-as-an-activity recontextualizes the space of advertising supplements the various

Figure 2.2 L&M's ballroom couple directly address the viewer. Commercial. Screen shot.

modes of direct address. Dancing also shifts the space of the L&M ad, in part, through reference to competitive ballroom dance. The allusion to the competitive form invokes a sense of dance as display and presentation, as an act performed for an audience, which is furthered by cultural notions of dance as spectacle, and carries with it the ideological positioning of direct address. In other words, the dancing itself invites the viewer to watch, and in doing so, it hails the viewer and positions him/her as audience. As noted above, this idea is confirmed, or reinforced, by the couple's ending pose with their smiling faces and bodies opening outward toward the camera.

Thus, direct address functions as a *line of flight* that ruptures disciplinary boundaries, connecting the hailing strategies of advertising with performance conventions and thus *deterritorializing* planes of discourse. This aspect of dance in advertising arises not only from dance's contributions to advertising but also from the history of television content and production practices. When television first emerged as a new technology its production practices were based on the limitations of its medium, which did not allow for prerecording broadcasts, and television's content was informed by its communication and entertainment predecessors, radio and the performing arts.[26] As a result, advertising's transition to television included not only the transferring of print's basic advertising strategies to the commercial format but also a merging of advertising conventions with developing televisual conventions and those of TV's early content, radio and live performance forms (e.g., theater, dance, music).

Furthermore, television has continued to incorporate new conventions as production practices, technology, and content have shifted over time.[27] As a result, the television commercial *formation* arises as a site of intersecting discourses that territorializes practices to create a recognizable genre (i.e., formation) *and* ruptures discourses that seek to distinguish advertising and television from other cultural forms. In advertising, the active presence of multiple, competing discourses is amplified through the incorporation of the dancing body.

DANCE-IN-ADVERTISING, TELEVISION PRODUCTION, AND THE PERFORMANCE OF LIVENESS

In an earlier publication,[28] I addressed how production history ties televisual conventions to live performance. Beginning in the experimental years of the late 1920s and 1930s, television programming drew on the practices established by broadcast networks' live radio shows.[29] As a result, television broadcasts up to the 1950s were often visual versions of radio programs, one early example being *The Fox Trappers Orchestra* (CBS 1928).[30] Because it was not initially possible to record the television signal, all television was broadcast live for the first three years of commercial network production.[31] While the technology to live broadcast filmed materials existed, procuring films was a costly process and networks feared losing control of station content, which resulted in the limited broadcasting of film.[32] In response to these limitations, early television developed much like radio, favoring live broadcasts, modeling its programming after radio, and broadcasting pre-existing radio shows.[33]

As a result, during the initial years of commercial network television (1948 to 1952) most programming consisted of various forms of live broadcasts, including sporting competitions, news-worthy events, operas, symphony concerts, and radio shows.[34] This emphasis on live presentation was reinforced by the practice of modeling other television programming after forms of live entertainment.[35] Adopting theatrical conventions, television often broadcast variety shows, dramas, comedies, music, and dance staged with a clear frontal perspective and employing forms of direct address. The TV show host, who introduced the acts, reinforced the sense of *liveness*, while also providing framing, context, and continuity within the show. These hosts, typically situated on a studio sound stage, employed direct address to speak and perform to and for the television audience. Other programming, such as news broadcasts and live sports events, echoed this presentation format. The following analysis demonstrates advertising's incorporation of these conventions.

The use of a host to incorporate direct address occurs in an Old Gold cigarette commercial, "Dancing Butts" (1950) (see video 2.1 ▶).[36] This black-and-
white TV spot begins with a shot of radio and television announcer Dennis
James, who would later become a television game show host,[37] walking into
frame and approaching the television in what looks like a living room. As he
lays his hand on the top of the TV set and looks toward the camera, he says,
"Say, it's time for my favorite dance team, so let's look," at which point, he
leans down and turns on the television. Standing, he backs away from the set,
while looking at the screen as the commercial cuts to what appears to be a TV
sound stage. The viewer sees a polished floor with a curtain backdrop upstage.
In front of the curtain stand two women (one tall and one short) dressed in
white ankle-high boots and boxes that entirely cover their torsos (i.e., from
just above their head to the top of their thighs), so that only the boxes and the
women's legs are visible. The two immediately begin to tap dance in unison to
a light, cheerful tune (see figure 2.3).[38]

The duet's light, crisp shuffle steps and quick turns fill the screen. Shortly
after they begin, the viewer hears James in a voiceover as he says, "Ah, a box
of matches and a pack of Old Gold cigarettes. That's all you need my friend,
and you're enjoying the smoothest, mildest, tastiest cigarette every created."

Figure 2.3 Dennis James watching Old Gold's dancing cigarette packs. Commercial.
Screen shot.

During a brief musical interlude, the two continue tap dancing in unison, and then James' voice returns, saying, "A treat instead of a treatment. That's Old Gold cigarettes. Made by tobacco men, not medicine men. They give you the cigarette that treats you better in every way, because in every way, it's a better cigarette." As he finishes speaking, the dancing duet chainé turns toward the left side of the screen to then paddle turn in place, at which point the commercial cuts back to the living room and an over-the-shoulder shot of James as he sits watching the dancing duet on his television.

The pair's dance number ends with a final pose, and the spot immediately cuts to a side shot of James in his armchair as he sits up and turns to face the camera. Speaking to the camera and the viewer, he says, "Good, huh? Yes, for a treat instead of a treatment, get a pack or get a carton of Old Gold cigarettes." He glances down at the cigarette he has passed from his left to his right hand, which brings the cigarette closer to his mouth as he gestures with it while finishing the ad copy: "Right now, this is Dennis James reminding you to keep smoking Old Gold cigarettes." As he says "Old Gold cigarettes," the commercial cuts to an image of Old Gold cigarette boxes arranged in a V formation, revealing the detail of the packaging design and creating the visual impression of boxes of cigarettes in a line that fades into the distance, like chorus girls on a vast sound stage.

This commercial demonstrates how television draws resources from radio and previously existing entertainment forms, as well as how it borrows theatrical conventions and employs direct address on multiple levels. Dennis James would have been recognizable and known as a radio host by many viewers, and as in radio, he speaks "directly" to the audience. Here, he also literally performs the *hailing* of the consumer through his use of "you" and by directly addressing the camera. His role as a radio celebrity would have amplified this sense of *hailing* because he was a familiar figure who regularly addressed broadcast audiences, thus his presence also would have created an expectation of direct address. In much the same way, his "favorite dance team's" performance of a choreographed routine with a clear frontal focus produces a form of direct address through its reference to live performance.

Both he and the dancers demonstrate how direct address often takes the form of embodied projection. Through the stylization of action, the intent of the body's movement is more precisely conveyed through a refinement of direction, shape, phrasing, and energy. In other words, bodily performance projects or directs actions to the audience, in part, by bringing a heightened clarity to the performer's movement, thus drawing the audience's attention to the body's choreography and its intent.[39] In the Old Gold ad, this stylization is visible in the actions of the dancers' legs, which have a bright, buoyant sharpness that is paired with a display of the line of the leg. This display of the legs is seen most clearly about halfway through the spot when the camera tilts, looking down the taller dancer's body, to frame her legs in a medium shot as she pauses in a closed parallel position with one leg slightly in front of the other, her body on a slight diagonal. The pose reminds one of the classic stance of Miss America contestants, legs together, standing tall, while still presenting the line of the leg for modest admiration.

I argue that on television this embodied direct address in combination with the deployment of other theatrical conventions reinforces the association of television with *liveness*, a televisual concept identified by Philip Auslander. He argues that the ideology of television includes a sense of *liveness* as a result of its relying on performance forms for content, its positioning of content as being performed for at-home viewers, and its initial role as a broadcaster of live events.[40] While the history of film includes the recording of both fictional and real events as they happen, film quickly developed conventions that positioned the viewer as a voyeur by maintaining the illusion of the "fourth wall" and, thus, the existence of a fictional world. Television conventions, on the other hand, tended to include both performing to and breaking the fourth wall.[41] Thus, while film invites its audience to peer into worlds other than their own, television programming often consciously directs its content to the viewers and emphasizes "its ability to bring disparate spaces together in the same time."[42]

However, within the context of television, liveness functions differently than in an actual live performance context. On television, liveness is linked to the medium's history of broadcasting events "*exactly when and as they happen.*"[43] As Auslander argues and more recent scholarship on reality television reiterates, television differs from film, in part, as a result of TV's association with live broadcasts, the television set's location in the home, and the resulting sense of "immediacy" and "intimacy."[44] However, television's *liveness* is also linked to the medium's appropriation of existing entertainment genres and discourses of theatrical performance.

While advances in recording technology allowed television to move quite rapidly away from live broadcasting to incorporating cinematic filming practices, television continued to include genres that consciously adopted theatrical codes and conventions for staging and filming events. Thus, the ideological connection to liveness has continued due to both its history as a medium for transmitting actual events and its engagement with theatrical presentation. On television, the dancing body activates theatrical discourse and allows dance to instill television, including television commercials, with a sense of performance. The discourse of performance activated by dancing bodies, in turn, functions as a form of hailing within advertising. This discursive function of dance has continued to operate effectively in digital media formats aired via the internet and viewed on digital devices such as phones and computers.

My purpose here is not to argue in favor of equating television, or other media forms, with attending live performances. Clearly, the two differ in how they frame events, and they offer audiences different experiences. Thus, the concept of liveness at play within dance-in-advertising differs from Peggy Phelan's argument about the ephemerality of live performance and the complexities of its political economy.[45] Rather, my goal here is to point to how dance operates inside of television advertising, the way it activates theatrical discourses within the discourse of advertising, and the *affective* power of dance's association with live performance.

THE APPEARANCE OF LIVENESS
IN DANCE-IN-ADVERTISING

Television studies has paid little attention to dance, but dance's value within the medium is inadvertently pointed out by John Thorton Caldwell's argument against an ideology of liveness in late twentieth-century American television.[46] Caldwell suggests that, by the 1980s, the sense of liveness found in television was nothing more than one of many styles employed at will within the medium.[47] I argue that dance, and often other forms of choreographed movement, functions as one means of producing liveness-as-style on television. Caldwell adopts a postmodernist approach to reading televisual styles, seeing them as a pastiche of styles employed at will and operating as spectacle and as a proliferation of free-floating signifiers. Extending and rerouting his analysis, I argue that by invoking liveness, either as style or ideology, commercials use dance to consciously break generic boundaries to construct a particular relationship to their television audience—one that allows for the production of *affect* in ways that are closely aligned with live performance. This kind of *affect* commonly occurs in film through the vehicle of film musicals, which also employ theatrical conventions.

The tap dance performed for Dennis James in the Old Gold cigarette commercial is also a performance for the television audience, who is sutured into position both through James' direct address and the collapsing of the television frame with that of the stage. It is this history of literally borrowing performance forms—both as content and as a source of framing codes or positioning strategies—that produces liveness as a style within the postmodernist practices of 1980s and 1990s television. As a result, liveness-as-style carries with it the weight of performance-as-discourse. Dance and choreography serve as a means of invoking liveness within television.[48]

My analysis of dance-in-advertising and its relationship to liveness thus aligns more closely with Auslander's analysis of television ideology, than Caldwell's. Auslander argues that the association of live performance genres with early television's production practices and its continued deployment of live performance (and its conventions) has allowed media forms to "displace and replace live performance in a wide variety of cultural contexts."[49] Extending his analysis, I argue that dance-in-advertising participates in this merging of performance and television discourses with the goal of demonstrating to television viewers that life is a performance enacted through the work of consumption. Dancing bodies generate an association with live performance through their performance of theatrical codes and conventions. In turn, dance hails the television viewer, in part, because dancing bodies interpellate the viewer as audience and thus engage the viewer first as the receiver of spectacle, or entertainment, and second as the decoder of the commodity-sign.

Furthermore, I argue that this operation of dance within television advertising works effectively both when ads employ additional signs of theatrical performance and when ads embed dance within normative social contexts. To demonstrate this aspect, I turn now to a discussion of advertising's incorporation of filmic conventions, looking at how it incorporates aspects of both narrative cinema and film musicals and how dance-as-discourse operates inside of these increasingly rhizomatic advertising strategies. By revisiting the formation of dance-in-advertising from different disciplinary perspectives, I demonstrate how dancing bodies facilitate advertising's *becoming (-dance, -film, -musical . . .)* and transform commercials into sites, or planes, of intersecting discourses.

TELEVISION, ADVERTISING, AND FILM CONVENTIONS

The site of the televisual has always been a plane of intricate articulations in terms of cultural ideologies conveyed through the codes and conventions of its various content. Up to this point, I have traced the lines of articulation within dance-in-advertising to reveal how commercials function as assemblages of advertising, dance, performance, and television conventions. Because television also incorporates film production practices and shows films as content, dance-in-advertising also articulates with filmic conventions, from both narrative cinema and film musicals.

Due to this blending of conventions, liveness and the real are conceptual assemblages that assume distinct configurations depending upon the lines of articulation active within a given advertisement. In other words, commercials vary in terms of which disciplinary discourses and socio-cultural practices they engage with through their positioning strategies and audio-visual content. In this section, I consider how established codes and conventions for incorporating dance within film genres are key to recognizing and understanding how dance creates lines of articulation and rupture within television commercials. Dance and film have a long history of interaction. Both dance and bodies-in-motion have been an ongoing source of fascination for film, dating back to Eadweard Muybridges's initial efforts to capture motion in a series of still photographs (1870s–1880s).[50] While the prevalence of dance in film genres has waxed and waned over the course of the twentieth century, filmic conventions have played an increasingly vital role in dance-in-advertising of the late twentieth and early twenty-first centuries.

When advertising features dance, the union of theatrical and filmic conventions is more prevalent than in most non-dance commercials and many television genres. While commercials featuring dance frequently adopt strategies commonly found in both film musicals and narrative dance films, they also articulate with music videos and screendance, each of which possesses a distinct relationship to film history. To demonstrate how dance in advertising discursively intersects with narrative dance films and film musicals, this section compares two Coca-Cola commercials. I also briefly address the relationship between dance in advertising and music videos within this section.

Both commercials are part of the "Coke is it!" ad campaign from the 1980s.[51] The Coca-Cola Company and its advertising agencies have employed a wide range of strategies for advertising Coca-Cola. The 1980s ads borrow techniques from and allude to the content of narrative films, musical theater and film musicals, music videos and pop stars, and television shows. I demonstrate the incorporation of musical theater strategies through one of these 1980s Coke commercials—one that draws on the popularity of musical theater, as well as television shows and films depicting the performing arts, such as *Fame* (1982–1987 TV show, 1980/2009 film).

The "Coke is It—Rehearsal" spot resembles an excerpt from a musical production (see figure 2.4 and video 2.2 ▶). In the one-minute version of the spot, the establishing shot zooms out to reveal a group of young male and female performers rehearsing on stage. The director walks on stage as the music ends and says, "Okay, kids, take a break." The ad cuts to a close-up of a young man drinking a coke and then to a wide shot as he sets the Coke down on the piano. The pianist plays the Coke-is-it jingle as other performers stand around him. Immediately, one of the girls at the piano responds by singing "Coke is it." The others reply in unison with an increase in tempo, "Coke is it!" At this point, the pianist begins to play the jingle at tempo and off-screen instruments join in to fill out the sound as cast members begin to sing. At times, the camera follows a soloist as he or she sings a verse, and at other times, the ad cuts between different groupings of the performers as they sing the jingle and perform a mix of actions: moving to the rhythm, stretching, engaging in pedestrian behaviors, or performing recognizable dance movements. Thus, their break consists of them singing the Coke jingle as they interact, drink Coke, and embody their enthusiasm for the soft drink by moving to the rhythm of the music. Much of the action lives in the realm of film musicals' "gestural anacrusis"—the space in which the shift between modalities of action occurs, or the in-between space where the actor transitions from pedestrian movement to dancing.[52]

Figure 2.4 Coca-Cola inspires song-and-dance during a musical theater rehearsal break. Commercial. Screen shot.

Placing the ad within the context of a musical theater rehearsal and the stage space associates the ad with films (e.g., *Dames* [1934] dir. Busby Berkeley) and television shows built around the performing arts in which musical numbers often arise out of rehearsals and performances.[53] The song's transformation of the actors' physicality (i.e., the gestural anacrusis) generates a line of flight that articulates the commercial to the backstage musical and its conventions for introducing musical numbers. Film musical scholars Rick Altman, Jane Feuer, and Martin Rubin have provided rich analyses of how the backstage musical plot revolves around the production of a musical theater show.[54] Their work demonstrates how the plot device of "putting on a show" provides a "naturally" occurring "self-enclosed and independent" space that is already distinct from reality, or "bracketed," and set off in a space of imagination.[55] In other words, backstage musicals facilitated the construction of the space of performance as a space of possibility a site in which make-believe, imagination, and expression are dominant, and as a space that lies in opposition to the narrative space, where realistic social interactions take place. Within the space of performance different "laws or ground rules" govern self-expression and social interactions.[56]

Thus, in the film musical genre, the number, unlike the narrative, allows characters to do two things: first, to step, temporarily, outside of the real to enter the imaginary, and second, to express themselves by sharing their thoughts and feelings with the viewer/audience.[57] The transition between narrative and number requires the transformation of the narrative film space. As the musical slides into its song and dance numbers, it brackets characters' conduct as expressive and excessive, as exceeding narrative cause and effect. The use of place, sound, and motion plays a vital role in both delimiting and linking the pedestrian, everyday world (i.e., the narrative) with the world of expression (i.e., the number). Often, dance in commercials alludes to this tendency to slip free of the narrative, allowing the ad's "characters" to go beyond the limits of normal social behavior and reveal their inner lives.

While backstage musicals establish the theater, as well as its rehearsals and productions, as the space of the dance number, other musicals, such as those of Fred Astaire and Ginger Rogers, do not always segregate the musical numbers from the narrative. Instead, these film musicals often transform everyday social places—parks, offices, hotel rooms, boats, and so on—into performance spaces. In these instances, the space of the narrative becomes the space of performance through the transition from dialogue and everyday action into song and dance. Sound and motion take precedence over narrativity and characterization. For example, the character's shift into singing is typically accompanied by the onset of instrumental accompaniment coming from off screen. Film theorist Rick Altman refers to this transition device as an audio dissolve.[58]

The merging of off-screen instrumental accompaniment with the on-screen character singing creates what Altman refers to as "supra-diegetic" music by blurring the border between two aspects of the soundtrack, and in doing so, it blurs the border between the space of the real and the space of the imaginary within the film.[59] Film theorist Jane Feuer describes this phenomenon in the following manner: "In becoming song, language is in a sense transfigured, lifted up into a higher, more expressive realm."[60] Correspondingly, Altman argues that this blending signals a shift in the logic of the film as music becomes the controlling force and reverses the conventional understanding of the relationship between image and sound in which sound is read as being produced by an event in the physical world. Thus sound, or music, appears to control or dictate movement. This dynamic visibly manifests when movement as rhythm and flow assumes dominance within the image and pedestrian actions become dance.

Thus singing and dancing function as lines of flight. They connect the linear world of the everyday/narrative to the world of *affective* meaning and perform a similar function to that of poetic expression, as found in the vertical film form of Maya Deren's experimental cinema. While film musicals often use the onset of off-screen orchestral music to signal this shift, singing and dancing outside of conventional social contexts also function as signs of this transformation. I argue that, as seen in the above Coke commercial, television advertising employs theatrical conventions in combination with dance, and sometimes song, to simulate the narrative/number codes and conventions of film musicals.

Over the course of the twentieth century, this opposition between narrative and number established itself as a recognizable convention of the film musical genre. Thus, when the Coke ad's musical theater cast takes a drink, "feels a song (or dance) coming on and bursts into [a] spontaneous, purportedly un-rehearsed, but perfectly executed performance,"[61] the ad's signifying image draws on film musical conventions to position the song and dance as existing outside of any realist, pedestrian space. Instead, the spot moves into the realm of the imaginary to capture the spontaneous expression of the joy of drinking Coca-Cola. While the filming of the ad primarily suggests that the viewer voyeuristically observes the spontaneous singing and dancing, the camera assumes the place of the audience, and the choreography stages the dancers with a frontal perspective. In addition, the commercial includes moments of direct address when cast members look directly at the camera as they sing. Thus, despite the ad's cinematic filming style, theatrical conventions rein-force the sense of performance instilled by the ad's allusion to musical theater productions.

While many dance commercials do not explicitly or completely employ the conventions of the film musical genre (i.e., narrative/number distinction and techniques for transitioning between the two), their strategies for including dance frequently build on film musical history and its production practices. In other words, advertising invokes the cultural positioning of dance as a form of expressive behavior, relying on its excess and the *affect* it produces to gen-erate meaning. Thus, film musical conventions often inform how commercials incorporate dance, even when such influences are not explicitly referenced in the image. Film musicals' transformation of the filmic space through song and dance corresponds to the roles that sound, dance, and editing play in televi-sion advertising positioning strategies. However, within advertising, film mu-sical conventions also intersect with those of music videos, reality television, and screendance to produce other forms of dance-in-advertising.

While "Coke is It—Rehearsal" incorporates dance in a manner that echoes that of the backstage film musical, a second Coca-Cola commercial, "Coke is It—Saxophone," from the 1980s follows a different model for incorporating dance (see video 2.3 ▶). In contrast to the musical theater conventions of the previous Coke commercial, which removes dance to a space of pure expres-sion, this second Coca-Cola ad keeps dance within the diegetic or everyday space, presenting dancing as a part of the social. This difference points to the genre of narrative dance films that rose in popularity during the 1980s (e.g., *Flashdance* [1983] dir. Adrian Lyne), which incorporated dance numbers into classic realist narratives. While this diegetic dance remains within the space of the narrative, the filming, editing and performing body often frame dance as

a performance for other characters and the film viewer. Narrative film sometimes increases this potential by borrowing the film musical strategy of gradually transitioning from diegetic music (i.e., when the acoustics support the
idea that the sound exists within the space of the narrative) to non-diegetic
music that dominates the visual image and cannot clearly be accounted for
within the narrative space.[62] Thus, the activity of foregrounding the soundtrack participates in signaling the characters' entry into a performance mode,
even as the dancing remains within the film's narrative.[63] These 1980s dance
films tied dance and music more directly to the film's diegesis instead of
allowing the number to carry the film into a space of pure excess and expression. Thus, dance in these narrative films plays a central role in the plot and
follows social conventions by occurring within appropriate settings such as
dance clubs, classes, street venues, and theaters.

Echoing the strategies of narrative dance films, the second Coca-Cola ad
consists of cinematically shot action. The actors and dancers are filmed on
location in everyday life situations and contexts rather than in performance
ones. The acting style adheres more to that of cinematic realism than theatrical performance, and the performers' use of explicit forms of direct address
is limited. The scenes vary widely in content, including shots of individuals
dancing and a variety of other kinds of social activity. These characteristics are
evident in the opening scene of the ad.[64] As the commercial begins, the viewer
sees an African-American man wearing a 1980s-style suit and a fedora with a
saxophone strapped to his chest; he dances on a sidewalk in front of a white-
washed brick wall bearing a painting of the Coca-Cola logo. While his back is
to the wall and the camera is directly opposite the wall, he does not perform
to the camera so much as simply dance while being filmed. He never looks directly at the camera, allowing the movement to change his facing without any
apparent effort to explicitly stage his body as a display for the camera's eye.
Rather, he *appears* to allow himself to be seen, dancing fully, but not engaging
in overt acts of projection.

In contrast, the opening scene is followed by a single shot of a group of
graduating students as they toss their caps into the air. Their gowns and caps
are red, and the caps have gold tassels, thus employing what is both a filmic
and advertising strategy of creating matching shots via color and tying the
first location/scene to this second one through the red of the Coca-Cola logo
and the red of the gowns. Further, the ad cuts from the saxophonist landing a
jump to the graduates as they are sinking down in preparation to rise up and
throw their caps; thus, the cut connects the two shots through a continuity
match on the movement.

This second scene is quickly followed by two more brief shots. First, the
camera captures Marines saluting, which picks up the gold of the gradua-
tion tassel while also providing a contrast in color through the blue of the
uniforms; second, the camera cuts to a woman in a yellow shirt who looks

away from the camera as she swings her arm across her body and up toward her head, an action that echoes that of the salute while looking more like a "rejection" of something. These two quick cuts are followed by a new scene, reminiscent of *Flashdance* (1983), featuring two shots of a dancer wearing tights and a crop top while dancing in a loft or warehouse space. The commercial continues in this manner, quickly cutting from one scene to the next, displaying a wide array of social actions, locations, and environments. The style of editing, framing of shots, and image content described here demonstrate filmic techniques and principles.

The "Coke is It—Saxophone" television spot demonstrates how commercials can present dance within the veneer of reality found in realist cinema by altering the mode of address and using narrative cinema's shots and editing conventions. This alteration creates a work that exists in a world unto itself, a world into which the viewer peers voyeuristically. In other words, by not acknowledging the camera, relying heavily on pedestrian action and filmic acting styles, creating the sense of a photographic montage of moments, largely avoiding direct address, and shooting on location, the director promotes a way of viewing in which the camera functions as a window through which the film audience is able to observe other worlds. The ad offers glimpses of other people's lives, as though looking in on other realities whose occupants are seemingly unaware that they are being watched.[65]

Only the opening and fourth scenes (described above) contain "dance;" however, the choreography of moving bodies, editing, and framing devices work together to compose the 30-second spot into a cohesive whole. The commercial consists of 19 scenes and 22 distinct shots, varying in length from 1 to 2 seconds. The only scenes consisting of more than one shot are the two employing a dance movement vocabulary, and the ad contains a disparate array of image content. Only five of the scenes show an actor drinking Coca-Cola. Thus, the ad is clearly organized around the filmic principles of montage, editing together a series of shots that differ in content and work to condense time, space, and information, so that they ask the viewer to construct meaning by reasoning out the relationship between images.[66]

Within the ad's montage, the jingle exists outside of the visual images, acting as a container or way of linking the disparate images together and coloring how the viewer reads the them. The use of the soundtrack is so prevalent in American film culture that audiences are accustomed to music that frames and permeates the visual image, even when the sound source is not readily identifiable. Thus, this ad demonstrates how the presence of non-diegetic music, or the transition of the music from diegetic to non-diegetic, is not sufficient cause for reading dance as bracketed—that is, as carrying the character from the real of the narrative into a space of excess, imagination, or expression in accordance with film musical conventions. Instead, by eliminating the convention of having actors/characters transition from talking to singing and setting the dancing in appropriate social spaces, the dance numbers in narrative films and some commercials effectively remain within the realm of reality, while still relying on dance's *affect* to move viewers in a manner similar to that of film musical numbers.

Stringing disparate moments together, this second Coke commercial draws on montage theory to produce Coca-Cola's *affect*. The montage editing works in collaboration with the ad copy (jingle) to function as a framing device that guides the viewer through the commercial, while also assisting in the construction of the commodity-sign. The shots are synchronized with the Coke jingle to create meaning not only through the syntax of the shots but also through the relationship of the visual content to the lyrics.

For example, the second line of the jingle consists of "a kiss, a glance, it's hot, it's cool, a king, a queen, it's breaking the rule," and each item listed is paired with a shot in which the visual content exemplifies the words being sung. For example, an image of a couple kissing is paired with "a kiss;" found footage of Elvis is paired with "a king," and a shot of a cop giving a ticket is paired with "it's breaking a rule." Both this Coca-Cola ad and the previous one convey the spirit and energy of Coke as a kinetic state of possibilities, out of which erupt moments of excess where the performers' actions are larger, more rhythmic, energetic, and stylized than most utilitarian pedestrian movement.

While "Coke is It—Saxophone" does not employ the full range of cinematic realist conventions, commercials do sometimes incorporate cinema's strategy of "invisible" editing and narrative film conventions to further reinforce the illusion of reality, creating an image that resembles how viewers see the world in their daily lives. Strategies that help achieve the naturalization of the medium's constructed reality include eye-line match devices, point-of-view, shot-reverse-shot, image quality, and camera movement to imbue a sense of the everyday. When these kinds of narrative film conventions are employed, the external (visible) signs of performance are diminished.

However, I argue that in mass media forms dance, whether seen in a social or theatrical context, is always already both a *performance* and the *real*. When television shows, commercials, and music videos are shot using realist film conventions, the presentation of intentional performance is replaced by the opportunity to *observe* dance as *though* it were a performance. In other words, as viewers watching television and film, we understand dancing bodies as a presentation or performance, even when they are framed in a way that suggests they are *real* behaviors. The dynamic is evident to a degree in this Coke commercial; however, I explore the notion in more depth in the following analysis of a Bacardi Rum spot.

In *Reading Ads Socially* (1992), Robert Goldman identifies a format within television advertising that borrows from documentary and narrative film conventions to disarm consumers by disguising the hailing mechanism of the commercial. According to Goldman, the *not-ad* is a television or print ad that exhibits an "avant-garde minimalism" by creating a "post-mortise format" in which the product is integrated into the ad's signifying image.[67] The *not-ad* disguises the ad as a documentary, narrative, or avant-garde film work by eliminating or masking framing devices and ad copy, forcing viewers to decipher the nature and purpose of the televisual text. In other words, by employing filmic codes and conventions, while downplaying or eliminating advertising positioning strategies, the commercial disrupts expectations, which, in turn, engages viewers in the act of decoding. Since the publication of Goldman's theory of the not-ad in the early 1990s, the genre of reality television has extended this concept of *not* to include a range of televisual forms that market the real by presenting themselves as unmediated, unscripted recordings of real people doing real things.[68]

A 40-second Bacardi Rum commercial, "No Bad Dancing" (2005),[69] demonstrates the use of documentary and reality TV codes and conventions to create a *not-ad* that hails the viewer by disrupting expectations and thus inviting the interpretive act of decoding (see video 2.4 ▶). The commercial consists of a montage filmed so that each shot appears to be "home" video footage of people dancing at parties or in bars. Each shot focuses on one or two dancers who possess unique, but not impressive (i.e., conventionally skilled or beautiful) movement styles. In other words, the shots feature soloists who appear to be "bad" dancers because their movements are clumsy, unmusical, stiff, out-of-control, or out-of-style. The perception of these individuals as odd, un-cool, and/or bad dancers is reinforced through their overall appearance and the way in which other partygoers seem to put a distance between themselves and the "bad" dancers (see figure 2.5).

For example, near the end, in a shot that appears to be taken in a bar or restaurant, the viewer sees two men dancing. The camera films them from the side as they face each other, while two women dance next to them but in the background. The dancers are surrounded on three sides by tables and a bar. Other men seated and standing in the foreground watch the two men dance, nodding their heads and appearing somewhat amused by the situation. One of the dancers wears jeans and a white button-down shirt, while the other wears a suit and tie. The one wearing jeans is more awkward. He stands in a wide second with his knees bent, almost as though he were going to squat, as he thrusts his bent arms back and forth in the sagittal plane vigorously, pulsating slightly in his upper body. The movement of his body creates the impression of parts that are not quite united in their endeavor and is vaguely

Figure 2.5 "Awkward" moves convey the value of drinking Bacardi Rum. Commercial. Screen shot.

reminiscent of an unskilled toddler "dancing" to music. His actions and energy gradually increase over the course of the 2.5-second shot, so that he appears both awkward and overly enthusiastic. Both dancing men seem to be paying no attention to the camera, the women beside them, or the men who are watching them.

One continuous soundtrack accompanies the "No Bad Dancing" Bacardi spot; however, as the ad cuts from one shot to the next, dramatic shifts in tempo, rhythm, accents, and/or timbre highlight various aspects of each soloist's movement. The first 30 seconds of the commercial consist solely of these shots of "bad" dancers. At 30 seconds, the viewer sees an adult male with a receding hairline holding a napkin or handkerchief as he snakes from side to side in a decidedly disjointed manner. The male dancer appears to be in a restaurant or bar, somewhat framed by other people dancing in the surrounding space. The viewer sees him dancing for a brief time and then the ad copy, "There's no Bad Dancing," appears near the top of the image, framing him as he dances and functioning as a caption. The ad then cuts to a shot of a Bacardi Rum bottle sitting on a bar as two silhouetted figures dance in the foreground. The image is accompanied by very fine print in the lower left-hand corner that states: "Enjoy BACARDI Rum responsibly," a web address, and information regarding the trademark. The silhouettes on either side of the bottle dance throughout the shot, and as they begin to move toward each other, the blackness of the silhouettes merges to frame the bottle. The next shot consists of an all-black screen with the following ad copy written in white lettering: "The way it should B." The final shot simply consists of this same image with the addition of the Bacardi logo at the end of the sentence.

The format and content of the Bacardi Rum spot correspond to Goldman's concept of the not-ad because the spot disguises its advertising nature on several levels: filming, dancing, visual framing devices, editing, and ad copy placement. Initially, the ad disrupts expectations by not providing any indication that it is an advertisement and by highlighting dancing rather than the product, rum. The ad further perpetuates this confusion by reproducing the image quality of a handheld video camera and by using shots that appear to be candid, as though the footage were shot by an amateur at a club or party. This appearance of candid, amateur footage is furthered by the fact that the people dancing in each shot do not appear to be performing for the camera so much as dancing for the sake of dancing. Additionally, most of the individuals who are the focus of each shot do not appear to realize that they are being filmed, nor do they appear to be self-conscious about, or even aware of, their bad dancing.

When the soloists do acknowledge the camera, they do not seem to be performing for the camera, so much as recognizing that someone is filming them. The solo figures appear to be blindly enjoying themselves, which reinforces the supposed reality of their dancing and thus the realness of their lack of skill. Thus, "No Bad Dancing" hails the viewer by presenting dancing bodies as real people rather than as choreographed or staged dancers. Because the dancers and the film footage appear to be real, the actors' movement produces a kind of self-conscious humor—dancing awkwardly in public is akin to being socially awkward—wherein the humor arises, in part, out of one's own fear of being that person. This humor has a disarming effect. The fact that the commercial aired on television, appearing unexpectedly within the television flow without appropriate contextual cues, means first-time viewers were more likely to engage with the images in an effort to decipher what they were seeing.

Avoiding any mention of the product until shortly before the end of the ad furthers its disguise. Even then, the first ad copy line ("There's no bad dancing") does not convey information about the actual product but instead seems to make an ironic comment about the image content. It isn't until the Bacardi Rum bottle appears in the third to last shot of the ad, not as a mortise but as a part of the signifying image, that the viewer becomes aware of an actual product, which is then reinforced by the additional ad copy and logo that appear in the final two shots. This combination of strategies works to entice the viewer into watching the complete commercial out of curiosity, amusement, or both until, finally, the work reveals itself to be an advertisement.

By putting the audience into the role of observer, incorporating home video filming aesthetics, and presenting the dancing within "real" social contexts, the ad encourages the audience to read the bodies and events as *real*, rather than as *fictional* or *theatrical* performances. Rather than include dancing that alludes to itself as performance, the ad presents a performance that denies its own performative nature. In other words, rather than stylized, choreographed movement that reveals dance training, this dancing appears "natural," though often awkwardly exaggerated. Thus, on the one hand, the commercial posits the dancing as authentic to those individuals and real, regardless of whether or not it is an intentional performance. This performance of the real allows the ad to connect the dancing and Bacardi to tangible social experiences and their *affect* (e.g., being a bad dancer or the fear that one is, being awkward, making fun of bad dancers, being stuck dancing with someone who is, etc.).

The ad copy seems to suggest that consuming Bacardi Rum at social events ensures that there are no bad dancers. However, the reasons why are more open to interpretation. The ad could offer a kind of acceptance—all dancing is good dancing because dancing is about enjoying and expressing oneself—suggesting Bacardi supports the idea that these are good things. In line with that idea, the ad also might suggest that Bacardi Rum makes things good by making them fun, regardless of whether one is a good or bad dancer. Dancing is dancing, and like rum, when we surrender to it, everything is better. However, one might also read the ad as suggesting that drinking Bacardi makes everything more tolerable and possibly more amusing, or simply see it as an ironic, amusing statement about the dancers that links Bacardi to a shared, humorous social experience, making the ad *and* the product memorable.

Goldman argues for the concept of the not-ad as part of a shift in advertising positioning strategies in the 1980s that corresponded to the rise of postmodernism. He identifies the strategy as part of an industry-wide effort to find new ways of attracting and holding the consumer's attention that responded to increasing consumer savviness and skepticism, as well as part of an ironic postmodern view of culture.[70] However, I argue that examining how dance has been utilized in television advertising reveals historical precedents for not-adness that draw on live performance as a model, revealing aspects of the not-ad strategy at work as early as the first decade of television. Furthermore, I extend his theory by looking at how dance has played a vital role in the development of the not-ad concept.

As I demonstrate in this chapter, not-ads simultaneously put into play the codes and conventions of dance and performance, film, and television alongside those of advertising. Now, not only does the disruption of the viewer's expectations function as a form of hailing, but the ad's self-conscious manipulation of codes and conventions has become an additional form of hailing. The ad itself becomes a kind of performance, which the dancing body amplifies. Even in instances when the ad disguises itself as the real, the dancing body creates a performance space by functioning as a spectacle that positions the viewer as audience.

MUSIC VIDEOS AS ADVERTISING, COMMERCIALS
AS MUSIC VIDEOS

An Apple iPod + iTunes commercial featuring U2, "the band" (2004), takes what was by that point the well-established look of Apple's iPod ads (e.g., silhouettes wearing white iPod earbuds dancing against solid, vibrantly colored backgrounds) and combines it with shots of the band U2 playing their song, "Vertigo" (see video 2.5 ▶).[71] The commercial initially alludes to music video conventions by including shots of the band. This allusion is reinforced by the fact that the "musicology of the image"[72] governs the content and editing of the spot. My analysis demonstrates the ways in which the ad employs many of the music video conventions identified by Andrew Goodwin in his analysis of the genre.

Goodwin identifies how aspects of the musicology of the image developed as part of the codes and conventions of the music video formation. The musicology of the image involves: 1) various interrelationships between music (e.g., tempo, rhythm, arrangement, harmonic development, acoustic space, composition/structure, and lyrics) and image; 2) three kinds of visual hooks (e.g., close-ups of the singer/band, the scopophilic male gaze, and visual motifs paired with musical motifs); and 3) the use of "double address" (i.e., singing understood as always implicitly direct address regardless of characterization or the form of address used in the lyrics).[73] The following close reading of the commercial employs Goodwin's concept. I argue that this incorporation of music video conventions is a variation on the not-ad concept identified by Robert Goldman—one that often employs the dancing body and choreography as visual content, positioning strategy, and framing device.

In the initial shots of the iPod + iTunes commercial, both the members of the band, who are seen playing their instruments, and Bono, who is singing, are lit to allow their faces to be visible enough to be recognizable as U2 (see figure 2.6). In contrast, the dancing figures remain entirely in silhouette[74] and their social identity is only visible through the outline of hairstyle, clothing, and dancing-body. Thus, the commercial features the band in much the way a music video would. The ad's framing devices then further emphasize its connection to the music video genre by highlighting the relationship between the music and the visual image (i.e., the musicology of the image).

The spot begins with a side shot of the drummer as he establishes the tempo and initiates the music by tapping his drumsticks four times before hitting the hi-hat cymbal. As the song begins, the ad cuts to a second shot, capturing one of the guitarists playing as he faces the camera. A shot of a dancer in silhouette follows, rather than a shot of one of the band members.[75] Shown

Figure 2.6 Apple's "the band" highlights U2's Bono as the lead singer. Commercial. Screen shot.

in profile, Bono first appears, singing, in a close-up in the fourth shot. This opening sequence allows the ad to be immediately recognizable as an Apple iPod or iTunes spot, but it quickly indicates to viewers that this one is unique or different. In addition, the sequence immediately establishes the musicology of the image, beginning with the shot of the drummer establishing tempo, cutting to the guitarist as he joins the drums and then to the dancer physically (e.g., through lip synch and gesture) counting down in time with Bono's voice as he sings "uno, dos, tres." The reproduction of music video conventions is furthered with the cut to a close-up of Bono in profile as he sings the "four" and gestures in time to the downbeat.[76]

The cut to him singing continues the synchronicity between image and music established in the opening shot, and this mimetic relationship continues throughout. In one notable example, Bono sings, "I'm in a place called vertigo," as the spot cuts to a wide shot of the whole band in an empty, entirely orange, virtual space while the camera appears to do a 360-degree pan around the band that swoops toward Bono as the circle ends, creating a literal spin that visualizes the vertigo of the song.[77] However, this mimesis and musical structuring of the commercial also continues through film cuts that include images where the band or the dancers' actions mirror accents in the music, or the band is seen literally singing the lyrics.

While the configuration of the band in space and the use of spiraling camera shots are reminiscent of the music video for "Vertigo," the ad's visual content differs significantly. Thus, the advertising spot does not reproduce U2's music video. Instead, it "parodies" the music video formation by merging the conventions of music videos with those of advertising,[78] while also employing the specific strategies of Apple's iPod/iTunes campaign. In doing so, the strategies used allow lines of territoriality to become lines of flight. Of course, the silhouette campaigns of Apple's iPod and iTunes ads were already employing music video conventions, so this ad simply makes that connection more explicit. This merger of discourses is particularly apt given that music videos began as a promotional form for music, and iPods and iTunes are both products for distributing and listening to music. Furthermore, music video's shift from promotional form to commodity form inhabits the ad, affecting its length—this version's duration being 2:22 instead of 0:30 secs—and its relationship to the consumer; it functions as a U2 music video in addition to being an advertisement.

Dance and movement play an important role in the ad. The performance by the band signifies the practice of live performance, linking the practice of listening to music via an iPod to the practice of attending music concerts and offering the possibility of carrying that experience with you, wherever you may go. While the viewer's ability to see and recognize the band contributes to this sense of performance, it is their physical embodiment of playing/singing the song that conveys the *affect* of liveness and the identity of the band members as performers. Bono moves like Bono. The kinesthetic qualities of his movement, the way he engages with the surrounding space, the way he directs his performance to the camera, and thus to the viewers, all work to create *affect* and *structures of feeling*[79] that enable identification with Bono and the music.[80]

The iPod/iTunes dancers that appear in silhouette in-between shots of the band support this identification by embodying the music in alternative ways. While different than Bono's movement, their actions still translate the music's tempo, rhythm, timbre, melody, structure, and lyrics into visible corporeal form. Thus, the dancing functions much the way it would in a music video: as a form of synesthesia, as a sign of authenticity, as a marker of identity, as a kind of spectacle, et cetera.[81] Additionally, these silhouetted bodies link the ad to previous Apple campaigns, hail viewers with their performance, and contribute to the commodity-sign by multiplying the levels of signification and social relations found in the image. The dancers offer alternative ways of moving to the music, suggesting individuality within the shared consumption of the song. At the same time, the markers of social identity visible in the outline of their hair and clothing, and the way they move, suggest cultural associations and forms of engagement in the world (i.e., agency) with which the consumer can identify.

ADVERTISING AS SCREENDANCE

Recent developments in the field of screendance have expanded how advertising positioning strategies employ the conventions of dance and film genres, making it possible for the dancing body to hold an even more prominent role within the signifying image. Similar to the iPod + iTunes commercial's allusion to music videos, advertising's adoption of screendance conventions creates yet another variation on Goldman's concept of the not-ad. The following example also stands out within this chapter, because, while produced by a branch of a US advertising agency for a US product, the commercial is an example of a global marketing campaign. The Levi's X Korea National Ballet commercial (2012) advertised their new line of "Stretch to Fit" jeans to the South Korean market (see video 2.6 ▶).[82] Significantly, the ad presents itself as a short film, specifically a screendance. Screendance as a cultural formation consists of dance made for the screen that explores the dance-camera relationship to create a work through dance and moving images that could not be achieved in a stage context.[83] This three-minute and forty-two second film is about five times longer than the average TV commercial airing in twenty-first-century America. Although designed for a specific television market, the ad was globally available via the internet, inspiring online viewers and receiving commentary from a broad range of consumers as well as the advertising industry.

The ad was part of Levi's Go Forth campaign, initially launched domestically in 2009 and then taken to a global market in 2011.[84] Constructed as both screendance and television commercial, the ad employs the filmic techniques of montage and continuity of action to allow the dancers and choreography to travel through six different locations in Seoul, Korea. The opening shot of an empty train station functions as an establishing shot, which is then contextualized first by the appearance of the Levi's X logo in the upper right corner and then by the appearance of the ad copy, "Korea National Ballet" in large text in the lower right quadrant of the screen. The logo and copy appear prior to the dancers and thus, like the initial establishing shot, participate in setting the context for the work. The placement and size of the text, "Korea National Ballet," results in the opening shot placing as much, or perhaps more, emphasis on the national affiliation of the two ballet dancers as on the product being advertised. In fact, this opening could almost be read as credits, providing the name of the company performing and its sponsor. In addition, the text provides key labels, identifying the style of dance for the viewer and reinforcing a Korean national affiliation.

The body of the commercial consists of a duet, beginning with the male and female dancers seated at opposite ends of a row of seats on a city train platform. Following both dance and film conventions, much of this opening scene is shot as wide shots filmed from a frontal, diagonal perspective, which allows viewers to see both dancers, their movement, and their relationship to each other. However, the ad's opening sequence also incorporates close-ups and alternate camera angles to reinforce the relationality of their actions and allow the audience to better capture facial expressions and intention.

At first, the dancers sit simply staring forward; they glance at each other and then look away. She attempts to motivate or woo him into dancing with her, sliding her left leg toward him until he looks at her pointed foot. At which point, she performs a little rond de jambe with her right leg before extending it in front of her to draw herself up to standing as her upper torso reaches back and up in a high arch.[85] He watches her as she continues to dance away and toward him, beckoning him to join. He starts to copy her initial movement but stops when she approaches him. Moving from a wide shot to a medium close-up, she chaîne turns away from him toward the camera and the right edge of the frame. At which point, the film cuts to a new location as she continues to chaîne but now moves away from the camera; this time she moves from a medium close-up to a wide shot. The cut on the movement creates continuity, linking the train platform to the next location. In addition, the cut reveals the dancers to be wearing different clothes, bringing the viewers' attention to the fact that they are both wearing jeans.

This basic strategy continues throughout the commercial: as the dancing and editing transport the dancers from one location in Seoul to another, the style of their jeans changes in each location. In the second location, the male danseur becomes more responsive. He begins to extend his pedestrian gestures into dancing and to follow her as she flits away from and toward the camera, up and down a narrow street. From this point on, with each shift in location, the choreography develops further, so that the structure of the dance resembles a cross between a grand pas de deux and a Fred Astaire and Ginger Rogers duet.

A zoom into her feet as she stands en pointe in soutenu becomes a zoom out to reveal her and her partner in a new location, a landing midway up a grand outdoor stairway, where they perform an adagio in unison. A close up of her back jean pocket cuts to a close up of her hips in a different pair of jeans as she walks away from the camera, revealing yet another new location, a city rooftop. Here the dancers perform versions of classical ballet's solo variations, sometimes joining briefly and, at times, directing their dancing to each other as though in conversation or competition (see figure 2.7). As they come into unison performing grand jetés, the commercial cuts on the action, carrying them and the viewers into a fifth location: empty traffic lanes on a bridge. The choreography of their relationship continues to develop. He is now fully engaged in dancing and moves more into the foreground as they perform simultaneous solos. They come into unison briefly in a sustained arabesque, before returning to their individual choreographies.

The cut to the final location—a sidewalk area bordered on two sides by busy streets—occurs as the dancers position themselves side by side to begin

Figure 2.7 On the rooftop, Kim Li Hoe and Lee Dong Hoon of Korean National Ballet continue their pas de deux in Levi's. Choreography by Hong Sejung. Commercial. Screen shot.

the next unison phrase. The camera establishes a front, and the two come together in what might be considered the coda, moving in and out of classical partnering phrases. In their final pose, he supports her as she stands on relevé with her left leg in a front attitude, after which they drop their dancerly bearings and walk out of frame. Following their exit, the ad copy "Jeans that stretch" appears across the screen. The female dancer returns in an out-of-focus medium shot of her hips and thighs. As she walks across the screen left to right she appears to erase the text. After a brief pause, the male dancer follows, and as he crosses the center of the image, the Levi's logo appears with the caption "Go Forth" just beneath it and the Levi's Korea web address at the bottom of the screen.

The first line of ad copy recontextualizes the duet, confirming that the work is an advertisement and drawing the viewer's awareness to the ability of the jeans to meet the demands of the athleticism, beauty, and line of the ballet movement, thus demonstrating the stretch and fit of the jeans. The ad copy suggests adaptability, as the does the ballet dancers' ability to dance in various locations and, in doing so, to temporarily (re)choreograph those city spaces.[86] In addition, the ballet vocabulary brings particular connotative meanings to the ad: Western culture, globalization, modernity, art, and heteronormative gender roles.[87]

The use of ballet, although Western European in origin, works in conjunction with the locations to connote South Korean nationalism. This sense of nationalism is supported by the Korea National Ballet ad copy, ongoing efforts within South Korea to bring ballet to the people, and the emphasis on globalization within the national agenda.[88] The second line of ad copy ("Go Forth") links the work to the larger Levi's campaign but also to a broad range of ideas summoned by the imperative: go forth and master a skill, pursue your dreams, "conquer" a city, take a chance on a relationship, be brave. The opening (i.e., the railway station) and the closing (i.e., city lights and traffic) shots reinforce connotations of travel, activity, and metropolitan life. However, even as the final ad copy and logo call attention to the fact that this filmic work is a commercial, the choreography, the dancers' presentation, even their breaking character to casually exit the frame, encourage the viewer to understand the content of the work as a theatrical performance.

Correspondingly, the movement vocabulary consists of classical ballet steps adapted to the city locations through the incorporation of stylized pedestrian actions, rather than the traditional pantomime, with occasional moments in which the vocabulary reflects a more contemporary approach to the genre through the modification of steps or the incorporation of non-traditional movement. The dancers' corporeality displays the bearing of classical ballet with its lift, effortlessness, verticality, line, and sense of reserve. As described above, the structure of the work is reminiscent of a classical ballet pas de deux but also of the film musical duets of Astaire and Rogers, conveying the development of a relationship through movement. The shifts in location contextualize this choreographic relationship, grounding the more abstract classical vocabulary within the city and linking it to everyday activities and movements. At the same time, the duet performs a physical journey through the city that complements the interpersonal journey of the dancers.

The sense of relationship and journey are further supported through the filming and editing's connecting of one location to the next through matching shots and editing on the movement. Meanwhile, the camera's placement in relationship to the dancers furthers the sense of performance by subtly defining a front, which is then largely reinforced in the staging of the choreography. The merger of film and dance within the work produces something closer to screendance than advertisement, thus producing a more contemporary version of a not-ad and requiring a reading that accounts for the rhizomatic nature of its construction and its articulations with the world.

The Levi's commercial clearly puts the dancing body in the foreground as the conveyor of social relations and product attributes. The dancing also functions as form of hailing through dance's ability to invoke the direct address of performance. The fact that the product can be worn allows the ad to foreground the product implicitly by foregrounding the bodies. In doing so, the ad further develops the not-ad positioning strategies. In addition, the fact that the dancers are professional ballet dancers means that their dancing can quite literally be both a performance and an authentic (i.e., "real") display of who they are, thus supporting an understanding of the work as simultaneously *becoming-dance* and *becoming-advertising*.

CONCLUDING THOUGHTS

The dance-in-advertising formation, as a site of disciplinary intersections, activates the conventions of multiple cultural forms inside a single work, creating lines of flight and territorialization. Dance-in-advertising, while not the only example of this shift, allows advertising to more easily elide its selling function with the entertainment and aesthetic functions of other cultural forms. By invoking advertising positioning strategies in conjunction with the codes and conventions of dance, live performance, music videos, and film, dance in advertising simultaneously anchors commercials to disciplinary territorialities and disrupts the stability of those disciplinary boundaries. In a sense, dance-in-advertising engages in an ongoing process of creating and disrupting expectations.

The primary disciplinary codes and conventions informing dance-in-advertising demonstrate how advertising's discourse draws on other cultural forms in its production of spectacle, *affect*, and meaning. The dancing body alters and enhances the basic strategies of advertising and how they operate within the commercial format. Each section of this chapter introduced a new aspect of advertising's *becoming* (*-dance, -performance, -film, -music video*) through its engagement with other cultural forms.

Thus, one aspect of the intersecting discourses found in dance-in-advertising is how they help to establish commercials as commodities as well as promotional texts, an echo of a similar shift that occurred within the music video industry. The dance-in-advertising formation as a plane of intersecting discourses consists of ads that position themselves as advertising *and* popular culture, as product *and* advertisement. In other words, as promotional forms, they both sell a product *and* themselves.

My goal in conducting this kind of analysis was to demonstrate how understanding the use of the dancing body in advertising is strengthened by examining dance-in-advertising from multiple disciplinary perspectives. Deleuze and Guattari's concepts of *assemblage, lines of territorialization,* and *lines of flight* offer what I find to be a more dynamic way of addressing commercials featuring dance as sites of articulating disciplines—spaces in which discourses and ideologies assemble to generate new possibilities, even as they reinforce the old. Close readings of commercials provide tangible examples of advertising's polysemy and production of *affect* through the dancing body as *spectacle*. The introduction of stylized movement and allusions to performance point to style as fundamental to product, brand, and consumer identity—concepts that inform the chapters that follow.

CHAPTER 3

Correspondence and Difference

Creating Rapport through Intertextuality

The video image, at first a solid black screen, transforms into the silhouette of a woman's mouth set against a sea of deep pink color. As she sings "La, la, la, la, la," the opening lyrics for the Black Eyed Peas' "Hey Mama" (2003),[1] the video cuts to a close-up shot of her head in profile, still in silhouette, revealing a white earbud and cord. The sound of the last "la" lingers, but the video is off and running as it cuts to a female silhouette against a light green screen; she holds an iPod as she dances a loose samba step in time to the music.

From this moment on, the video cuts quickly through a series of colored screen shots (e.g., pink, green, yellow, and lavender), each featuring one of four silhouettes—two male and two female ones—dancing to the song (see figure 3.1). Some shots play with contrast and depth by featuring two related but different silhouettes of the same dancer—as though the dancer's shadow is dancing with its shadow—creating a kind of choreographic echo. Each dancing silhouette wears white earbuds whose cords lead down to a white iPod that she/he holds while dancing. The dancers are identifiable as individuals not only by the style of their hair and clothing—as revealed in the outline of the silhouette—but by their choreography. Thirty-six seconds into the video, a lavender backdrop with the copy "iPod + iTunes" in bold white lettering appears center screen. The image of the copy lasts for only a second before the video slips back into shots of the dancers, only to be interrupted once again by a pink screen with the copy "Windows" in bold white lettering (at 41 seconds) and then again by a white Apple logo and the copy "iTunes.com" against a green screen (at 43 seconds), which stays through the remainder of the 45-second video (see video 3.0 ▶).

Figure 3.1 Apple earbuds visible, a silhouette dances to the Black Eyed Peas' "Hey Mama." Choreography by Hi Hat. Commercial. Screen shot.

The video of dancing silhouettes set to the Black Eyed Peas' "Hey Mama" (2003) is one of a series of commercials created by Apple Inc. to advertise their iTunes and iPod products.[2] The Apple spot, "Hip Hop," announced the compatibility of iTunes and the iPod with the Windows operating system. The ad was part of a larger, serial campaign in which Apple commercials advertised iPod + iTunes, new features, or new products such as the iPod shuffle. The initial ads featured black silhouettes against colored backdrops, but later ads featured a range of colored silhouettes (blue, purple, red/orange) against light-colored backdrops.[3] These dancing silhouettes quickly became a key positioning strategy for Apple's iTunes and iPod commercials and an important sign of the Apple brand.

For example, one iPod + iTunes ad, "Wild Postings" (2005),[4] features footage of a man with the iconic white earbuds and an iPhone walking down the street (see video 3.1 ⊙). The silhouettes on a series of Apple iTunes posters dance as he (and his music) walks by them. While the silhouette campaign proved highly profitable,[5] as Apple continued to diversify its product the iPod commercials continued to evolve. "Nano Colors" (2006),[6] features dimly lit dancers in an all-black space, each holding a different color of iPod Nano as they sweep their arms through the space, leaving trace forms that match the color of the Nano (see video 3.2 ⊙). Further varying the idea, two iPod Nano with video commercials sacrifice the silhouette strategy, but spotlight the dancing, focusing on the video function of the Nano. Apple's "Capture" (2009)[7] is a montage of individuals dancing in an all-white space (see video 3.3 ▶). In each shot, the dancer is filmed twice, once by the camera filming the commercial and once by an iPod Nano visible in the foreground. The viewer sees part of the dancer on the Nano's screen and part of the dancer within the space of the ad (see figure 3.2).

Apple's "1234" (2007)[8] demonstrates the Nano's ability to play videos in iTunes (see video 3.4 ▶). The ad begins with a shot of a white Nano resting on a white surface as it plays the music video for Canadian Indie singer/songwriter Leslie Feist's "1234" (2007). A hand comes into view and removes the white iPod Nano to reveal a red one underneath—match cuts on the movement maintain choreographic continuity, which consists of dancers in red, yellow, green, and burgundy moving in and out of unison as they shift between formations. The hand returns to remove the red, revealing a light blue one, as Feist joins the dancers in a unison sequence of turning steps punctuated by a clap on the 2 and the 4. Hands continually remove one Nano after another—revealing the options of white, red, blue, and black—before arriving on a blank screen with the copy "A little video for everyone." A shot of Feist bowing, as seen on the iPod Nano screen, follows, and the ad closes with a shot of the Apple logo next to the copy, "iPod Nano." The spot's reproduction of Feist's music video highlights not only the self-referential component of serial campaigns but how this strategy enables "media's negation of their own mediation" by collapsing distinctions between reality and appearance.[9]

In 2005 Apple joined Motorola and Cingular in the launch of the first cell phone with iTunes. Cingular marketed the iTunes-capable phones with

Figure 3.2 The Apple iPod Nano captures dancing bodies. Commercial. Screen shot.

commercials that follow an everyday person who listens to music on her/ his phone as she/he walks down the street, rides the subway, and so on (see videos 3.5, 3.6, and 3.7 ⓟ).[10] While the music plays, her/his shadow and/or reflection dances to the music; when the phone rings, the music stops and the shadow/reflection reverts to echoing its owner's pedestrian behavior (see figure 3.3). These Cingular commercials continue to promote the Apple brand through the dancing shadows and reflections, which allude to Apple's silhouettes, reminding viewers of the original positioning strategy. While the silhouettes function somewhat like a mortise by creating "blank" spaces that allow consumers to articulate themselves into the ad, the introduction of "real" locations and bodies highlights the incorporation of iTunes into mobile phones and furthers the idea that everyone can have her/his personal sound-track to accompany the narrative action of day-to-day existence.

I begin with this abbreviated history of Apple's marketing strategies for iPod and iTunes because it aptly introduces concepts central to this chapter. Apple's silhouette campaign marketed iTunes and iPod through distinctive visual framing devices, eye-catching choreography, and catchy music. Dance and music function as spectacle that helps the ads stand out in the flow of media texts, "hooking" viewers.[11] Additionally, the strategic use of color,

Figure 3.3 With Cingular + iTunes, silhouettes become reflections as the dancing enters the everyday. Commercial. Screen shot.

design, and imagery function as "hooks" and as ways of linking one ad to the next. Thus, these strategies initially serve to catch consumers' attention and then, through repetition, they become associated with the product and help create brand identity. Dance scholar Sherril Dodds argues that these repeating elements not only create a unique "look" for the brand but produce "serial" marketing campaigns. Thinking of each ad as an "episode," the repetition of elements across the series produces a sense of expectation that further promotes the brand. As Dodds argues, "each episode promotes the following episode, yet is self-contained."[12] Apple, like The Gap, produced highly distinctive serial campaigns that viewers learned to recognize.

While the creative, atypical advertising positioning strategies created a unique "look" for the Apple iPod/iTunes brand, the choice to create an abstract space, to highlight choreography and music, and to delay ad copy and logo until the end echoed The Gap's not-ad strategies.[13] By highlighting music and dance the ads assume the appearance of entertainment media, particularly music videos. The Apple campaigns illustrate how dance-in-advertising creates ads that entertain by building on the marketing history of music videos, which evolved from a music promotional form to an entertainment form that also promotes music. Thus, in positioning the commercials as serial not-ads, Apple created marketing that initially hooks and then retains viewers' attention through a combination of eye/ear-catching strategies and entertainment. They offer consumers the pleasure of recognizing the ads as Apple ads, as well as recognizing the music, musicians, or dance forms.

As I demonstrated in Chapter Two, a central aspect of dance in advertising is its incorporation of choreographic, filmic, and theatrical conventions, as well as a tendency to allude to, parody, or otherwise cite specific works from both popular culture and the performing arts. Through dance, advertising borrows everything from specific choreographies to movement styles; whole works from film, television, and/or dance; directorial styles and star personalities; narratives; and other advertising campaigns. These borrowings produce nostalgia and authenticity through correspondence, which hails viewers and produces pleasure, while differences between original sources and the ads create puzzles to decipher.[14] The sense of familiarity engages viewers in decoding the ads as ads. In addition, the pleasure of recognition is reinforced by the production of *affect* as dance and music work with cultural references to produce *structures of feeling*.

In this chapter, I examine how advertising appropriates and reorganizes cultural images (i.e., signifiers) and values (i.e., signifieds) to create new signs (i.e., commodity-signs or preferred readings). Through dance, I explore connections between advertising campaigns, popular culture, cinema, and the performing arts, identifying forms of self-referentiality that collapse distinctions between appearance and reality.[15] In reading individual ads and campaigns, I demonstrate how advertising incorporates and copies existing cultural works to produce spectacle that *hails* viewers and produces pleasure by creating relationality, *affect* through recognition, and *nostalgia without memory*.[16] Consumers, or viewers, actualize *affect* and activate specific meanings depending on their knowledge and experience.[17] By examining lines of flight, mapping the intertextuality and polysemy of commercials, I highlight how they function as planes of discursive meaning-making in which corporations and consumers engage in producing what are often competing and contradictory cultural and social meanings.

SELF-REFERENTIALITY AND SERIALISM

Goldman argues that the not-ad format in television advertising began as a response to the over-saturation of advertising and a resulting consumer skepticism during the postmodern culture of 1980s United States.[18] However, some not-ad hooking strategies, such as dance, have played vital roles in marketing campaigns since television advertising's beginnings. Choreography often works in tandem with media's self-referentiality and advertising's serialism to generate *affect* by engaging viewers in deciphering meaning and recognizing brands via contextual clues.

Apple's serial advertising strategy builds on earlier models. As demonstrated in the introduction, ad campaigns strive to develop "hooks" or elements that capture the viewer's attention and are memorable, including catchy jingles or the use of well-known songs, striking visual compositions, well-known stars or personalities, or references to popular culture or the arts. Even in early television, advertising used the repetition of one or more of these elements across a series of ads within a single campaign, or with variations across a series of campaigns, to help companies successfully brand and market their products. These products are often widely recognized by consumers, regardless of whether a given consumer decides to purchase the product. Take for example the controversial and well-known figure of the Marlboro Man. In the 1950s with help of the Leo Burnett Company, Marlboro cigarettes created an iconic figure that made the brand recognizable to smokers and non-smokers alike. By the 1970s, the company had successfully made smoking a way of life and associated it with the image of the solitary, rugged, "masculine" cowboy.[19] Like the Marlboro Man, iconic choreographies and performers have helped advertising create successful serial campaign structures. To demonstrate this idea, I examine two deceptively charming examples.

Lucky Strikes and Old Gold are brands of cigarettes that have used dance as a repeating, identifiable element and branding tool across multiple commercials. The Old Gold commercial discussed in Chapter Two demonstrates serialism through a form of self-referentiality by using repeating "characters"—the dancing boxes of Old Gold cigarettes and matches and the well-known radio host Dennis James.[20] I use the term "self-referentiality" here to indicate the media practice of incorporating elements in the ad image that refer to other ads and/or media. By using the same figures or elements across a series of ads, commercials build off one another to create an ongoing experience. This strategy can create a kind of narrative through-line, build on character familiarity, or produce variations on a theme that engage viewers through the play of correspondence and difference. I argue that advertising's serialism and references to other media function as forms of self-reflexiveness, because they call attention to advertising's place within mass media and/or marketing discourses. The Old Gold commercial performs this concept on more than one level.

The presence of James in the ad demonstrates mass media's self-referencing nature as his career as a popular radio host preceded his appearance on television. Featuring James in the ad as himself, Dennis James, and having him seated in a living room, smoking a cigarette as he watches the dancing Old Gold characters perform on television refers back to reality and American media, because he is a real person. Even though his radio personality is a performance, Dennis James the radio host is a real person, who, like the at-home viewer, is watching a cigarette box dance on television. He becomes a source of familiarity, and recognition of him becomes a potential site for producing pleasure—either because viewers associate him with positive *affect* and experiences, or because his familiarity brings an increased sense of belonging. Furthermore, his response to the dancing boxes ("it's time for my favorite dance team") transfers this familiarity and sense of belonging to the brand characters, even when viewers are seeing them for the first time. Furthermore, the dancing boxes serve as a mnemonic device. The next time viewers see a dancing cigarette box, it may prompt them to wonder if what they are seeing is an Old Gold commercial and how it might vary from this one.

The Old Gold dancing cigarette box built on the association between dancing and cigarettes established by one of the earliest television commercials. Lucky Strike's "Barn Dance" (1948) captured viewers' attention by animating and personifying the cigarettes (see video 3.8 ▶).[21] In other words, actual cigarettes dance. Product and signifying image merge through choreography. The repetition of this strategy produced a serial Lucky Strike campaign featuring animated cigarettes in large-scale group choreographies, prompting viewers to recognize the brand and find pleasure in their ability to do so, as well as to find pleasure in the choreography and humorous personification. However, the 1948 "Barn Dance" employs intertextuality to produce recognition and *affect* in other ways as well.

LUCKY STRIKE AND THE POSSIBILITY OF "NOSTALGIA WITHOUT MEMORY"

Lucky Strike's black and white commercial uses stop-action animation to film cigarettes square dancing in a barn. The caller is a smoking cigarette who stands on a small, raised platform and calls out a mix of advertising copy and square dance directives.[22] Arranged into couples, the cigarettes promenade and do-si-do around their partners, forming a series of group shapes (e.g., circles, crosses) (see figure 3.4). The potential to produce *affect* exists on several levels, as the ad potentially activates the social relations and cultural meanings associated with square dancing. On one level, the ad abstracts human social relations to attribute them to inanimate objects (i.e., the process of abstraction and reification). This abstraction and reification makes the familiar unfamiliar and creates humor. However, this association also opens the door for viewers to feel a sense of recognition to varying degrees depending on their relation to, and knowledge of, square dancing. This process potentially produces positive *affect* through forms of memory. For example, square dancing potentially evokes "Americanness" and the conflation of humans and objects works in conjunction with parts of the choreography and filming to call to mind cinematic dance director Busby Berkeley's film musicals.

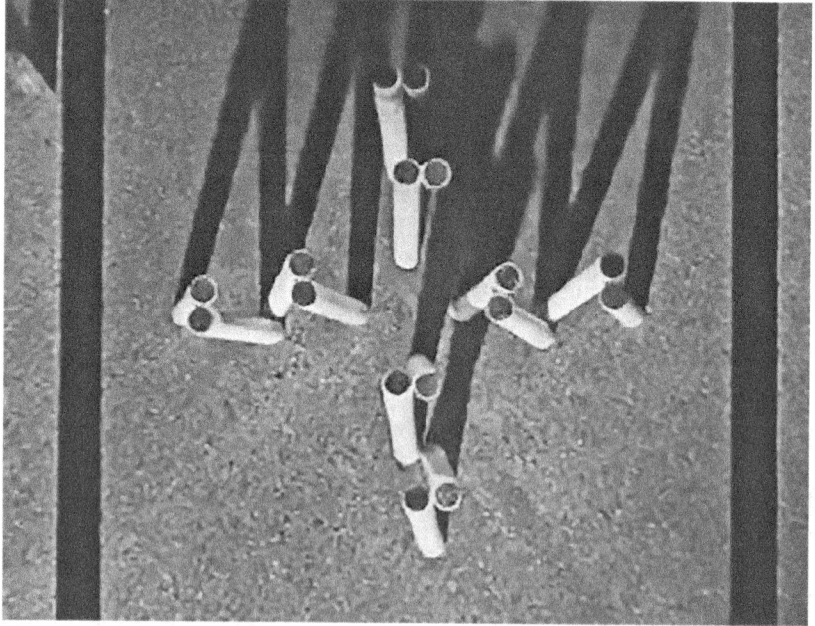

Figure 3.4 Lucky Strike cigarettes square dance. Commercial. Screen shot.

Thus, the commercial references American cultural history through dance, placing disparate aspects of American culture in relation to one another to form a commodity-sign for Lucky Strike. In doing so, the ad activates nostalgia as it reconfigures cultural values and actively (re)constructs historical memory. Colloquially, the concept of nostalgia encapsulates a sense of absence, a longing for what is absent, and a desire for the past as a source of both the familiar and the "real."[23] As an aspect of postmodernity, Fredric Jameson describes nostalgia as a longing for cultural homogeneity that offers a normative foundation for understanding experience, a ground from which to differ.[24] By linking the product to national identity through the histories of social dance and film, the Lucky Strike commercial taps into nostalgia to add authenticity to the cigarette brand.

While the following analysis examines the role nostalgia plays in the advertiser's preferred meaning, I recognize that individual viewers may construct divergent, localized meanings as well. In this case, "Barn Dance" produces nostalgia for a recent past. For example, the square dancing in the Lucky Strike spot generates a kind of utopic nostalgia that imagines the United States as a nation grounded in a unified folk culture derived from European immigrants. Alternatively, it associates the brand with the importance of community as a shared cultural value and highlights social dance as means of affirming social relations. While for many Americans in 1948 square dancing would have been a popular pastime, what the ad activates is the notion of square dancing as American folk culture and as a source of authenticity— one in which the importance of community is a shared value and social activities are about building this sense of community. By associating cigarettes with square dancing—a form that requires harmonious group participation and adherence to a specific set of "rules" that govern steps, pathways, and interactions with partners—the ad suggests that cigarettes are also a form of social interaction with the potential to build community structures or bonds.[25] For those living in urban environments, the ad might also generate nostalgia for an imagined time and place where communities are strong and harmonious wholes. Nostalgia also summons up square dancing's link to the larger history of American social dance as a marker of race and class.[26]

In a similar manner, the spot generates a host of possible associations by alluding to the first generation of film musicals. More specifically, the spot calls to mind Busby Berkeley's 1930s choreography and cinematography for his Warner Brothers film musicals.[27] Midway through "Barn Dance," the camera cuts from a high angle frontal shot of the "smokes" promenading in a cross formation to do-si-do around their partners to an overhead crane shot of the same action. The overhead shot captures the dancing cigarettes as they work together to alternate between a cross formation and a circle, emphasizing the pattern of the coordinated pathways of the group. By introducing a bird's eye view the crane shot draws attention to square dancing's group formations and geometric designs, calling to mind its choreographic lineage.[28] In addition, the camera angle transforms the dance by calling attention to it as visual display and performance.

The ad's use of stop-action animation to achieve inventive visual content and editing corresponds with Berkeley's "spectacularization of the camera" and his tendency to produce kaledeiscopic designs and cinematic illusions.[29] In many of his musical numbers, Berkeley's camerawork and editing reduce the female chorus to that of objects—or sometimes into one big object or inanimate design—either by cutting from a shot of live women to a two-dimensional picture, or by using lighting, camera angles, and long shots to make the women appear to be animated objects. The Lucky Strike commercial uses stop-action animation to reverse this idea, creating the illusion that the objects are the dancers. Thus, unlike Berkeley, Lucky Strike completely eliminates the chorus to allow the object to take precedence. Furthermore, the allusion to Berkeley's crane shots promotes cigarettes as harmless and playful by capturing the viewer's attention with spectacle, illusion, and humor. The ad directs focus away from the more troubling equivalence of people and cigarettes—just as Berkeley's illusions and kaleidoscope designs distract viewers from his disconcerting equating of women with inanimate objects. Correspondingly, the literal equivalence of people and objects allows the ad to quite literally transfer the *affect* and values of square dancing and Berkeley's 1930s film musicals to the product, Lucky Strike cigarettes.

The connection to Berkeley's film musicals potentially produces a "false" memory of abundance (via spectacle) by associating America in the 1930s with the *affect* of Berkeley's dance cinematography rather than the socio-economic strains of the Great Depression. While Berkeley was still making films in the late 1940s, he had left Warner Brothers to work at MGM in 1939. Berkeley historian Martin Rubin notes that MGM's "integration-oriented" musical aesthetic was less receptive to Berkeleyesque spectacle.[30] Thus, in 1948 the era of Berkeleyesque film musicals was the recent past, not entirely gone, but no longer what it once was. Given the inherent contradictions of the ad's allusions (e.g., spectacle vs. community, spectacle at a time of economic depression), the ad holds the potential to enact nostalgia as a form of forgetting as much as one of remembrance. In this sense, the ad potentially demonstrates nostalgia as a desire for an imagined past, rather than a *lived* one.

Paul Grainge, Andrew Wernick, and Fredric Jameson identify similar concepts of nostalgia at work within postmodern, late capitalist culture.[31] I find within the era of neoliberal capitalism the concept has, if anything, become more prominent and established rather than less. American Studies scholar Paul Grainge offers an analysis of how postmodern advertising functions based on the concept of "nostalgia without memory."[32] For Grainge, the phrase, "nostalgia without memory," refers to a form of nostalgia that does not require consumers to recognize a literal, shared cultural or historical memory, rather it refers to the construction of an imaginary, shared cultural history.

Grainge demonstrates consumer culture's use of "nostalgia without memory" in an analysis of a 1993 Gap print campaign. In this instance, by using images of historic artists and cultural figures, the ad campaign linked The Gap's basic khakis and jeans to a classic sensibility that could then be labeled as retro-chic and seen as a marker of hip individuality.[33] Grainge's concept extends Andrew Wernick's analysis of the role of memory in consumer culture in the following way: "Nostalgia, in Wernick's case, is set in a cultural moment where the past has developed a particular discursive power . . . when the past has become increasingly subject to cultural mediation, textual reconfiguration and ideological contestation in the present, memory has become a new locus of both cultural identity and commercial style."[34] In other words, as the past and history have come under scrutiny as a result of shifts in the academy and in culture (postmodernism, Civil Rights movement, feminism . . .), memory and its ability to reframe and reconstruct, as much as preserve, has stepped up to fill the gap.

Following Grainge's lead, I temper colloquial notions of nostalgia with the conceptual sense of a constructed memory or history. Grainge, and the theorists whose work he draws on, argues that "nostalgia without memory" is symptomatic of postmodern culture. By applying his concept to dance-in-advertising, I demonstrate how advertising's production of nostalgia as a longing for a past that is more real due to its intangibility precedes and extends beyond the advent of postmodernism, continuing on within neoliberal capitalism. Rather than a longing for home or a moment in one's past, nostalgia reveals ambivalence in its construction of past times, places, or identities.

In memory's capacity as a tool for smoothing over history's dilemmas, nostalgia comes into play as a way of creating a whole and grounding identity in an untroubled past. I return to this concept in Chapter Four to look at how advertising's appropriation of dance and its production of nostalgia engage with the construction of social identity in neoliberal consumer culture. For now, I employ Grainge's concept in an analysis of how advertising uses intertextuality as a means of engaging viewers. Drawing on the discursive power of the past, commercials use dance to manufacture communities of memory as a means of claiming authenticity and generating *affect* through "nostalgia without memory."[35]

NOSTALGIA WITHOUT MEMORY AND INTERTEXTUALITY

Intertextuality, including serialism and media's self-referentiality, play key roles in the production of nostalgia without memory. Many ads are intentionally highly intertextual in their image content; however, ads incorporating dance, as examined in Chapter Two, typically activate a wider array of codes and conventions from other genres. While intertextuality occurs in multiple ways, dance also often participates in this activity by referencing works that lie outside the commercial text, generating *affect* and binding the ad's polysemy to move toward the advertiser's preferred meaning.

Thus, intertextuality facilitates advertising's efforts to reroute cultural meanings in the creation of new ones. Through intertextuality, advertising produces nostalgia without memory by triggering recognition and engaging the viewers in deciphering the text. Though viewers occupy and read ads from distinct, varying perspectives—making each ad's meaning locally actualized—understanding the richness of possible localized meanings and their various inflections requires looking at ads as intertexts. As with any text, ads can fail to produce the desired reading, be taken at face value, or produce negative responses. Understanding how advertising engages viewers in thinking about and responding to ads-as-texts in productive ways requires looking at how ads use dance in relation to other media to generate *affect* and meaning.

Postmodern literary theorist, Linda Hutcheon argues that allusion's goal—as a kind of intertext—is to highlight correspondence; in other words, allusion emphasizes the similarities between two works.[36] Drawing on previous literary studies, she argues that allusion is commonly employed in order to "hint without directly stating [or] . . . to parade one's knowledge or to use the texts of others for authoritative support."[37] By simultaneously activating two texts (the original and the borrower), allusion allows the borrower—in this case the advertiser—to put ideologies of past/other works into play in the creation of its own meaning without literally reproducing a significant portion of the other work.[38] Within advertising these types of allusions can also bring with them the pleasure of recognition, as viewers become cognizant of sites of correspondence and difference.

This pleasure of recognition can take several forms as pleasure can be found in possessing the knowledge necessary to recognize the allusion, finding affirmation in the repetition of one's experience or knowledge, or experiencing a positive *affective* response (e.g., a sense of familiarity or belonging, a recalling of an emotional response, a connection to a positive time or experience in one's life, etc.). Intertextuality might be said to produce a "phase space" out of which emerge meaning and *affect*.[39] I find that dance-in-advertising offers a way to watch theory at work, to see concepts such as emergence and *affect* in action, so to speak—highlighting advertising's relevance to cultural theory.

A serial campaign by eBay that employs film musical codes and conventions to create spectacle employs dance in each of its ads. The "Do You Know the Way to Use eBay" (2003) spot from that campaign employs intertextuality to create a commodity-sign that produces nostalgia without memory and *affective* meaning through correspondence and difference (see video 3.9 ⊙).[40]

The jingle for "Do You Know the Way to Use eBay" alters Dionne Warwick's 1968 hit "Do You Know the Way to San Jose?"[41] Warwick sings of leaving the glitzy lifestyle and struggle that comes with trying to make it in the entertainment industry of Los Angeles to return to "her" hometown of San Jose, where she hopes to find some "peace of mind" and space to breathe.

Playing off the song's premise of asking for directions on how to get to San Jose, the jingle modifies the lyrics to make the song about how to use eBay, describing aspects of the online bidding site and what it offers consumers. The jingle never addresses anything practical such as "how" to bid. In contrast to the "escape" of the original song, the lyrics of the jingle express the ease with which "millions of people" use eBay to actively participate in consumer culture by purchasing a wide range of goods, directing the song's audience toward consumerism and the spectacle of excess rather than away from it.

While consumers can grasp the point of the commercial (i.e., what it is advertising and why one might want to use the online site) without analyzing its intertextuality, the jingle's relationship to the pop song interacts with visual allusions to create a cohesive commodity-sign and *affect*. Recognition of the song deepens the effectiveness of the ad, because the sense of familiarity reinforces the *affect* of "home" and acts as "hook" that *hails* the viewer. The ad then rewards viewers for engaging by creating humor through difference and producing spectacle. In an additional, though perhaps subtle, ironic twist, the sense of San Jose as "home" conveyed in the original lyrics is transformed into the visual space of the home that opens and closes the commercial. Furthermore, like Bacharach's song, the ad posits a relationship between two places, the home of the consumer and the online shopping/bidding site. Dance facilitates this sense of "home" through its allusion to other mass media works.

The commercial first establishes a "normal," everyday home space. In film musicals, this space would be the space of the narrative or diegesis. Following that, the ad disrupts the home space by transitioning into the space of the musical number—the non-diegetic space of expression and spectacle.

The camera reveals an average-looking den in a suburban home. A computer sits on a desk that faces a wall and a large combination cabinet and bookshelf. The husband sits typing at the computer with his back to the camera, while his wife dusts the bookcase. As he finishes typing, the camera cuts to capture him from his wife's perspective as he says, "Okay, I'm on. How do I get started?" The shot-reverse-shot structure continues as the camera joins him in watching his wife as she turns around to face him. Replying to his query, she begins to sing the opening bars of the jingle as she slides into a pose and slowly pulls her glasses off her face. As she sings, the bookcase cabinet slides apart behind her to reveal a film musical sound stage (see figure 3.5). The reveal of an alternative space echoes the narrative/number structure of film musicals, creating two filmic spaces connected through aural and visual devices: the diegetic

Figure 3.5 The wife sings about eBay as she backs into the space of the musical number. Commercial. Screen shot.

space of the commercial versus the expressive, imaginary space of the musical number.

The world of the musical number comes to life inside the walls of their home. The eBay musical number contains a mishmash of elements that call to mind several very different film musicals through a mix of choreography, set design, and props. As the camera moves into the interior space of the number, it reveals a pyramid-shaped staircase with lines of male chorus dancers arrayed across it in a wash of blue lighting. Four columns, each with a female dancer atop it, frame the sides of the stairs. The back wall of the sound stage resembles a blue sky with white fluffy clouds painted on it.

For me as a viewer, the staging is a hybrid of the dream sequence in *Grease*'s "Beauty School Dropout" number and the opulent set of "Diamonds are a Girl's Best Friend" in *Gentlemen Prefer Blondes*.[42] These two films are not the only ones to employ large choruses or elaborate staircases, but they resonate most strongly for me in terms of production elements and content. These associations are grounded in details within the number. For example, the blue-sky background, blue lighting, and sliver-clad female dancers arranged alongside the stairs are reminiscent of the "angels" and heavenly all-white setting of "Beauty School Dropout." Meanwhile, the male chorus that forms a backdrop for the wife's song, which references money, and the game show opulence of the consumer products featured near the end of the number (e.g., a film/video camera, a shovel, a car, etc.) invoke a capitalist-sanctioned middle-class, married version of the gold-digging fiancé. Thus, the ad alludes to Marilyn Monroe's performance in "Diamonds are a Girl's Best Friend." However, the shift from jewelry to consumer goods blends the musical reference with an allusion to the long-airing game show, *The Price is Right*, creating a parallel between the audience participation of the game show and the interactive nature of eBay's online bidding wars.

Furthering the web of musical references, the ad's 1950s convertible T-bird calls to mind the "Grease Lightning" number from *Grease*, though the car featured in the film's drag race is a 1948 Ford De Luxe. While the car references the 1950s, the attire of the female dancers, their choreography, and their position atop the columns calls to mind the go-go dancers of the 1960s. The reference to the 1960s is further reinforced by the male chorus's choreography, which consists of a cross between modern dance choreographer Ted Shawn's hypermasculine body builder gestures and Bob Fosse's "The Rich Man's Frug."[43]

While these allusions may not resonate with all viewers, the diversity of musical references parallels the diversity of goods to be found on eBay, creating an obvious sense of abundance and pastiche that echoes what eBay offers. As a source of abundance and excess, eBay offers consumers access to a world of potential purchases—many of which are no longer possible to find at retailers, such as classic cars and collector's items, instilling a sense of the aura of the "original"—just as musical numbers offer access to an imaginary world of possibility and expression where everyone can dance and sing the fullest expression of their feelings. The musical narrative/number structure parallels eBay's convenience, highlighting the idea that the world of possibility (i.e., eBay and the musical number) is just a transition, or a computer, away from the everyday world of one's home.

However, on a "deeper" level, the collection of references to the 1950s and 1960s brings a subtle reminder of shifts in consumerism and images of normative American middle-class families during this period.[44] While the wife is savvy in the sense of being computer literate, she is still positioned in a traditional role: for example, the viewer first sees her dusting while the husband sits at the desk. In the ad, the wife facilitates the transition from pedestrian action to spectacular expression, which occurs through her performance of the *gestural anacrusis* (i.e., transitioning speech into song and everyday action into dance).[45] Her performance carries the ad from its representation of the couple's day-to-day reality to the imaginary, spectacular, theatrical world of consumption. In doing so, her role echoes the 1950s positioning of the housewife as the family consumer and reinforces hetero-normative capitalist ideologies of the American middle-class family in which the husband earns the income and the wife spends it. She is positioned as the knowledgeable consumer, the one who has taken responsibility for purchasing the goods necessary to create a comfortable home.

The film musical and television references in combination with the allusion to the rise of consumer culture offer multiple points of entry into the ad's meaning. Additionally, allusions to cinema and pop songs create *affect* and nostalgia without memory in ways that are effective even when viewers fail to consciously grasp the references. The ad promotes nostalgia for the American Dream (i.e., hetero-normative, middle class consumer culture), which was always already a construct and thus exists as a longing for something imaginary. It does this through surface imagery first: the den, the couple, and the lyric/dialogue references to purchasing power.

Likewise, the spectacular excess of the musical number implicitly furthers notions of consumption and money as it details possible purchases. The allusions to film musicals further amplifies this effect by potentially increasing the *affective* power of the ad through its production of qualitative excess. Furthermore, the choreographic quotations and allusions potentially trigger recognition, which activates the *affective* power of the source material, while engaging viewers in teasing out the correspondences and differences. These varied lines of discursive flight ultimately unite within the commodity-sign of eBay, re-routing previous associations and meanings as they join to produce the brand's image.

INTERTEXTUALITY AND *BECOMING-CELEBRITY*

The eBay ad effectively joins the spectacle and entertainment of theatrical performance with the act of consumption, linking the excess and abundance of the musical number with the experience of shopping on eBay. In addition, the ad fosters a nostalgia for being in the limelight and a concept of theatrical performance as a metaphor for being a star or celebrity—for one's life being *special*. In other words, I argue that the eBay brand depicts consumption-as-performance and gestures toward the notion of consumption as *becoming-celebrity*. One way it produces this effect is through its participation in mass media's self-referentiality. I want to look now at examples of dance in advertising that use intertextuality to create *affect* by promoting consumption as *becoming-celebrity*. By treating mass media as the *real*, these ads work to produce consumer pleasure through familiarity that is tied to an increased sense of belonging and/or access to *being-celebrity*. Pop stars in combination with dance in advertising produce this effect.

Arguably, since the 1980s cross-promotional efforts and self-referentiality in mass media have increased, though seriality in advertising predates this increase and can be seen as form of self-reference. Serial structures, cross-promotion, and self-referentiality work effectively together to build brands by catching consumer interest and increasing brand recognition. However, the role of dance within these practices seemingly increased significantly around 1998 with the premier of The Gap's khakis campaign. Preceding this shift, the 1980s saw the rise of music videos and their development from advertising form to cross-promotional vehicle to entertainment, providing a new fertile ground for dance in mass media. As Sherril Dodds argues, dance serves several functions in music videos, including providing visual spectacle, serving the "musicology of the image," and enhancing the authenticity of music stars.[46] Correspondingly, beginning in the 1980s advertisers increased their use of the music video format and music artists in advertising campaigns, particularly those for soda/cola products.[47]

The 1970s Dr. Pepper's "Be a Pepper" serial campaign featuring David Naughton created a strong brand identity using the hooks of a catchy jingle, a recognizable figure, and ad content centered on dance. In the 1980s Pepsi Cola, Coca-Cola (Coke), and Dr. Pepper all created serial ad campaigns using catchy jingles and dance to effectively catch viewers' attention and brand their products. The success of music videos and their initial proliferation on channels such as MTV and VH-1 created an opportunity for cross-promotion that built on the use of existing song and dance in soda advertising. Both Coke and Pepsi built campaigns around well-known music stars. The 1989 Madonna-Pepsi cross-promotional collaboration featuring her single, "Like a Prayer," consisted of a two-minute Pepsi commercial-as-music video and a 30-second commercial advertising the premiere of the two-minute television spot (see videos 3.10 and 3.11 ▶).[48] The Pepsi commercial featured some restaged elements of the music video without literally including any of its footage (for example a church, a black gospel choir, Madonna dancing with the choir). Instead of the video's attempted rape scene and Madonna's interactions with the black saint/Jesus, the ad consists of flashbacks between present day Madonna and Madonna at her eighth birthday party, creating an "intergenerational" exchange.[49]

The ad opens with a shot of white female pop star Madonna sitting in an armchair watching black-and-white film footage of a birthday party. A boy in the film holds up a sign that says "Madonna's 8th Birthday." Eight-year-old Madonna meets the camera's gaze, seemingly looking at adult Madonna. When the camera cuts back to find the singer returning that gaze, the film dissolves to black and white, transporting the adult pop singer back in time to her childhood and carrying the girl into the 1980s. The remainder then consists of the girl watching Madonna perform on television, first surrounded by a racially diverse group of dancers on a city street and then in a soda shop. Madonna eventually appears in an all-black church as the choir transforms "Like a Prayer" into gospel music. At this point, she appears to sing less and instead lets loose, relaxing into dance as the chorus sings and the members of the congregation rise to clap along as they let the music move through them.

Madonna's performance places the commercial in dialogue with her music videos through its reliance on her "gestural idiogest."[50] It is Madonna's corporeal style and its relation to the music that holds the various scenes together. Her easy relation to the music's rhythm and the deceptive casualness of her carefully crafted movement allow her idiogest to live, suspended, inside of the gestural anacrusis. She seems to forever exist on the verge of breaking into dance, even when she performs alongside her backup dancers, or embodies a version of the charleston in a hallway full of schoolgirls. This aspect of her idiogest creates a site of potential, positioning her "dancing" body as the locus of the ad's *affect*, so that she seems to resonate with the vitality of the bodies surrounding her (see figure 3.6).

This transfer of vitality includes that of church members and the black gospel choir. Historically, the embodiment of spirituality through song and dance, the call and response relationship, and the ebullient freedom of expression captured in the ad are attributes of black Christianity that distinguish it from much of white Christianity—where, for example, some branches actively forbid and/or discourage dancing.[51] Madonna, and Pepsi, draw on black culture as a source of authenticity, linking nostalgia for the innocence of youth with the spirituality of African-American Christianity. Her single becomes spiritual expression as the ad's images associate it with religious experiences often found in black Southern Christian churches, much like Alvin Ailey's representation of this cultural space in the last sections of *Revelations* (1960).[52]

Intertextuality in the Pepsi ad merges with cross-promotion and self-referentiality to negate mediation, collapsing differences between appearance and reality. On the one hand, by having one media form (i.e., consumer advertising) reference another (i.e., music videos) the ad builds authenticity by treating Madonna and her video as the real. Taking this logic further, Madonna-the-celebrity refers to Madonna-the-person through the trope of her eighth birthday, merging the world of performance with that of the everyday. By appearing to ground Madonna-the-celebrity in the wishes of her

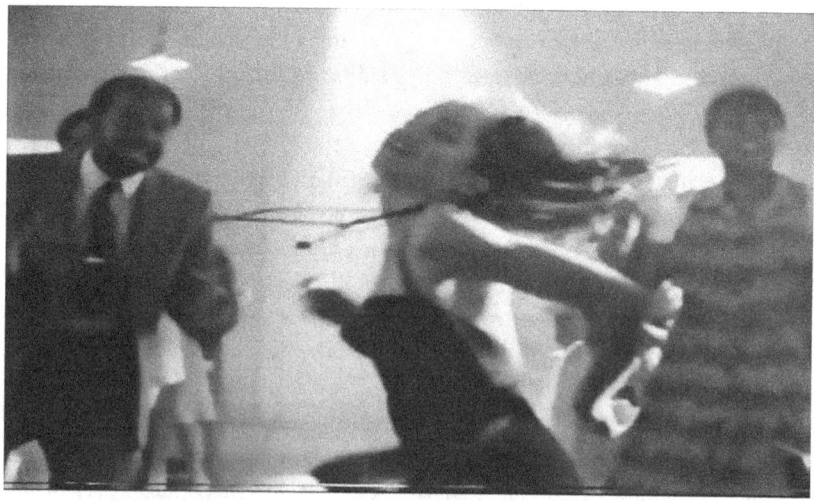

Figure 3.6 Madonna dances in church in Pepsi's "Make a Wish" commercial. Choreography by Vincent Patterson. Commercial. Screen shot.

eight-year-old self, the fictional space of mass media performance merges with "real" world of consumers, blurring the distinction between performance and life. This negation of mediation suggests the reverse is true—that the everyday is like the mediated. Thus, through my consumption, I place myself in relation to *becoming-celebrity*.

THE *AFFECT* AND POLYSEMY OF *BECOMING-CELEBRITY*

This merging of intertextuality and cross-promotion also enables ads to engage viewers in thinking about and responding to ads in productive ways as they attempt to decipher the media text. On a surface level, cross-promotion uses celebrities to hook viewers, produce pleasure, and associate the *affect* of the star with the brand. All three soda brands have practiced this kind of collaborative, cross-promotion by featuring popular music artists in their commercials. These collaborations typically involve singers who also dance, encouraging consumers to watch—rather than only listen to—the ad, and even when the artist is not a dancer, the ads feature dance and/or choreographed action to some degree. Pepsi has worked with a variety of artists including Madonna, Michael Jackson, the Jackson 5, Aretha Franklin, Britney Spears, Christina Aguilera, Beyoncé, Mariah Carey, and the Black Eyed Peas. While many of the various Coke campaigns have featured dancing as the bulk of the image content, a few also have featured music celebrities, such as Paula Abdul, Christina Aguilera, Whitney Houston, and Elton John. Like Coke, Dr. Pepper has often included dance as key image content in its commercials and, at times, has featured popular music artists.

For example, the "Be You" (2002–2003) Dr. Pepper campaign[53] produced a series of commercials featuring current pop stars paying tribute to past music artists. Most of the ads include dance as a major component of the signifying image, and through cross-generational promotion they amplify advertising's polysemy. The ads in which dance plays a central role include the following artist pairings: Anastacia and Cyndi Lauper (2003), the Black Eyed Peas in tribute to Billie Holiday and Louis Armstrong (2002), LL Cool J and Run DMC (2002), Mark McGrath of Sugar Ray in tribute to Buddy Holly (2002), Paulina Rubio in tribute to Celia Cruz (2003), and Thalia in tribute to Tito Puente (2002) (see videos 3.12–3.17 ▶).

Each commercial combines a then-current pop star with one of his/her predecessors, connecting the present with the past, amplifying the potential for meaning and pleasure based on recognition and familiarity, and encouraging viewers to look for moments of correspondence and difference. The range of content across the ad campaign demonstrates an effort to have the campaign-as-a-whole account for socio-cultural diversity, potentially maximizing its ability to generate nostalgia without memory for a wider audience. To demonstrate this intensification of the ad's polysemy, *affective potential*, and possible points of recognition, I look at two of the ads from the campaign: one featuring Mark McGrath and the other featuring the Black Eyed Peas.

The campaign posits Dr. Pepper as a part of American cultural history. The artists featured and referenced in each ad act as points of access for each other, in essence introducing one another to their existing fan base. Nostalgia for earlier periods in American music history is linked to contemporary artists, who in turn lend their celebrity personas to the past and are contextualized by a range of visual signs that gesture toward the historical period; this composite sign is then transferred to Dr. Pepper through the ad's jingle and images of the product and logo. Viewers potentially experience the pleasure of recognizing the artists and are encouraged to seek out who they are, if they don't already know. In addition, once the first ad aired it established a precedent and expectation, prompting consumers to anticipate new pairings in future commercials.

The 2002 Dr. Pepper "Be You" commercial starring Mark McGrath in tribute to Buddy Holly takes the form of McGrath literally stepping back in time to assume Holly's style (see figure 3.7). The television spot opens with a medium close-up of McGrath singing into a 1950s microphone.[54] McGrath sports black chinos and button-down shirt, loafers with white socks, a gold jacket with black lapels and pocket, and black horn-rimmed glasses. His hair is more Elvis than Buddy, loosely modeled after the pompadour. Behind him, a gold curtain and members of a rock band wearing suits and ties are partially visible.[55]

Figure 3.7 Mark McGrath as Buddy Holly at the prom in Dr. Pepper's "Be You" commercial. Screen shot.

At one point, the camera cuts away from him to reveal a male teenager pulling a "girl's" light blue skirt up around her head to reveal the white crinoline underneath as other teens dance and hoot in the background; she struggles and pushes him away. Another cut-away catches a dancer as he slides across the floor on his knees toward a pair of legs that end in red high heels. As he comes to a stop, the camera assumes her perspective, looking down on him as he thrusts a Dr. Pepper can toward her. By this point, it is possible to see the lines on the floor indicating that this dance takes place in a gymnasium. The wide shot that follows confirms this impression as it captures the slightly raised stage where the band performs in front of a curtain decorated with balloons.

"Teenagers" dressed in 1950s-style clothing dance as McGrath pops up from the floor. Black-and-white images of Buddy Holly adorn the bass drum of the rock-n-roll band and the floor of the gym. McGrath moves from one woman to the next as they try to win his attention. At one point, a stack of Dr. Pepper cans arranged on a refreshment table take the focus. A top shot catches the dancers as they rapidly pony across the space in two lines, crossing over the image of Buddy Holly; another shot captures McGrath drinking from a Dr. Pepper with Holly's image visible on the bass drum behind him. As the ad draws to a close, the dancers perform the hand jive, which culminates in them posing in the center of the space.

For those unfamiliar with *Grease*,[56] images of the 1950s, or early rock-n-roll, the ad offers a puzzle to be worked out as choreography, set, and costumes trigger a kind of recognition without memory. Clearly, there is something being referenced, and for younger audiences who easily recognize Mark McGrath, part of the puzzle is figuring out why he is represented in this way. However, for those *Grease* fans out there, this commercial is rife with opportunities to reminisce.

References to the film include the following: the guy pulling the girl's skirt up (happens to Patty Simcox, who ran the decorating committee); the slide on the knees (happens during the dance competition and Danny does it twice while dancing with Cha-Cha); girls fighting over McGrath (references both the bickering between Rizzo and Cha-Cha over Leo, leader of the Scorpions, and Cha-Cha's stealing Danny away from Sandy); a shot of one of the girls pulling up the bust of her strapless dress (Marty does the same action at one point); the lines of dancers crossing the space (happens in the middle of the hand jive); and the hand jive itself. While the reference to Buddy Holly requires some knowledge of rock-n-roll history, it rests primarily on the reproduction of his image via the graphics and McGrath's attire. The moments of correspondence bring pleasure to viewers as they affirm their knowledge of film and music history. The allusions trigger a recall of the *affective* viewing experience, validate consumers' taste, and tap into nostalgia for 1950s America and the birth of rock-n-roll. The overall 1950s aesthetic echoes the embrace of retro fashions as a contemporary stylistic choice; for example, the revival of swing and lindy hop in the late 1990s triggered a similar trend.

Given the lyrics of the jingle and the slogan, "Be You," which appears in the lyrics and at the end as ad copy in the lower right corner of the screen, it is possible to understand the ad's intent without attempting to piece apart the commodity-sign. On a surface level, the ad encourages consumers to embrace their individuality and suggests that Dr. Pepper's taste is unique compared to Pepsi and Coke, like the consumers who drink it. While it is possible to simply take the ad at face value, looking more closely at differences between the ad (2002), film musical (1978), and music references (1950s and 1990s–2000s) deepens the effectiveness of the message. Buddy Holly is a rock-n-roll icon, credited as being a "seminal white voice" in rock-n-roll with a distinctive vocal style.[57] His untimely, accidental death by plane crash in 1959 immortalized him, and his wholesome boy-next-door looks combined with his musical talent made him unique as an artist.

This notion of individuality and being oneself is a central theme of *Grease*. During an era known now for its emphasis on conformity and the establishment of solid, middle-class values, the teenage characters in the musical struggle to find and be true to "themselves." Both Sandy and Danny resist and then succumb to trying to fit the other's image of the ideal mate. Their friends face similar struggles: Frenchy tries to figure out her skill set, Rizzo defends her life choices as a woman, and so on. Ultimately, the ad's intertextuality summons up the teenage angst and efforts to fit in versus being oneself as found in the film, as well as the sense of rebellion and individuality found in Holly's music. Holly lends his singularity to McGrath; *Grease* lends its portrayal of the 1950s to the singers, and together they promote Dr. Pepper. In the end, nostalgia for the *past-as-imagined* takes the form of a celebration of music and culture grounded in notions of innocence, youth, and individuality. To be fair, Dr. Pepper has a distinctive flavor, but the irony, of course, is that the ad promotes drinking Dr. Pepper, a mass-produced consumer product, for its individuality because you, like a million others, are unique.[58]

The irony of the individuality pitch is furthered by other ads in the campaign as they work to diversify the brand's image. The "Be You" (2002) commercial featuring the Black Eyed Peas (BEP) pays tribute to two African-American musicians, blues singer Billie Holiday and trumpeter/singer Louis Armstrong. As in the other ads, the commercial provides historical and cultural context for the music icons via dance. While the BEP ad directly acknowledges Billie Holiday and Louis Armstrong in the opening lines of the jingle's lyrics, which is reinforced when a curtain opens to reveal pictures of their faces, it is the dancing that provides historical context for the musicians. The set design consists of a two-tiered theatrical stage space with a red curtain across the upstage and in front of that a split staircase that arcs down to the main stage.

Instead of rows of seats, there are small cabaret tables with room to dance in front of them.

The ad opens with two lines of chorus girls streaming out of the upstage curtain and prancing downstairs as they holler and wave their hands in the air. Their entrance is accompanied by the sound of the men from BEP singing the jingle, who are revealed entering from under the staircase as the camera cuts to a wide shot to capture the whole stage (see figure 3.8). The chorus appears to consist entirely of long-legged, light-skinned black women wearing red briefs and bra tops draped in black fringe. The costumes are augmented by red-heeled tap shoes, black cloth chokers with large red flowers, and headpieces that combine a large red flower with long, thin black-and-white striped feathers. They call to mind Josephine Baker and the black chorus lines of vaudeville and early Broadway.[59] The overall simplicity of their largely unison choreography (e.g., prances, hip shimmies, and stylized walks) captures the feel of early twentieth-century chorus lines.[60]

This dancing creates a composite allusion. Chorus line floor shows were part of cabaret culture, which might remind one of Armstrong's ensemble work in cabaret venues. In addition, shortly after the introduction, the ad includes shots of the dance floor in front of the stage where black "audience members" dance, performing Charleston steps. This participatory element calls to mind Armstrong's contributions to jazz, Holiday's experiences singing with big bands, and popular dances in African-American expressive culture (1920s–1940s).[61] The naming of the two singers also makes a nod to music history by calling to mind Armstrong's influence on Holiday's development as a singer.[62]

Figure 3.8 Three members of the Black Eyed Peas pose in front of chorus girls in Dr. Pepper's "Be You" commercial. Choreography by Michael Rooney. Screen shot.

The journey through time to the present day is anchored by the members of the Black Eyed Peas singing, particularly will.i.am, who at one point dances down the thrust stage in his signature style.[63] Shots of him performing his loose-legged, sliding, kicking steps are juxtaposed with shots of the audience members' Charleston kick steps, inviting the viewer to find the similarities between then and now. The link between BEP, Louis Armstrong, and Billie Holiday relies on race and musical influences. The syncopation, scatting, and unique vocal phrasing employed by Armstrong and Holiday make the BEP's contemporary R&B style possible. Correspondingly, the dance styles generated in response to jazz music inform contemporary hip hop styles.[64] In this ad, as in the others, the jingle's lyrics suggest a comparison between Dr. Pepper and the musical artists based on both being representative of what it means to be an "original" and an "individual."

The Dr. Pepper "Be You" campaign creates commercials that consist of a pastiche of historical and contemporary references; this use of pastiche incorporates nostalgia metonymically, using signature elements to refer to a larger history.[65] The ads highlight similarity (i.e., music artists noted for their individual style and unique contributions) across time based primarily on race and music genre.[66] However, the ads rely on choreography to evoke the feeling of the historical periods they invoke. Thus, the combination of dance and the contemporary pop stars featured in the ads work to produce a form of nostalgia without memory for consumers, particularly those not already familiar with the historical referents. The reverse is true as well. Older generations of consumers may find the ads introducing them to contemporary artists, so that their nostalgia for a known past colors the present. In both cases, the mixture of old and new triggers recognition and the possibility that consumers will find pleasure in investigating the correspondences.

The Dr. Pepper campaign's tribute to past artists and its construction of nostalgia without memory through dance is not without historical precedent. For example, a 1992 Coca-Cola television spot uses stock footage and the magic of editing to feature Paula Abdul dancing with Gene Kelly and Groucho Marx while Carey Grant admires her from the audience (see figure 3.9).[67] Advertising's creative use of stock footage leads me to the last section of this chapter and the role of parody as a meaning-making strategy in advertising's use of dance. Here I look at how citations and the use of existing choreography in advertising enables localized meanings and participates in the (re)construction of cultural memory.

PARODY AND DANCE IN ADVERTISING → Use in essay

Linda Hutcheon explains parody as "ironic 'transcontextualization' and inversion," as "repetition with a difference," in which a "critical distance is implied

Figure 3.9 Paula Abdul dances with stock footage of Gene Kelly in a Coke commercial. Screen shot.

between the background text being parodied and the new incorporating work, a distance usually signaled by irony."[68] In her genealogy of parody, she identifies what she argues are the essential elements of parody: imitation and/ or borrowing, transformation, differentiation and/or difference, and the tendency to produce a relationship to the model or "original." Countering notions of parody that wed it to ridicule, Hutcheon argues that the "pleasure of parody's irony comes not from humor in particular but from the degree of engagement of the reader in the intertextual 'bouncing' . . . between complicity and distance."[69] Thus, the ability to understand a parodic work is dependent upon the "coincidence" of decoding (i.e., "recognition and interpretation") and encoding. Parody requires that the creator superimpose texts in a manner that incorporates the old in the new and that the work's audience must likewise interpret this superimposition.

She argues that in twentieth-century art parody is a self-reflexive form that employs irony, calling attention to its relationship to an earlier work in order to create new meaning through the interplay of correspondence and difference.[70] In that respect, parody resembles carnivalesque subversion in its relationship to established conventions—both rely on the existence of an established and widely acknowledged set of conventions and cultural forms in order to make their point, because both rely on difference as a means of generating meaning.[71] As a result, parody performs the role of challenging and/or commenting on forms and conventions while simultaneously contributing to the preservation and continuation of those very forms and conventions.

Drawing on Hutcheon's analysis, I explore the idea that advertising sometimes employs a *kind* of parody in which choreography is key to the *transformation* of an "original" work. Typically, these ads either recreate sections of musical numbers, or incorporate stock footage, that metonymically stand in for a larger whole (i.e., the complete work, the star persona . . .). In advertising's choreographic parodies, the original work acts a medium of transmission. The parody acts as a *hook*, or *hail*, that captures consumers' attention and engages them in reading the ad to puzzle out the relationship. Many of these ads are self-reflexive purely in the sense that they call attention to themselves and ground their preferred reading in this form of "repetition with a difference." They activate the original work's *affect* in a new context to produce new meaning(s).

These parodies do not mock or critique the original so much as alter its *affective* resonance and reshape its place in cultural memory. These acts of borrowing position dance and dancers as vehicles of transmission that offer access to the *real* by generating a notion of authenticity grounded in a kind of nostalgia without memory. In this sense, the ads perform or embody a kind of *ambivalence* as they engage in a desire for the past while displacing it. They both draw on cultural memory—generating nostalgia in those who are familiar with the original—and produce it as they introduce other consumers to the work for the first time. Furthermore, parody in advertising works in correspondence with dance to reinforce the genre conventions of dance and film by breaking the conventions of advertising.

My extension of Hutcheon's concept of parody corresponds to Goldman's concept of not-ads and their proliferation during the 1980s. The not-ad is ironic in that it is an ad that is not an ad—just as many of my examples are musical numbers that are not musical numbers, or music videos that are not music videos. In not-ads, as in parodies using dance, meaning relies on the doubling of conventions. In doing so, they remind viewers of the legacies of various media forms and their interwoven histories, and they restructure cultural meanings through their intermixing of various codes and conventions.

While not all not-ads are parodies by Hutcheon's definition, because they do not all rely on establishing a relationship between the ad and a previously existing work, they do employ a kind of double-coding that plays off consumers' knowledge of various media conventions and requires them to engage in decoding the visual text to understand the work's meaning. In doing so, commercials create cultural puzzles that often engage consumers in researching the visual text. This relationship between advertising text and consumers is facilitated by and evident in product websites, online journalism, and internet postings dedicated to calling out these references and making the original material available.

Sometimes these parodies take the form of borrowing the likenesses of the performers to circulate them in service of the product's identity (i.e., commodity-sign). These works are not always successful, but even the failures demonstrate how they participate in a reworking of cultural memory. In 1997 Dirt Devil created three Super Bowl commercials that combine archival footage of Fred Astaire from *Royal Wedding* (1951)[72] and *Easter Parade* (1948)[73] with new footage (see videos 3.18–3.20 ▶).[74] The ads use digital editing to transform solo and prop-oriented numbers into numbers where he dances with Dirt Devil products (see figure 3.10). According to online news stories, fans of Astaire were less than thrilled, and the ads resulted in a drop in sales, as well as criticism of his wife's decision to lease rights to his likeness.[75] One article suggests that the "general feeling was that replacing Ginger Rogers with a vacuum cleaner was in poor taste."[76] In fact, none of the original choreography features Astaire dancing with a human partner, much less Rogers.

Instead, the ads quite cleverly play off his talent for dancing with *props*; I find them to be apt in their allusion to his creativity and performance style. In fact, consumer responses to the ad reflect not only our understanding of advertising's ability to transform cultural history but also the ways in

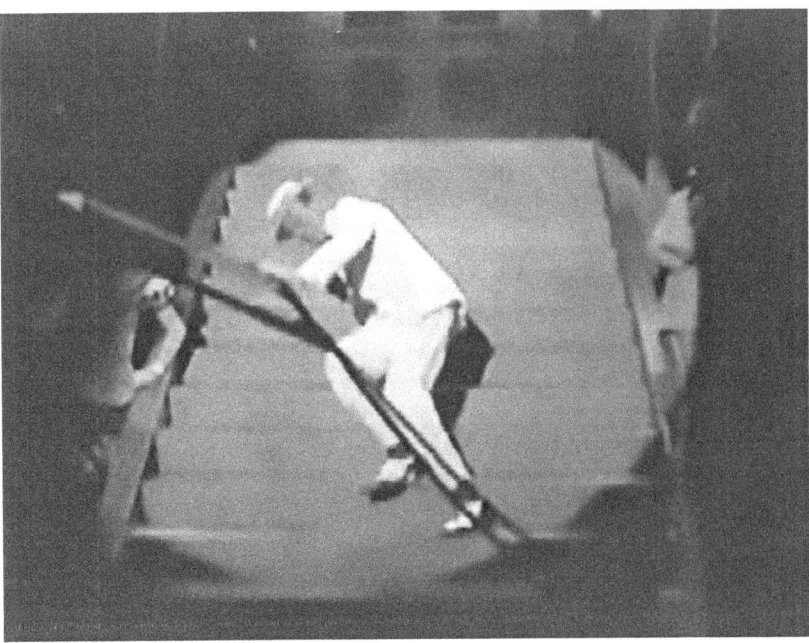

Figure 3.10 Fred Astaire *appears* to dance with a Dirt Devil vacuum in an excerpt from "Steppin' out with My Baby" in *Easter Parade* (1948). Commercial. Screen shot.

which nostalgia is inflected by capitalism's culture of promotion. Memory is selective and promotional forms have residual tendencies; they seem to linger longer than the actual works. Furthermore, celebrities function as promotional forms that employ repetition in much the way advertising does. For example, as seen in this example of the Astaire/Dirt Devil "collaboration," Astaire's celebrity persona, which includes his long-standing partnership with Rogers, retains its vitality better than the details of his musical choreographies. Advertising redirects the performance style and choreographic *affect* of celebrities, transferring it from performer to product and brand.[77]

In a 2011 Volkswagen commercial, the magic of post-production editing transfers a small section of a longer sitting duet—performed by Gene Kelly and Donald O'Connor on an episode of the 1959 Pontiac Star Parade— to the backseat of a 2011 Volkswagen Jetta (see figures 3.11 and 3.12, and video 3.21 ⏵). The ad essentially creates the impression that the two are, say, out car shopping and decide to check out the legroom in the backseat. In this instance, the archival footage from the variety show functions as a part that stands in for the whole of the choreography, the whole of the TV episode, and then, I argue, for a much larger whole, that of Gene Kelly and Donald O'Connor as film musical stars.

Figure 3.11 Gene Kelly and Donald O'Connor tap dance while sitting during a 1959 episode from the *Pontiac Star Parade*. Screen shot.

Figure 3.12 Gene Kelly and Donald O'Connor perform their 1959 sitting tap dance in the back of a Volkswagen Jetta. Commercial. Screen shot.

On the one hand, Kelly's and O'Connor's backseat tap dance, performed entirely while sitting, demonstrates the ample leg room available to passengers, and this intent is made evident when the ad copy "Best-in-class Rear Legroom" appears across the lower half of the image at the "end" of their dance. Compositionally, the "original" dance is a longer work that begins when the two joke with their live audience about how much easier Frank Sinatra and Perry Como had it because as singers they could sit while they performed. The joke leads to the idea of sitting down to do a medley of their film musical dances.

Tap dancing-while-sitting functions as a choreographic ploy to create novelty, as does the wholesale abstraction of the footage and its insertion into the back of a Jetta. The ad puts nostalgia for the golden era of film musicals to work and creates nostalgia without memory by triggering viewers to decipher the puzzle and thus (re)encounter the historical work. While there are, potentially, numerous connections to be made, depending on the viewer's familiarity with the dancers' work, the decision to associate Jetta with the sitting tap dance aligns with previous efforts by Volkswagen to link the brand to popular culture "classics" and key figures in American performance history.

Here, the *real* takes the form of stock or archival footage that serves as *authentic* American culture. Coincidentally, the sitting routine does begin with a medley of Kelly's and Connor's film musical performances, making nostalgia an aspect of its performance on the television show as well. For younger audiences who encounter the ad without previous knowledge of the two performers, the obvious use of stock footage provides an entryway into this discovery of the "past" and potentially an *affective* response based on the value of a cultural history grounded in mass media representations. Volkswagen used a similar tactic to appeal to younger consumers in its 2005 spot featuring Gene Kelly.

The Volkswagen 2005 Golf GTI commercial parodies Gene Kelly's "Singing in the Rain" number from the film musical *Singing in the Rain* (1952) (see video 3.22 ⓟ).[78] In the original, the number begins as Gene Kelly's character, Don, leaves his love interest, fellow actor Kathy, at her door. As their dialogue ends, off-screen (i.e., extra-diegetic) orchestral music begins to slowly fade in. Though it is raining steadily, Don/Kelly waives his taxi away and begins to walk home, umbrella in hand.

As he walks down the rainy city street, high on love, he hums to himself and allows his body to gently sway. At a sudden swell and phrase break in the music, he stops, plants his feet in a wide stance, and opens his arms. Shrugging, he closes his umbrella and allows the rain to pour down on him. As he begins to walk again, he starts singing ("I'm singing in the rain, just singing in the rain") and stepping in time to the music, holding the umbrella over his shoulder as his left arm gently swings back and forth. With each musical swell, his pedestrian walk becomes more stylized and rhythmic, mirroring accents in the music, as it gradually becomes a traveling dance. Singing and tapping intermittently, he continues down the street until, finally, he stops singing and erupts into an extended dance sequence. As he taps, he manipulates his umbrella and interacts with the rain water and the city street. The number climaxes as he jumps off the curb into a large puddle and stomps around, kicking the water, until a policeman walks over, stops, crosses his arms, and stares at him. At this point, Don/Kelly steps back up onto the curb and smiles. Closing his umbrella, he shrugs, sings "I'm dancing and singing in the rain," and begins to walk away quickly as he waves goodbye.

In the film musical the set is designed to resemble a city street and sidewalk of the 1930s/40s with storefronts and lampposts, and periodically, Don/Kelly passes other pedestrians as he travels. The Volkswagen commercial reproduces the set design with certain key exceptions; however, the ad's set is still recognizably that of the film musical number. Like the number, the commercial follows Don/Kelly as he dances down the street to "Singing in the Rain." However, the ad differs in key ways, and these differences allow it to function as a form of parody.

The contemporary flows into the past through the dancing. Don/Kelly is played by three different dancers (David Bernal, Crumbs, and Jay Walker), who wear replicas of Don/Kelly's suit and have been made to look like him through a combination of make-up and CGI effects.[79] Thus, at first, on the surface, the commercial appears to literally be the film musical number, simply lifted out of the film and placed in a new context. However, the differences soon become apparent. In the ad, at the moment when film musical Don/Kelly normally breaks into song, the ad's off-screen music abruptly "scratches," as though being manipulated on a DJ's turntable. Rather than singing, he begins to dance to a big beat remix of "Singing in the Rain" by Mint Royale that includes digital samples of the original music and vocals.[80] Occasionally the ad's Don/Kelly appears to join the soundtrack and sing along. From this point on, the choreography, like the music, is altered significantly, while still retaining the essence of the original. Now, instead of mixing the stylized pedestrian actions with tap dance, the ad's dancers combine pedestrian movement with liquid popping, inversions, somersaults, aerials, and break dancing. In addition to altering the choreography and music, the entire commercial only lasts one minute, whereas the musical number lasts almost four.

Despite these differences, the basic structure of the number remains the same, and several movement motifs from the film appear in the commercial in an updated form. While the ad replicates the set design, the walk is much shorter, so that several storefronts are missing, and the dancing infiltrates the walking (via a popping-influenced movement style) as soon as the music breaks. Instead of giving his umbrella away at the end of the number, Don/Kelly hands it off to a gentleman passing by at the beginning of his traveling dance, freeing up his hands and enabling the introduction of acrobatic vocabulary. Much of the movement that was once subtly stylized, rhythmic pedestrian movement is now obviously dancing, as movement travels successively through his arms and torso. Rather than hopping up to stand on the base of a lamppost, he grabs the post with both hands and hauls his body up, kicking into an inversion. Unlike the original, this Don/Kelly touches the ground with more than his feet, cartwheeling and somersaulting to bring him to the end of his journey.

The two versions converge, and yet still differ, as the ad finds its resolution. In the film, Don/Kelly encounters a policeman just as the dance climaxes with his puddle jumping, at which point he regains his composure and returns to walking. In the ad, the camera/crane dollies back and up to reveal a white Golf GTI as Don/Kelly somersaults into the street, cartwheels into a backflip, rights himself and then drops into a hand spin (see figure 3.13). A policeman watches his entrance, crossing his arms over his chest as Don/Kelly spins. When the dancer pops back onto his feet and turns around, he stops suddenly as he sees the car (arms opening out to either side as though surprised) and tips his hat toward it. The cop watches the whole thing, but Don/Kelly does not seem to ever look directly at him. Thus, while the police presence in the original suggests the reintroduction of social order and norms, in the ad his role is less clear.

Rather than oppressive social forces, such as policemen and normative social behavior, bringing an end to Don/Kelly's foray into the world of excess and expression, the car brings him to a halt. In this final sequence, the cop is on the left-hand side of the screen, while Don/Kelly is toward the right side; the car sits between them. What was a moving crane shot taken from above,

Figure 3.13 Volkswagen's "Gene Kelly" performs a hand spin beside the Golf GTI. Commercial. Screen shot.

cuts to a wide shot from the front that allows the viewer to see the Volkswagen symbol on the front grill. In the last shot, the viewer sees an all-black screen with the Volkswagen logo, first with the ad copy, "The new Golf GTI." After a moment, a quick dissolve reveals a second line, "The original, updated."

The ad copy provides a contextual clue to let consumers know there is a puzzle to be solved, directing them toward discovering the original "Singing in the Rain" and Gene Kelly, as well as what the two have in common with the 2005 Golf GTI.[81] For viewers unfamiliar with the musical, the combination of the set design, opening bars of music, and the soundtrack's remix suggest a blending of old and new. When the ad aired, deciphering the ad's content was furthered by other media, as press releases and news articles identified the original material and explained the process of making the commercial.[82] The relationship between the original film musical number and the commercial reflects historical shifts and developments in movement vocabulary, technology, and style/aesthetics; however, the relationship extends beyond surface comparisons. Gene Kelly's tap dancing is indebted to Africanist movement practices, which also inform contemporary forms like popping and breaking. Linking the two together points to the influence of Africanist movement aesthetics on both "street," or social, and theatrical dance forms. Thus, on one level, the ad alludes to the history of jazz dance, linking tap dance and breakdancing through their histories and the role of city streets and clubs in the development of the two forms.[83]

Tap dance developed out of the mixture of European and African step dances brought to the United States through immigration and slavery and incorporates Africanist aesthetic principles and values. Improvisation, vitality, and the aesthetic of the cool (i.e., calm detachment within virtuoso displays of skill) alongside quick, nimble articulation of the feet and rhythmic sophistication are all valued qualities and skills.[84] While the form and movement vocabulary in breakdancing and popping differs from tap (e.g., nimble articulation transfers from the feet to the whole body), they share Africanist movement principles.

In addition, dance and film musicals posit movement as an *expression of interiority*. In musicals, the stylized, rhythmic movement of dance is understood as an outlet for an excess of feeling.[85] As a vehicle for expression, dance manifests what the individual is otherwise unable to fully articulate in words. The inclusion of hip hop reinforces this concept, associating the choreography with the *corporeal orature* of African-American expressive culture.[86] By tapping into the musical's narrative/number structure, the ad reproduces the transition from the practical, everyday world to the theatrical world of expressivity, creativity, and imagination. In the world of imagination, the *possible* outweighs the *probable*.[87] The connection to this world of possibility and expression buoys the ad's concept of "updated" by associating it with the concept of innovation, a term associated with originality built on tradition.[88]

For those who recognize or discover this history, the ad validates contemporary practices, grounding them in tradition and authenticity. In addition, the use of a loved icon (i.e., Gene Kelly), a film musical viewed as an American classic, and the connection to African-American culture encourages consumers to view the German Volkswagen Golf GTI as "American." The ad manipulates nostalgia for America's cultural history and the currency of American popular culture into *affective* currency.

Thus, the ad suggests the car is not only technologically updated and functional but also hip (i.e., youthful, vital, and cutting-edge) and authentic (i.e., steeped in tradition). How the commercial differs from the original musical number points to the vehicle's value—updated technology and aesthetics paired with the compact dependability, versatility, and the power of a Volkswagen Golf GTI. It retains the essence of Volkswagen (a German brand known for its durability) and of the Golf GTI's style (its *itness*).

CONCLUDING THOUGHTS

Both the ad's content and positioning strategies clearly evoke the original with the intent of highlighting the differences between the film musical and the commercial in support of the commodity-sign. To not consider the relationship between the number in the film musical and the number as it appears in the ad is to fail to fully grasp or appreciate the ad's intended meaning. While the ad copy conveys the preferred meaning in a literal way (i.e., this version of the Golf reflects current values and/or needs), the visual and aural content of the commercial fully expresses the commodity-sign, and the dance and music bring the relationship between original source material and its reproduction to light.

Thus, Volkswagen's parody of "Singing in the Rain" demonstrates how advertising and mass-media's intertextuality often incorporates self-referentiality. While the musical is fictional, it is a part of people's lived reality, which allows it to generate nostalgia for earlier periods in American history but also for earlier periods in consumers' lives. The incorporation of the film musical into the commercial merges fictional and lived realities, enabling consumption to become a mechanism for participating in the worlds of film and television, as well as merging past and present.

I argue that this form of borrowing is a kind of parody because its recuperation of the past performs a kind of ambivalence.[89] The ad's metonymy uses Kelly's likeness to repeat the cultural history of white bodies displacing black ones.[90] Kelly stands in as a source of originality despite the ad's choreography originating in other bodies. In a similar way, Volkswagen uses *Singing in the Rain* to stand in for a nostalgic vision of American culture, one that it constructs anew, building Volkswagen into the history as it links the 1950s to the 2000s. For younger generations, the ad's puzzle allows them to participate in this construction, building their concept of Americanness and potentially producing a nostalgia for a history they never knew. The ad's vision of American national identity produces a kind of authenticity and a ghost of the transcendent *real*.

Advertising models the production of new meaning built on *correspondence to* and *difference from* prior cultural products, introducing consumers to the pleasure of deciphering a work's connective tissue and creating meaning through complex webs of association and the practice of remixing existing work. Dancing bodies inhabit past and present simultaneously, pulling the two together to live within them. Through dance, bodies become the locus by which meaning and *affect* transfer to the product and brand. Offering a potential point of identification for consumers, dance-as-*affect* and dance-as-agency engage consumers in the production of localized meanings. In this sense, the spectacle of dance-in-advertising participates in the construction of social and personal identity.

CHAPTER 4

Consumer Culture and Appropriation

Advertising, Dance, and Social Identity

Suddenly, to the sound of the Black Eyed Peas' "The Boogie that Be" (2003)[1] the television screen flashes to a picture of a digital screen, slightly blue in tint and bordered on each side by black, with the word "You" and an arrow pointing toward the right. To the beat of the music, the digital screen appears to slide left as though being swiped or wiped away, each new screen revealing a new word: "Let," "Musical," "Worlds," "Collide." When "collide" slides to the left, it reveals a shot of a country-western bar and a mixed-age group of white dancers in Western-style clothing line dancing to the "Boogie that Be." Over the course of two eight-counts the camera captures the line dancing in five wide shots, each taken from a slightly different angle, including the last shot where an older gentleman steps away from the wall at the back of the room to join the crowd in a hand clap and double-tap isolation of the hip to the right just as the BEP sing, "get your booty bumping."

Just after the next downbeat, the screen suddenly begins to slide rapidly through a blur of images before settling on a new scene. A packed crowd of punk rockers pogo dance to the sounds of "Mr. Lee" (1957) by the Bobbettes. A short series of wide and medium-wide shots captures different details of the crowd, including a "skinhead" madly shaking his head side-to-side as he bounces. The screen blurs, sliding rapidly, and comes to a stop on the image of a "sweet" older lady with white hair, wearing a white dress and cropped black jacket, as she sits at a table along the wall. Other men and women of a similar age are seated around her; the men wear button down shirts and the women, dresses. She begins to "air drum" along to the percussion of DJ Assault's "Work it, Shake it" (2003), and then a cut to an extreme wide reveals her location in a hall where the 73rd Annual Polka Festival is taking place. The center of the room, arranged longways, is filled with male-female couples polka dancing. The lyrics provide a frame for the dancing. As a male voice says, "I like when you shake it, work it, shake it," a medium shot captures a woman pivot turning as her male partner holds one of her hands overhead, while swatting her skirt as she spins.

Again, images slide by in a blur before suddenly landing on a medium-wide shot taken from behind a DJ at a turntable. One arm raised and pulsing to the beat, he faces a sea of bodies at a house party. The three shots that follow reveal black Americans getting down, bodies pulsing to the music, which just happens to be Jimmy Sturr's "I Love to Polka" (1995). In contrast to the previous scene's female polka dancers in full, knee-length skirts, shots of the house party reveal women in tight-fitting terry cloth jumpsuits, shorts, and tube tops. Another blurring swipe of the screen reveals an alley where a cypher is taking place. In a series of wide shots, the dancers solo and/or duet in the center, breaking and popping to the sound of the Charles Daniel's Bands' performance of "Orange Blossom Special" (1974) (see figure 4.1).[2] The rapid-fire bluegrass fiddle matches the seemingly endless reservoir of energy coming from the dancers. The image begins rapidly sliding through all five scenes to land on a shot of the actual iPod screen as it scrolls through a list of musical genres (electro, hip hop, country, polka, pop, rock . . .).

Figure 4.1 A b-boy spins to "Orange Blossom Special" in the cypher that ends HP's "Mash Up" commercial. Screen shot.

The list is rapidly followed by a quick, animated digital zoom out to a graphic representation of a white iPod against a black background with its tell-tale earplug cord curling next to it. The Apple logo and the ad copy "iPod+HP" appears below it and then slides to the left as "you+HP" slides into its place. The iPod image animates, transforming into the blue concentric circles of HP that expand out to reveal the HP (invent) logo and the URL, "www.hp.com/music," at the bottom of the all black screen. Beginning in the final moments of the cypher scene and continuing through to the end of the ad, the voiceover states: "You have all your favorite music living happily together in one place. Introducing the Apple iPod from HP. Your PC will never be the same again. HP invent." Finally, in the very last moment of ad, the viewer can just barely hear what sounds like a male voice from one of the music/dance scenes say "whoa, that's hot."

This 60-second HP Apple iPod commercial, "Mash Up" (2004),[3] clearly hails the viewer (see video 4.0 ▶). The camera's framing of the iPod screen places the viewer in the role of navigating the device's various menus, creating the impression that the viewer already holds the product in his/her hand and positioning him/her as subject/consumer of the iPod. The sliding of dance images across the screen mirrors the way the iPod screen transitions from one menu to the next. This positioning suggests that the range of dance and music genres displayed in the ad "belong" to the viewer. The positioning strategies work with the ad content to suggest that the iPod is an extension of the consumer, an electronic miniature version of the individual's personality as reflected through musical taste. However, the ad also suggests that Apple's iPod is for everyone, regardless of musical taste or social group.

I begin with this commercial because it introduces key concepts operating through dance in advertising and their relationship to social identity in the era of neoliberal capitalism. The ad's hailing, on the one hand, enacts the Althusserian concept of subjectivity, the subject as consumer being called into existence by and in relation to external powers/forces.[4] At the same time, the ad also elides music choices and social categories, presenting social relations and identity as a series of pre-fabricated options. This elision occurs through the mismatched music and dance genres captured in the swipe of the iPod. In other words, while the ad's image content conveys the fictional user's interest in a range of music genres, the humorous, clever juxtapositions of music and dance rely on assumptions about social groups that are tied to racial and ethnic stereotypes.

The consumer's ability to mix and match genres suggests a subject that stands outside of these stereotypes—the consumer as imperialist—even as it reproduces *static* social identities. So while, on the one hand, the commercial suggests consumers are not bound by their group affiliations or social identities—defining themselves through consumption rather than biology or social relations—the ad also points to consumer society's *appropriation*, or borrowing, of social relations in the service of capitalism. In this manner, I argue, HP and Apple's "Mash Up" explicitly demonstrates how advertising employs dance to simultaneously perform race as natural *and* as constructed.[5]

As the HP Apple iPod ad demonstrates, contemporary advertising promotes a concept of "conspicuous consumption"[6] that performs social status as based not only on gendered class and economic power but also on race and cultural knowledge. The ad engages with neoliberal capitalist discourses that value and use cultural knowledge as social and economic currency. "Mash Up" introduces how advertising models the appropriateness of appropriation as a tactic for living in a neoliberal capitalist society, demonstrating the subjection of social relations and culture to economic laws. Drawing on dance historian Pallabi Chakravorty's analysis of interculturalism in dance, I argue that dance in advertising "highlights the availability of all cultures of the world for consumption."[7] Correspondingly, the ad points to how mass media, as a whole, participates in the defining, maintenance, and transformation of social categories. The ad opens the door to considering how consumer culture liberates social relations from lived experience and puts cultural meanings into circulation as a system of unmoored signs.

Dance in advertising plays an important role in the promotion of constructed categories of social identity. While concepts of blackness and whiteness are often subtly instilled in advertising through dance, ideological subject positons based on gender, sexuality, and class intersect with race within these constructs. A key part of this dynamic is how dance-in-advertising often associates products with popular culture in ways that invisibilize its social origins, liberating cultural products from their practitioners and social contexts. Thus, dance in advertising participates in a complex interplay of social formations. While advertising sometimes employs dance to *recognize* social groups, it continues to participate in defining and reinforcing social identity categories in ways that serve consumerism, neoliberal capitalism, and hegemonic ideologies. In other words, advertising's borrowing of marginalized groups and their cultural products points to the heterogeneity of United States culture embedded within the hegemonic discursive structure of whiteness.[8]

Thus, in this chapter, I take up the question of how dance in advertising participates in this conflation of social identity as both essential and constructed, examining advertising's relationship to neoliberal capitalist economic ideology, concepts of appropriation and transmission, *affect*, and cultural values. My analysis concentrates on a recurring racial relationship evident in advertising and dance in the United States. The "Mash Up" commercial points to the deep influence the African diaspora has had, and continues to have, on US consumer culture. Approaching social identity through the lens of this relationship, I examine the performance of blackness and gender through dance to explore advertising's participation in cultural discourses.

"MASH UP" AS A MODEL FOR THE COLONIAL CONSUMER

The HP Apple iPod "Mash Up" spot offers a productive entryway into a deeper consideration of dance-in-advertising's relation to appropriation and interculturalism. The commercial puts ideologically-defined subject positions into play as the ad reinforces racialized understandings of social/popular dance. The humor of mixing dance and music genres arises from the juxtaposition of the social categories associated with them. For example, the ad plays off associations between polka's European heritage and white, older conservative Americans and contrasts it with youthfulness and the "now" of early twentieth-century dance music and its ties to African-American culture. These juxtapositions implicitly tie Africanist movement aesthetics to black bodies and Europeanist movement aesthetics to white bodies.

Additionally, "racial" movement aesthetics are promoted through choreography and casting. White bodies are shown enjoying country line dancing, polka, and pogoing.[9] The polka and line dancing emphasize order, form, and contained energy, minimizing torso and hip articulation and reinforcing an overall attachment to verticality. While the pogoing breaks from this sense of order and form, it does so through rebellion via lack, emphasizing the disarticulation of the body's relationship to rhythm and the production of "chaotic" energy. In contrast to these three, in the freestyle house dancing and b-boying, torsos and hips articulate, and grounded bodies engage in syncopated rhythms. Dancers break from rigid verticality to allow energy to flow freely and visibly while still retaining form. Thus, each of these dances participates in maintaining an understanding of white bodies and their dancing as inherently different from that of black bodies.

These racially marked differences in movement styles are often maintained in advertising content, even as they are disrupted by the consumption and appropriation of black cultural practices. Cultural discourses within US history have marked black bodies as having natural rhythm and an inherent ability to dance while also denoting African-American dance practices as "vulgar"[10] and less refined than white ones.[11] "Mash Up" reproduces the former notion, emphasizing the rhythmic complexity and "polycentrism" of African-American dance as well as implying a heightened and more explicit sexuality (via women's clothing in the house party scene) in comparison with the white dance forms.[12] Thus, the juxtaposition of dance and music forms highlights the racial markers of American subcultures while reinforcing heterosexual gender roles.

Even as the ad posits the "I" of the iPod consumer as not reducible to socio-cultural markers of race, ethnicity, gender, class, or age—or for that matter clothing, dance, or music preferences—it reproduces social categories based on these markers. Thus, the ad strategically employs static understandings of social categories to mobilize individual identity.

Correspondingly, the commercial demonstrates how communities and their cultural practices and products are subject within neoliberal capitalism to consumerism.[13] The iPod acts as a physical form of assemblage, as a site wherein the various sides, or interests, of one's personality merge through one's consumption of culture.

Thus, I argue that the ad's tactics for creating humor model how dance in advertising participates in the preservation of ideological notions of racial identity *in conjunction with* a growing emphasis on the transferability of racially marked attributes, as well as other markers of identity. The mixing and matching of dance and music genres serves as a metaphor for the idea of a privileged subject position from which an individual may consume cultural products at will. In my analysis, I draw on post-colonial theory's concepts of cultural appropriation and interculturalism, examining advertising's appropriation of dance in relation to practices of borrowing where a dominant, typically Euro-American cultural group assumes use and/or ownership of the cultural products of a subordinate, often non-white, group.[14]

Drawing on the work of Pallabi Chakravorty, I find a parallel between advertising's *borrowing* of social dances and the cultural appropriations undertaken in the West within practices of "interculturalism."[15] While advertising promotes a form of interculturalism among consumers where the power distribution is potentially more equitable than it is between advertisers and social groups, it sanctions cultural borrowing without attention to how the implications are not the same for all social groups or individuals. Technology and globalization continue to complicate forms of cultural borrowing outside, but also within, the United States where race, gender, and sexuality still inform access to class and power. Chakravorty suggests that the form of appropriation found in interculturalism is "subsumed under the master narrative of capitalism."[16] In correspondence with Chakravorty, I argue that dance in advertising, such as in the "Mash Up" commercial, is evidence of the equivalence of cultural practices and consumer products. This construction of the world-as-product corresponds to neoliberal economic ideology.

In his *A Brief History of Neoliberalism*, David Harvey argues that neoliberal politico-economic theory "proposes that human well being can best be advanced by liberating individual entrepreneurial freedoms and skills within an institutional framework characterized by strong private property rights, free markets, and free trade."[17] Correspondingly, as a political and economic system, he argues that neoliberalism assumes that the freedom of the market ensures the freedom of individuals. This return to free market ideology, according to Harvey, positions "market exchange as 'an ethic in itself'" and "seeks to bring all human action into the domain of the market."[18] His extension of neoliberalism's politico-economic ideology posits a hegemonic function that pervasively infiltrates cultural discourses, informing everyday thinking and living. My analysis of dance in advertising demonstrates this discursive operation, suggesting that ads model capitalism's relationship to culture and the individual as capitalist.

Correspondingly, "Mash Up" positions the viewer as the iPod user, who has access to a wide variety of music and dance genres, and thus, the commercial models a privileged, unmarked subject position and offers the possibility that within neoliberal capitalism all consumers can assume "white privilege." The ad's visual metaphor produces a notion of the individual as a unique, distinctive collection of interests. Furthermore, the emphasis on the consumer's eclecticism suggests a liberation from social identity as a determining factor of personal identity. However, its positing of identity as relational and emergent relies on reductive representations of dance forms abstracted from their social contexts and put into a system of equivalence and exchange. Thus, the ad suggests that neoliberal capitalist economic ideology translates, at the level of the consumer, to a kind of cultural appropriation or mimicry—the colonial consumer.[19]

Dance facilitates this ideology through its association with the construction of personal identity. Dance theorist Thomas DeFrantz identifies this notion at work in late twentieth-century dance discourse and argues: "Social dance is inevitably tied to the construction of personal identity, by dancers and the participating audiences who observe them."[20] While DeFrantz identifies this link between dance and identity in hip hop, dance historians have identified similar connections across Western genres at different historical moments. Dance in advertising enacts a kind of metonymy in which stylized movement vocabulary stands in for the totalities of both product/brand and marginalized social bodies and practices. This dynamic produces the effect of abstracting qualitative aspects of dancing bodies and "transferring" them to product and consumer. For example, US advertising facilitates the spread of black social dances beyond their communities of origin and stresses their appropriation by, and transformation within, a capitalist political economy.[21] I argue that "Mash Up" is just one example of how advertising's borrowing of African-American dance vernaculars plays a role in the ongoing construction of American national identity.

I am tempted to say that "Mash Up" is an example of advertising's borrowing of dance as kind of *fetish* in which movement vocabulary and style work with compositional form to stand in for African-American dance practices, which in turn stand in for socio-cultural values that are linked to discourses of American nationality. In the ad's use of black social dance, there is (as in parody) a kind of "intertextual 'bouncing' . . . between complicity and distance."[22] The dancing echoes the complicity of parodic forms by demonstrating similarities between its dancing bodies and those of the social bodies who practice it. However, at the same time, the ad distances the dancing from its African-American so-cial history—a distancing that DeFrantz points to in the spread of black so-cial dances within American popular culture. The difference created by this distancing functions not as a critical distance by which to comment on either the ad's conventions or the source of the movement, but rather as means of si-multaneously evoking and disavowing Africanist aesthetics and social values. Dance as a site of contestation in which communities negotiate shifting values, identity politics, or generational relationships is reduced. Within "Mash Up," the corporeal orature of the b-boy cypher becomes a literal and metaphoric representation of the iPod's potential versatility and its role as metaphor for the consumer's perceived individuality.[23]

In the context of this chapter, I show how the presence of black social dances in advertising often functions based on a kind of ambivalence. Reproducing dance outside of its social context allows dance forms to facili-tate both desire and displacement as traces of bodily difference stand in for marginalized social bodies. In essence, mass media's transmission of black social dances beyond their communities of origin reproduces ideologies of race in America even as it seemingly embraces Africanist aesthetics.[24] The ambivalence lies in the simultaneous apparent desire for and disavowal of African-American culture, as is evident in the widespread use of black social dances in mass media alongside the upsurge of racial violence in the twenty-first century. I argue that this embrace reflects a desire for the appearance of unity in retrospect, a retroactive unifying vision of American national identity that lays claim to the contributions of African-American culture as property. In this way, the ad offers consumers a kind of nostalgia without memory, a nostalgia or desire for a reconstructed and imagined shared cul-tural history.[25]

Thus, the role of dance is to provide access to an intangible *real* that stands beyond the consumer's reach. Here, I use the term *real* to refer to forms of authenticity and *affect* that dancing bodies lend to products. Advertising employs dance to create authenticity through apparent (i.e., imagined) access to social communities and cultural values that once were, or might otherwise be, held at a distance. As I move through the remainder of the chapter, I examine examples of advertising's cultural appropriations and how they abstract dancers and dance forms from their original social context, ignoring their histories and cultural complexities, to utilize the aesthetics of movement in a production of meaning that serves product and brand identity. Thus, as I show, advertising employs the spectacle of abstracted movement in ways that rely on essentialized, reductive notions of social identities. Within US advertising, blackness as a cultural construct works in tandem with the construction of whiteness to create representations of race that mobilize specific attributes and values while reproducing binary constructs.

I step "backwards" here to a historical example of dance in advertising to il-luminate the concept of ambivalence in relation to consumer culture. The potential jarringness of Red Rose Tea's "Savoy Ritz" commercial (1960) for a modern critical audience makes it an effective foil to much contemporary advertising (see video 4.1 ▶),[26] because it demonstrates the appropriation of dance and music indebted to marginalized social groups as a sign of inclusive-ness.[27] This jarringness arises from its combination of chimpanzees and jazz, which amplifies the sense of ambivalence operating within late twentieth- and early twenty-first-century advertising.

Even as the ad embraces the influence of jazz culture on American national identity, it relies on the implicit reproduction and circulation of a racial stere-otype. The novelty and humor of the chimpanzees' performance participates in both the invisibilization of African Americans and their cultural practices and demonstrates how advertising's appropriation of culture reveals a form of post-colonial ambivalence within constructions of national identity. Here, I gesture back to Paul Grainge's use of Arjun Appadurai's concept of "nostalgia without memory," which I introduced in Chapter Three. Appadurai's use of the phrase points to global capitalism's construction of the past and how it enables people to consume images from a cultural history that is not their own.[28] However, I use the term more broadly here to refer to a constructed sense of a shared past and a shared longing for a constructed past. While Appadurai seeks to theorize globalization, my analysis aligns with Grainge's in that, like him, I seek to explore how advertising functions as a site of the constitution and "reconstitution of American national identity."[29] More spe-cifically, I aim to show how dance plays a fundamental role in advertising's (re) constitution of Americanness.

The Red Rose Tea ad depicts the Marquis Chimps at the "Savoy Ritz," using a catchy jingle and the anthropomorphic humor of chimpanzees performing jazz music and swing dance to capture the viewer's attention.[30] An establishing shot reveals the outside of a building with an overhanging marquee that reads "Savoy Ritz."[31] With the help of editing, the black and white image appears to part at the middle and open to reveal the interior of the club. A jazz quartet of chimpanzees, wearing suits with plaid jackets, occupies the stage: featured are a pianist, drummer, trombonist, and bass player. Shots of the band are intercut with shots of a male/female chimpanzee couple swing dancing: she wears a white dress with black polka dots; he wears a black suit jacket and white pants (see figure 4.2). There are two shots of the dancers: one shot in which the boy holds the girl's hand as she spins and one in which they hold each other in a ballroom embrace and turn in place. At about the midpoint (32 seconds) of the 55-second ad, the camera cuts to a shot of the lead vocalist at a microphone as he appears to scat, singing: "Eeeee, Yowww Yowww, Red Rose

Figure 4.2 Two of the Marquis Chimps dance at the "Savoy Ritz" in a Red Rose Tea commercial. Archived on the Detroit Kid Show website. Screen shot.

Tea! Red Rose Tea! Red Rose, Red Rose!."[32] A series of band shots follows, including close ups of each of the four musicians. The TV spot comes to a blaring finish with the sound of a cymbal crash and a close up of the drummer waving his drumsticks as he appears to scream "Red Rose!"

While the chimp's performance alludes to swing dancing more than it accurately reproduces it, the dance and music are central to the ad's production of *affect* and Americanness.[33] In the case of Red Rose Tea, the chimps' mimicry (i.e., being "almost the same, *but not quite*")[34] of humans produces a site of ambiguity and nostalgia without memory that allows the ad to serve the (re)construction of Americanness in localized ways. Despite the Marquis Chimps' origin as a British theatrical group,[35] the group was known in the United States by the time the ad aired.

Their popularity and success in England had led to an invitation to appear on the Ed Sullivan Show in 1958, as well as on comedian Danny Kaye's show and in his Broadway production, The Danny Kaye All-Star International Show. The group went on to appear in American film and television during the 1960s, including a total of eleven appearances on the Ed Sullivan show. Their appearance on American television in other formats suggests that for some viewers the group would produce a sense of familiarity, or recognition, that would have acted as a form of hailing. However, regardless of the troupe's origin or familiarity, the allusion to swing music and dance associates the ad with American cultural history and its debt to African-American contributions in music and dance.

Within an American context, the name "Savoy" alludes to New York City's Savoy Ballroom in Harlem, a historic site in the development of African-American vernacular dance known for being the home of Whitey's Lindy Hoppers. The Savoy was open from 1926 to 1958 on Lenox Avenue and sought to provide the predominately African-American community of Harlem with a luxurious entertainment and dancing space.[36] The popularity of the club and its notoriety as a site of innovation in vernacular dance made it a popular destination for both black and white couples from outside Harlem, including celebrities.[37] Dance at the Savoy became a locus of cultural exchange and integration, contributing to the spread of Lindy Hop and the rise of swing dance in mainstream, white American culture.[38] The chimp couple's very basic choreography in combination with the Savoy marquee, costumes, jazz quartet, and scatting to swing music work to construct an image of a moment in what was then the recent past of American cultural history.

Through the allusion to jazz and big band leaders, the chimp's scatting furthers the association with African-American cultural contributions and their invisibilization due to segregation practices. I am thinking here of someone like Cab Calloway and his Cotton Club Orchestra, who are featured in one of the first Hollywood films to star an all African-American cast, *Stormy Weather* (1943). However, while film musicals and shorts provided a venue for black performers in the 1930s and 40s, blacks were typically confined to musical numbers that could be edited out in the South.[39] In 1960 Americans would rarely have seen black stars in narrative films, and when they did appear they were confined primarily to roles that reproduced racist stereotypes. Though the 1950s saw the rise of Sydney Poitier (who won an Academy Award in 1963) and tap dancer Bill "Bojangles" Robinson (who appeared in several films in the 1930s and 40s, including *Stormy Weather* as well as in other films as partner to well-known child-actor Shirley Temple), blacks were largely excluded from the industry. The presence of blacks on television was severely limited also, and black actors were largely confined to racial stereotypes, except for performers on variety shows in the 1950s.[40] I revisit this aspect of film-television history to point to how the chimps' mimicry enables a cultural nostalgia grounded in ambivalence. The representation of black bodies by chimpanzees allows the ad to embrace a desire for African-American music and dance as part of a shared American cultural history while displacing the "problem" of race.

I am not arguing that the racial implications of the decision to feature chimpanzees in this ad, or the others in the campaign, were necessarily intentional. However, regardless of intention, how the casting perpetuates existing ideologies and facilitates *affective* engagement with the commercial is informative in understanding advertising's appropriation of black dance in the late twentieth and early twenty-first centuries. The chimps implicitly link the ad to colonial practices in which indigenous, non-whites were treated as less than human and seen as emblems of the primitive.[41] In addition, the first half of the twentieth century saw jazz music and dance linked to the concept of primitivism.[42] Dance scholar Brenda Dixon Gottschild examines modernism's construction of primitivism within art and culture in the twentieth century, demonstrating its role in the appropriation and assimilation of Africanisms into American mainstream culture. Gottschild offers several examples of this exchange and how they participated in the simultaneous embrace and disavowal (i.e., "invisibilization") of African-American contributions.[43]

The casting of the chimpanzees permits both desire for and disavowal of black cultural contributions while avoiding the need to confront the history of race relations in the United States. While accounts of US race relations and African-American cultural contributions have been more fully addressed by other scholars working in various disciplines, I revisit them both to establish dance-in-advertising's role and to highlight how the ad's generation of *affect* allows it to participate in the construction of a shared sense of nostalgia that fails to account for this history. This production of *affect* and nostalgia is evident in online comments about the commercial.

The *Detroit Kids Show* website devotes a whole page to the Red Rose Tea "Savoy Ritz" commercial. The website's author, Detroit television archivist Ed Golick, recalls seeing the ad as a child, notes its "cult" status, and refers to it as his "personal holy grail."[44] In 2013 Richard Kienzle wrote an article about the popularity of the ad and its original soundtrack for the Pittsburgh *Post-Gazette*.[45] Both sources cite how the song's popularity led to it being recorded and sold as a single in 1968.[46] Journalist Doug Krentzlin also recalls staying up late with his friends to see the ad on WRC in the DC Metro area during the Friday night Late Movie, which aired at 1:00 am.[47] The apparent enthusiasm of these accounts is reiterated in online commentary by people who remember watching the ad as a child.[48] Much of the commentary citing the ad as a favorite of childhood either does not address the potential racial stereotype or outright denies being aware of it in the 1960s. While the ad's audience may or may not have been aware of the ad's connotations at the time, the commercial's positive reception then, and enthusiastic responses to it by people seeing it for the first time online, reveal the ease with which advertising often divorces black cultural expression and its history from the social bodies that produce it.

This absence is particularly troubling given the history of race relations in Detroit, notably the riots of 1943 and 1967.[49] Additionally, this ad aired during a period of civil unrest, at a moment when black civil rights were being contested on a national level.[50] The depth and breadth of the possible connotations I outline and the sense of nostalgia expressed by consumers online points to the complexity of advertising's reception. However, I argue that this ad's ambivalence, its simultaneous embrace and invisibilization of African-American cultural products, demonstrates how contested culture can function as fundamental to constructions of national identity and personal histories.[51]

THE COMMODIFICATION OF CULTURE

While this chapter's analysis of dance in advertising looks at the commodification of black cultural expression, one of my larger goals is to use the ads in this chapter to examine the "discursivity of the commodity"[52] and its relation to constructions of social identity. In her Marxist analysis of appropriation and exploitation in US consumer culture, cultural theorist Miranda Joseph extends his work to theorize consumptive labor. Her re-examination of what qualifies as labor and its relation to the "discourse of private property" troubles understandings of appropriation within capitalism. Drawing on Amy Robinson's work, Joseph argues that the "logic of appropriation reinvokes and relies on a discourse of private property, which is precisely the discourse that functions to separate subordinate groups from social goods. According to Marx, exploitation is not appropriation; it is not the taking of property that properly belongs to someone else."[53] There are two aspects of this argument that I want to engage with here.

Joseph's analysis draws attention to how cultural critiques sometimes threaten to perpetuate the discourses and systems they attempt to disrupt. Thus, on one level, the attempt to look critically at capitalism's exploitation of social groups may end up reifying capitalism. While my goals are to put dance in advertising into conversation with cultural theories and disciplinary analysis, I realize that in doing so, on one level, I am assigning it significance and weight—in a sense affirming its power. However, advertising's pervasiveness and intersection with other forms of cultural expression warrants substantial consideration. Correspondingly, I often fear that in identifying ideologies or categorizing social identities I participate in the oversimplification and codification of a complex and ever shifting event in which the choreography of ideology encounters self-organization and the tactics of improvisation at play in individual performances of identity.

Joseph's argument that appropriation, defined as a dominant group's taking of and profiting from cultural forms of a subordinate group, assumes a capitalist perspective by invoking a discourse of private property points to how shared social relations and cultural forms are implicated into the capitalist system as exchangeable entities. Adopting Marx's distinction between appropriation and exploitation, or the control of production within an asymmetrical power relation, Joseph argues that, for example, the "problem . . . with the incorporation of hip hop into sneaker ads, is not that someone has stolen a cultural form that properly belongs to one group but that corporate appropriation of the given form or style make it at least in part alien to and against those who generated it."[54] She argues from a perspective that asserts culture is not an object subject to ownership. However, her argument is potentially problematic in its move away from questions of appropriation given the tendency of capitalism to equate bodies with things, the history of the "propertization of black persons," and the objectification of women.[55]

In her study of choreographic copyright, dance theorist Anthea Kraut highlights the complexity of dance's relationship to capitalist structures and the concepts of private property. While choreography was not legally copyrightable until 1976 and social dance is not included within the scope of the law given that it would limit public access to expression, Kraut's analysis offers two important counter-arguments to previous scholarship on copyright.[56] First, she establishes how "choreographic copyright has served to consolidate and to contest racial and gendered power."[57] Second, she argues that "copyright's value for choreographers lay in the way it enabled them to position themselves as possessive individuals and rights-bearing subjects rather than as commodities and objects of exchange."[58] She then connects this tactic to crises of reproduction, arguing that dance's corporeal nature results in dance having "strong ties to the bodies that generate them" and suggests that "dance-maker's bodies are deeply implicated in the circulation of their choreography."[59] By analyzing specific instances of dance's circulation, she demonstrates how they can result in the commodification of bodies and the objectification of subjects/producers.[60] While my goal here is not to delve into the copyright status of advertising, or the dances within it, I concur with Kraut's assessment. Given advertising's discursivity, advertising's borrowing of dance, ultimately, has critical ramifications for consumers as subjects and the construction of social identities.

The power of advertising's discursivity is captured in philosopher Brian Massumi's analysis of neoliberal capitalism's *affective* power as grounded in the "decoding (rendering immanent of signs as vectors of indeterminate potential) and deterritorialization (the drawing off of the event from its general-particular spaces of expression)."[61] This dynamic is evident in the Red Rose Tea ad, which dislocates African-American cultural contributions from their historical context and communities of expression to put them into circulation within consumer culture. The liberation, or deterritorialization, of African-American cultural expression enables divergent readings that participate in advertising's mobilization and production of ideologies and social relations in ways that affect lived realities.

While the Red Rose Tea commercial provided an entryway into an analysis of appropriation in advertising and its reproduction of social ideologies related to race, the ad makes limited use of dance and so offers little in terms of looking at corporeality's role. To examine the conceptual complexities of advertising's appropriation and exploitation of social groups and their corporeal cultural expressions, I look to Brenda Dixon Gottschild's articulation of the "Africanist aesthetic" in American culture and performance forms. By returning to her use of the term to denote the five basic principles[62] of the Africanist aesthetic and "concepts and practices that exist in Africa and the African diaspora and have their sources in concepts or practices from Africa,"[63] I highlight how the transmission of dance in advertising continues to integrate African-American culture into the national imagination. However, I, also acknowledge that twentieth and twenty-first-century advertising operates in a world informed by mass media where imbricated social groups and subcultures merge and intersect to form the everyday fabric of people's lives. In the next section, I trace an example of advertising's corporeal borrowing from marginalized groups and its contribution to the construction of white masculinity.

MOBILIZING SOCIAL IDENTITIES: MASCULINITY AND AFRICANIST AESTHETICS

The following Dr. Pepper commercial from 1998 demonstrates how dance in advertising mobilizes Africanist principles in the construction of white masculinity (see video 4.2 ▶). The ad begins by immediately placing the viewer into the middle of a scene. In a medium shot, a young (8–10-year-old) boy holds an apple in his left hand and looks up at someone as he approaches the camera. Behind him rows of desks with children seated at them reveal him to be in a classroom. As he approaches, he sweetly says, "Happy Birthday," before the camera cuts to a shot of his teacher, who wearily says, "Oh, good, another apple," and adds the apple to the already sizable pile on her desk. Looking up, she scans the room and with an expression of concern, or possibly curiosity, and brightly asks, "Where's Danny?" A quick cut reveals a close up of a hand running a comb through water. Then, a quick series of shots reveal Danny (another young white boy conservatively dressed in dark trousers and a white oxford shirt with tie) in the bathroom, looking in the mirror as he slicks back his hair with a comb. The cut to Danny brings on the onset of the music soundtrack, the Bee Gees' hit "Staying Alive"[64] introduced to US audiences in the popular film *Saturday Night Fever* (1977), which catapulted John Travolta to fame in part due to his magnificent strut.

Danny finishes combing his hair and sharply turns toward the bathroom door. The ad cuts to a medium-wide shot of the closed classroom door a second before it swings open to reveal Danny jauntily leaning in the doorway—legs crossed, one arm propped against the door frame as the other holds up a can of Dr. Pepper. On the lyric, "Oh, you can tell by the way I use my walk, I'm a woman's man, no time to talk," Danny struts into the room, nodding his head and swinging one arm in time to the music. Pausing at the center of the aisle, he pivots sharply and heads up the aisle to the teacher's desk. A series of quick medium close ups captures students as they stare at him, singling out individual responses. As he walks, three different black girls smile at him admiringly. A white, blonde girl gapes at him in shock as he works his way up the aisle. In the back of the classroom, a black boy grooves (i.e., he sits at his desk, rhythmically leaning side to side) along to the imaginary (i.e., non-diegetic) music embodied in Danny's walk. A shot of the teacher reveals her standing, arms crossed, smiling resignedly, rolling her eyes, and shaking her head, as though this behavior is typical of Danny, the "ladies' man."

Just as he reaches the teacher, Danny smoothly transitions into a triple turn, stopping quickly at the end to thrust the Dr. Pepper can toward her. When she says, "Thank you," he winks, and a cut to a new shot reveals one of the black girls in the back dancing in her seat and smiling broadly (see figure 4.3). After a shot of the teacher taking a drink and smiling at him, the camera cuts back to Danny as he backflips down the aisle and slides into his seat, folding his arms across his chest. The chorus sings "Dr. Pepper" (in place of "staying alive"). In the final shot, as Danny slides into his seat the ad copy "This is the Taste" appears across the screen, and Danny slouches, smiles smugly, nods, and performs a "back at cha'ya" gesture with both arms.

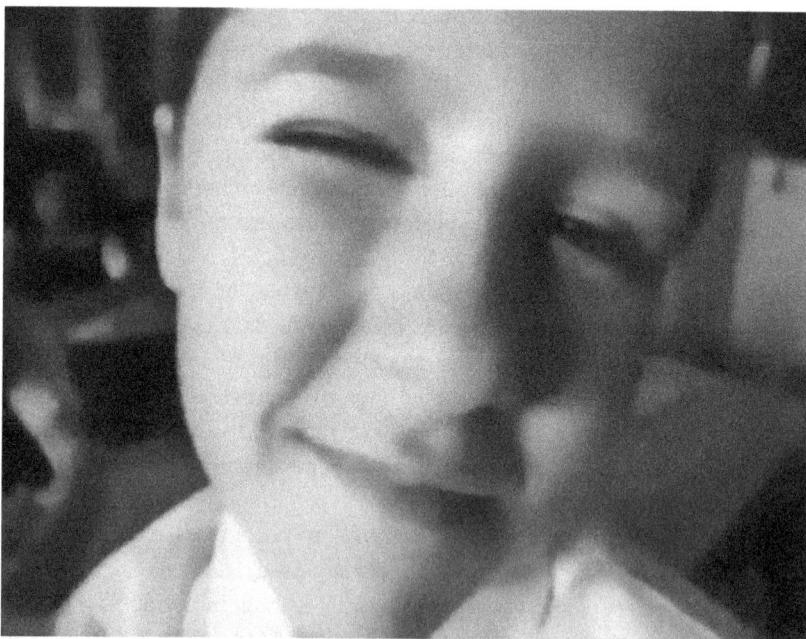

Figure 4.3 Young Travis Payne winks at the camera and commercial audience in Dr. Pepper's "play" on John Travolta's machismo. Choreography by AC Ciulla. Screen Shot.

Created as part of the 1998 "This is the Taste" Dr. Pepper campaign,[65] the ad underscores the contributions from American subcultures while simultaneously displacing these contributions onto a white male body. Key to this displacement is Danny's embodiment of Africanist movement values. His calm, confident manner that easily slides from strutting through the classroom to a smooth, triple turn into a casual backflip taps into the aesthetic of the cool. The sudden, unexpected insertion of the flip into his walk produces a high-effect juxtaposition, moving from verticality to rotating inversion with little transition. This sense of attention-getting contrast is furthered by the relationship between his movement style, age, and elementary school setting. Ultimately, his virtuosic moments demonstrate ephebism,[66] bringing a vital energy to the orderly world of the classroom and breaking the dull repetition of the properly prim apple-for-teacher tradition. The traces of Africanist movement aesthetics within his choreography, in contrast to the restrained bodies of the other students, aligns the classroom with traditional constructions of whiteness.[67] The location's sense of confinement juxtaposes the stylized, expressive, rhythmic body of Danny. His performance manifests excess as black culture infuses white and helps to refine Danny's display of masculinity as a form of patriarchy-in-training.

This Dr. Pepper commercial provides a productive site for examining capitalism's incorporation of expressive forms developed within marginalized social groups and the *affective* power of these associations. As Richard Dyer noted in the 1970s, capitalism is adept at finding ways to profit from social forms regardless of ideological compatibility.[68] The transformation of "Staying Alive" from pop song to ad jingle links Danny's dancing in the ad to disco and Travolta's character in *Saturday Night Fever*. The filmic allusion in relation to Danny's body—as a vehicle of transmission—constructs masculinity as white and heterosexual, through a kind of fetishism that invisibilizes the homosexual African-American and Latino bodies that were central to disco's development. Disco music arose in the 1970s as a kind of "commercial offspring" of funk music, borrowing the rhythm track style from funk to create a "hypnotic steady pulse" centered on two alternating bass phrases that continually loop back to a musical hook.[69] Disco's debt to music forms developed within and for African-American communities is also noted by Dyer who notes its rhythmic connection to soul music.[70]

Notably, disco music was developed to feed the desire to dance, extending the commercialized "single" format to allow for more uninterrupted dancing and to facilitate the DJ's ability to smoothly transition from one single to the next. The form enabled the birth of a club culture where ongoing streams of dance music dominated the scene. Music historians note the genre's connection to African-American musical values, identifying its "insistent" rhythm and the resulting physicality as distinct from traditional Western (i.e., white, European-American) music.[71] This format grew in popularity within the urban African-American, Latino, Italian-American and "visibly gay" communities of New York City and San Francisco.[72]

As industrialization and the move to a capitalist economic system fostered new urban spaces, they facilitated the development and liberation of marginalized groups, allowing them access to spaces where they could build communities based on alternative social identity criteria.[73] In his account of the emergence of contemporary club dancers, Tim Lawrence describes the development of disco as fundamentally interwoven with that of gay club culture in New York City: "Contemporary disco dancing emerged out of the dual context of African-American social dance and the rise of the discotheque and was propelled forward by the sudden influx of gay men into these social dance spaces at the beginning of the 1970s."[74] He credits this development to the 1970 opening of two dance spaces, the Loft and the Sanctuary: "Both venues were unique in that gay men—who required special protection until Mayor John Lindsay repealed New York City's laws governing the admission of gay men to cabarets, dance halls, and restaurants in October 1971—were dominant on the floor (even if straights were present), and the energy and expressivity of these dancers, many of whom faced the double marginalization of being black as well as gay, kick-started 1970s dance culture."[75] Thus, while city laws initially restricted gay men's access to dance halls, capitalist ventures found ways to create spaces where gay cultural expression could thrive and foster contemporary club dancing.

Disco initially introduced a new form of solo dancing driven by its relation to the crowd. This solo form emphasized improvisation, high energy, an articulate body that incorporated isolations, circle formations where dancers took turns displaying their skills, and a kind of call-and-response between crowd and DJ.[76] Thus, initially, disco's body aligned itself with corporeal freedom and excess rather than codified structure and restraint. However, in the late 1970s, *Saturday Night Fever* helped bring disco, and the hustle, into the popular mainstream music and club scene.[77] The formation of the Hustle led to the incorporation of white Euro-American ballroom dance conventions,[78] reintroducing an emphasis on heterosexual partnering with a more presentational, posed, and controlled dance style[79] and, thus, a more restrained corporeality. Additionally, the film linked disco to Travolta's character (Tony), who initially displays an aggressive, showy, physically dominant, sexual relationship to his female partners, creating a representation of Italian-American heterosexual machismo. I argue that the Dr. Pepper commercial uses the Bee Gees' hit to explicitly allude to Travolta's character and implicitly connect Danny's choreography to the larger history of disco. In doing so, the commercial fetishizes racially and sexually marginalized bodies and reveals an ongoing cultural ambivalence surrounding their social formations.

This layering of allusions occurs through Danny's choreography, which combines elements of hetero-normative masculinity with corporeal values found in early disco, including a sense of power (or energy) and sensuality aligned with ephebism and the aesthetic of the cool. For example, Danny's rhythmic strut, flirtatious wink, and enthusiastic reception by the black girls in the class work collectively to make this layered allusion. The layered allusion is furthered by the fact that, while the white girls his age seem shocked, his teacher almost seems pleased by his physical display as much as by the Dr. Pepper he hands her. One way or another, he knows how to please a *woman*. The teacher's response seems to reinforce the connections to Travolta's representation of a macho, but ultimately somewhat sensitive, man; whereas, I argue, the racially-defined student responses point to the implicit allusion to disco's larger history. They suggest that the approval and appreciation of his "performance" is a recognition of his successful appropriation of black culture; however, the emphasis on the girls' appreciation furthers the disavowal of gay culture.

Danny's body acts as a medium of transmission, conveying the desire for and the disavowal of disco's dancing bodies. By abstracting the movement aesthetics of disco and casting a young, white boy as the corporeal bearer of this cultural knowledge, the ad employs marginalized social identities in the construction of white masculinity. The transferal of disco's social formation from the urban club scene of the 1970s to the body of Danny invisiblizes social relations and identities to selectively activate their corporeality in new ways. This aspect of the ad's meaning production opens the door to Joseph's discussion of how capitalism performatively enacts relationships between subcultures and product branding to facilitate the transformation of self-organizing social formations into circulating ideological subject positions.

This dynamic of capitalism is one that cultural theorists, such as Dyer, Massumi, and Joseph, recognize as a form of control. Joseph views this form of control through a Marxian lens, thus identifying it as exploitation, rather than appropriation. By addressing consumption as a form of labor, Joseph extends Marx's analysis of capitalism's relationship to social relations. She argues that consumers freely express identity and community through consumption, which functions as a form of labor in that it ensures the continuation of production, but that in doing so, they "contribute to the accumulation of capital—and thus to the power of the owners of the means of production—and enact the cultural and social formations in which their choices are embedded but which they do not control. The consumer's free choice is constrained and productive of further constraints."[80] Thus, while she sees consumption-as-labor as a form of agency, she also argues that it is a form of agency severely limited by the logic of capitalism.

Potentially, any positive effects achieved by marginalized groups in establishing new social identities are countered by capitalism's cooptation of new communities and lifestyles. Brian Massumi goes so far as to suggest that the "current capitalist mode of power could be called control: neither coding nor codification, neither regularization nor regulation, but the *immanently encompassing modulation of both*."[81] I argue that advertising's deployment of social relations and cultural forms as abstracted elements placed into new, *affective*, polysemic contexts visibly manifests this capitalist form of power.[82]

To fully demonstrate how advertising visibilizes this form of capitalist power, I turn back to Joseph one more time. Joseph extends this notion of control and its relation to social formations in a critical way, arguing that in its most extreme form capitalism controls agency and cultural meaning because "the very differentiations that communities may seek to enact with their consumptive production may not be external to or oppositional to capitalist production but may very well be the elaboration of its own necessarily increasingly dense articulations of difference, of niches, and of communities of consumers and producers."[83] In other words, what begins as an alternative practice of consumption grounded in an unorthodox lifestyle, once embraced by the capitalist market, (potentially) becomes yet another articulation of difference employed as a marketing strategy.

As advertising struggles to access and create new markets, it turns to subcultures and marginalized lifestyles. This dynamic echoes that of colonialism and its accompanying ideologies in which the Other becomes a source of the new. Continued growth within consumerism requires the constant manufacturing of new products and new markets. The appropriation and modification of marginalized social groups functions, at least in part, as a means for generating new markets and innovation in product lines. Thus, while the Red Rose Tea and Dr. Pepper ads embrace expressive forms developed in marginalized social groups, lending a kind of authenticity to the product, this recognition requires a loss of control as markers of social identity freely circulate beyond the immediate communities of production.

In tracking how this dynamic operates through dance in advertising, I recognize a conceptual connection to colonialist ideology. As dance in advertising borrows from marginalized social groups, it reveals a kind of ambivalence, performing both complicity and distance and simultaneously acknowledging and invisibilizing subordinate groups within its articulation of Americanness. This dynamic allows dance in advertising to take part in an ongoing project of constructing and reconstructing social and national identities. Often, it consolidates and reinforces normative categories of race, gender, class, or sexuality. However, sometimes advertising's discursivity employs dance to alter, adapt, and transform those identities, simultaneously embracing and disavowing difference. Sometimes, dance in advertising participates in moments of minor relational shifts.

Giant billboards featuring shirtless men in jeans with "ripped abs" fill the black-and-white wide shot of a New York City street skyline, but the image is accompanied by a voiceover saying, "Come on, a six pack?" As music plays, the camera arcs downward to the right, revealing a car where a young woman in the driver's seat smiles/laughs in response to something the thin young man, with a prominent nose, sitting in the passenger seat has said to her. The voiceover returns with, "Who needs a six pack, when you got the nose?" As the spokesman finishes, the young man turns to look at the camera with a confident smile.

The screen shifts to color as the camera cuts to a close up of a man's feet clad in brown leather dress shoes as they hit the pavement. As the camera tilts, scrolling up his body to reveal a blue-pinstriped suit and white Stetson cowboy hat he is placing on his head, the voiceover says, "Or a nose, when you got the suit." The voiceover continues, "Now you don't need a suit, when you got the moves," as the image cuts to the only black man in sight at a gym as he literally dances on his treadmill while others walk or run. The voice continues with this theme of celebrating difference, "or moves when you got the fire," as the image cuts to a "carrot-topped"[84] young man in a locker room as he looks in the mirror to box an imaginary component.

With the next cut, spectators form a runway and cheer for male dancers, who execute "Machiavellis" or "death drops"[85] while wearing four-inch heels, as the voiceover announces, "Or fire, when you rock those heels." The dancers' attire evokes a cross between "feminine" and "masculine" fashions that display the body, beginning with the heels. For example, one wears long, black dangling earrings with a button-down shirt of multi-colored squares and high-waisted black briefs—a look that recalls an emphasis on bare midriffs and legs commonly seen in women's fashion as well as the return of high-waisted women's swimwear and jeans. The dancers, cheering crowd, and judges holding up point cards suggest the context is a contemporary vogue ball.[86]

The images and voice continue in this manner, depicting a series of scenes that portray a variety of men, each of whom is desirable for a different reason: a wheelchair-bound young man wearing a blue tux with a blond girl on his lap in a prom-decorated gym ("or heels when you ride those wheels"); a shy red-headed boy holding an album with the image of a gorilla on it surreptitiously looking at another red-headed boy holding a book, "The Power of the Banana" ("Looks, man, who needs looks, when you got the books"); a naked young man and woman "wearing" signs made of sheets as they run from a police squad in riot gear ("or books, when you got some balls"); and a guy kicking open the car door and helping his girlfriend out of the passenger seat in the courtyard of a rundown tenement building ("and who needs all that when you get the door").

The final series of scenes are single shots that capture one moment, creating a series of portraits: a muscular guy working dough in a pizza shop ("when you got the dough"), a young man standing at a chalkboard full of mathematical equations ("the brains"), a woman lying on a bed in the throes of orgasm by cunnilingus ("the touch"), and a heavily-bearded guy in a black leather jacket sitting on a couch as kittens climb on him ("the hah . . . aww"). The ad finally returns to the opening city shot and the young man sitting in a car with his girlfriend. He looks at the camera with a knowing, confident gaze as the voice continues: "That's right. Who needs some other thing?"

The voice pauses as the image cuts to a home bathroom sink with men's grooming tools arranged along the edges, as the voice says, "when you've got your thing." The camera tilts up to reveal Axe body products on the counter above the sink as the voice commands, "Now work on it." The ad copy, "Axe grooming products for men," appears near the top of the image. Two shots of a man using Axe body wash in the shower lead into one last round of images and text: the word "FIND," a shot of the suit guy using a body spray, "YOUR," a shot of the carrot-top fighter applying deodorant, "MAGIC," and a second shot of him using hair gel. The final image in the one-minute commercial is an all-black screen with the following ad copy in the center: "Axe. Find your magic."

As the ad copy reveals, the "Find Your Magic" (2016) commercial advertises the Axe brand of men's grooming products (see video 4.3 ▶).[87] The brand is known for creating ironic ads that riff on advertising's tendency to link consumer products with intangibles such as beauty, popularity, athletic prowess, family, or love by creating extreme, over-the-top scenarios. For example, an ad from the early 2000s advertises Axe body products by having an average-looking man fall through the floor while showering to land, naked and soapy, in an aerobics studio. He recovers quickly and leads the women's aerobics class through a series of moves before turning to escape into the locker room. As he leaves, the women look on and confirm his desirability with some solid hip thrusts—reinforcing the sexual connotation, just in case someone missed it— as he walks into the embrace of a stunningly beautiful woman in a towel. As this earlier commercial demonstrates, Axe is known for promoting its brand based on highly stereotypical, exaggerated representations of heterosexual masculinity.

However, in a critique of the hyper-masculine, muscular, semi-naked male models and heterosexual stereotypes commonly found in advertising, the more recent "Find Your Magic" ad appears to offer a range of masculinities and sexualities as desirable. This move is complicated by the ad's representation of gay culture. For example, the image of the male model that the ad counters reflects a shift in representations of masculinity already linked to alternative male sexualities.

The public display of the male body as erotic object in advertising and the construction of the "beefcake" image in contemporary American culture owes a debt to gay culture and the depiction of homosexual desire in art photography. In the mid-to-late 1980s celebrity and fashion photographer Herb Ritts and controversial art photographer Robert Mapplethorpe helped to popularize this image of the (semi-)nude male body, promoting a version of masculinity that embraced its role as erotic object.[88] In 1994, journalist Mark Simpson identified the crossover of these representations into mainstream mass media: "Advertising, film and magazines have for more than a decade offered the male body in poses which are taken straight from gay erotica. But this depiction always depends upon the assertion that it is not homoerotic."[89] Simpson points to how these kinds of images tended to be heterosexualized through visual and textual links to women and masculine activities (e.g., sports). Thus, the Axe commercial works to counter a heterosexual image of the male body as an erotic object that arose out of homoerotic counterculture.

Furthermore, this image of the hyper-masculine body and its "disguise" as heteronormative masculinity in American culture pre-dates its widespread distribution via mass media. The introduction of the physical culture movement to the United States in the nineteenth century promoted strong, physically active, toned (lean muscular) bodies.[90] In an effort to counter associations between dance, effeminacy, and homosexuality, seminal modern dancer Ted Shawn promoted a hyper-masculine image for himself and his male company members in the 1930s by linking the display of the lean, athletic, toned male body with labor and sports themes.[91] While weight-lifting and the heavily-muscled body types did not rise to prominence in popular culture until the 1970s,[92] the late twentieth- and twenty-first-century iconic image of the naked, muscular male body with six-pack abs continues this representation of the hyper-masculine body as a counter-measure to effeminacy. The success of this image in American mass media suggests that it appeals to both homosexual and heterosexual audiences—in the case of heteronormativity, as an object of desire for women and as a role model for men.[93] In this sense, this stereotypical image reaches a wider audience by addressing homosexual men without asking heterosexual consumers to confront difference.

Arguably, the Axe commercial plays on this history as it claims to offer alternative masculinities. Grounding masculine sex appeal in concepts of individuality and uniqueness, the ad promotes the idea that being successful in love (or sex) has more to do with selling what you've got than with trying to fit a mold. However, it closes with the idea that one needs to "groom" what one has—making consumption of things like body wash and hair gel a necessity—to achieve the fullest version of oneself. Furthermore, despite the ad's apparent appeal to self-defined masculinity, many of the scenes continue to link masculinity to heteronormative behaviors and attributes. For example, getting the door for a woman, or being gruff and tough on the outside but sweet and gentle on the inside, or knowing how to sexually please a woman—all things still marked by heteronormativity, at least if popular paperback romance novels are any indication.[94] Thus, while the ad counters certain heteronormative ideologies, it upholds others.

This juxtaposition proves productive. The inclusion of what have been nonnormative, invisiblized masculinities demonstrates how dance in advertising participates in the reshaping of social identity. The juxtaposition creates a conflict that can only be resolved by the viewer's reading of the commercial, and it does so through the commodification of popular culture and subaltern identities. In this sense, the ad reveals how capitalism responds to and participates in social and discursive change.[95]

A locus of the ad's participation in discursive change lies in the shots of the dancers in heels, which reference the Harlem balls that emerged within LBGTQ African-American and Latino drag culture in the 1960s, largely in New York City, and which entered mainstream popular culture with the release of Madonna's music video, "Vogue" (1990), and Jennie Livingston's documentary, *Paris is Burning* (1991).[96] The dance form, voguing, developed out of the competitive performance of gender roles in an imitation of high fashion models, as well as cinema and television celebrities.[97] In the 1980s–90s, the practice emphasized the performance of "realness" and included a variety of gendered categories, including BGTQ men performing both heteronormative female and male gender identities.[98]

To vogue meant to move seamlessly through a series of poses modeled after hegemonic cultural representations of gender and class. The competitive nature of the dance meant that it included its own form of battling, "throwing shade," an embodied way of "talking trash" or "signifying."[99] While voguing entered heteronormative popular culture in the 1990s with Madonna's video, the form did not remain widely known outside of LGBTQ and TQPOC communities.[100] Scholars such as Thomas DeFrantz and Marlon Bailey identify the continuation of voguing and ball culture within "underground" Queer culture in the 2000s, as well as its spread through globalization and the occasional resurfacing of voguing within popular culture.

In an ethnographic study of ball culture in Detroit, Bailey notes how twenty-first-century versions of the form create extreme juxtaposition by combining vogue's "fluid hand and arm movements" and "stop-action movement sequences" with dramatics (i.e., hard, fast, aggressive executions of spins and dips performed on the beat).[101] While ball culture and voguing dropped out of American mass media for a time, they returned in the 2000s through vehicles such as *America's Best Dance Crew*, music videos, and the rerelease of Livingston's documentary. Voguing, arguably, influenced the dance style of the all-male music group Kazaky and the popularization of "heel choreography."[102]

The Axe commercial's incorporation of ball culture's voguing and dramatics—which I read as a reference to ball culture due to the mixture of choreography, runway composition, costuming, and the panel of judges scoring the performance—points to how the appropriation of subordinate social groups into mainstream media leads to the construction of social formations as categories of identity that circulate freely within consumer culture. Analyzing consumption as labor, Miranda Joseph argues that capitalism both perpetuates normative social identity categories (e.g., heterosexuality, masculinity, etc.) and participates in the construction of new or alternative ones (e.g., homosexuality, transgender, etc.).

Joseph argues that consumer culture positions these identities as separate entities "over and against the subjects who produced them."[103] Within consumerism social groups founded on shared social identity, practices, and/or lifestyles appear to be ongoing, self-generating categories represented as organic, natural, ethnic, national, and so on, or become social formations discursively positioned as distinct from the alienated realm of production. Through this process these social identities appear to be independent of larger socioeconomic forces. In his analysis of branding and authenticity within neoliberal capitalism, David Savran echoes Joesph's concern; brands "must be rooted in a world which, 'consumers believe [. . .] is not entirely fictional,' a world that need not—and arguably cannot—exist, which transcends and cancels the sphere of commodity production."[104] In other words, commodity-signs establish and maintain brand identity through the appropriation, or representation, and exploitation of social formations, which are distilled down to markers of belonging that exist at a distance from their lived social relations.

These advertising-constructed social entities become access points allowing consumers to express their personal identity through imagined communities of relation. Product consumption becomes a form of self-transformation.[105] In commercials, corporeality plays a vivid and central role in this process, highlighting the importance of social choreographies and performance. While Joseph argues that using the term "appropriation" wrongly applies the notion of private property to the social, when the issue is more one of control rather than ownership, dance scholars Anthea Kraut and Thomas F. DeFrantz offer critiques of dance's relationship to capitalist structures and argue in support of further scholarship that addresses the appropriation of social formations. DeFrantz aptly points to how capitalism and the globalization of culture "allow[s] these social dances to be appropriated and repurposed as intellectual property to generate profit . . . [and] that neoliberal discourses of freedom encourage the spread of black social dance" beyond their community.[106] There are two effects of this repurposing of social dance that I address here in relation to advertising.

First, while social formations and the dances that arise from them may not be forms of private property, they operate within distinct political economies and social relations. Second, capitalist "borrowings" of social formations, or their dances, fundamentally raises the issue of appropriation because they put social relations and practices into circulation within cultural and economic systems governed by private property's discursive structure. The fact that the social groups do not profit from the practices and lifestyle choices that define them does not alleviate the problems raised by neoliberal capitalist ventures using them to turn a profit. The move from their social origins to consumer culture increases the potential loss of meaning and history as they begin to circulate beyond their community. As DeFrantz argues, in the case of black social dances: "These are dances that forward ideologies of *corporeal orature*—expressive body talking—as a productive means of group formation and social connectivity; they are embodied structures of playful musicality, understanding, and questioning cast in terms that involve active physical exploration."[107] Black dance plays a significant role in linking individuals to particular social formations, defining relationality, and functioning as a form of social discourse/dialogue.

DeFrantz identifies several examples of this phenomenon within black dance, including the fact that "contemporary voguing by queer youth of color actively tease[s] out and confirm[s] sexual identity within a frame of social dance practice."[108] He argues that "African Americans consistently invent social dances that confirm an apparent 'outside' to market forces,"[109] which have been coopted by neoliberal capitalism and linked to the concept of freedom. Drawing on David Harvey's analysis of an encompassing, "unexamined concept" of freedom operating within neoliberal discourse, DeFrantz posits that neoliberal capitalism links black social dance to the freedom to "move as one wants to," resulting in consumer culture's circulation of these dance form(s) to a "global public with little understanding of its aesthetic histories or varied social contexts within black communities."[110] DeFrantz's concerns regarding the distribution and cooptation of black social dance corresponds to Joseph's concerns about exploitation and my argument that dance in advertising activates *affect* and participates in the formation of social identities, ideology, and cultural discourse.[111]

Drawing on Joseph and DeFrantz, I argue that dance in advertising often participates in the production of social identities as static states of being; they become things-in-themselves that define categories of belonging within consumer culture. However, I also recognize how dance in advertising creates the potential for change in cultural discourses. For example, the Axe ad brings voguing and its construction of sexual identity to the mainstream in way that potentially serves to expand concepts of masculinity operating in popular culture. The ad introduces a counter-narrative, seemingly modeling an alternative way of being attractive (or sexy) and male. Unfortunately, I find the politics of the ad complex and problematic given how it (re)presents voguing.

The problem lies in the viewer's (in)ability to read the dance scene in its fullest sense. Of the three men in the ball scene only one is captured in shots that allow the viewer to really *see* him and the five-second ball scene consists of seven distinct shots. For viewers familiar with ball culture, the shots convey

Figure 4.4 A dancer performs at a New Way Ball. Axe commercial. Screen shot.

the reference through key markers. The first dancer *appears* biologically male,[112] but he wears large dangling earrings and four- to five-inch heels (see figure 4.4). The movement vocabulary employs the catwalk format along with the dramatics of contemporary voguing, and judges seated at a table hold up score cards. The other two performers are more difficult to see clearly, since they are in frame for shorter periods of time, don't always face the camera, and move quickly. The ability to recognize the scene as a ball is further complicated by the audience, which includes what look to me to be white men and women in club apparel. My point here is not that all ball participants look the same but that the staging helps support alternative readings of the context. As a result, the social practice of voguing loses much of its discursive power as it is reduced to *spectacle* and *style*.

However, the possibility of alternative sexuality resurfaces two scenes later when the two young men encounter each other in the bookstore—one holding a gorilla album and the other a banana book. The shot captures their acknowledgement of each other and recognition of a "commonality." Thus, the scene is suggestive rather than explicit in its challenge to heteronormativity. Outside of these two scenes, the men are all shown either alone or in relation to a woman. One gets the sense that, since the whole point of the ad is to highlight the unique ways in which "men" are sexually attractive, the goal is not to completely upset the categories of "men" or "masculinity" but rather to broaden them. At least, the goal seems to be to broaden them enough to expand the market for Axe products.

Thus, the ad offers the possibility of change, proposing potential identities consumers can align themselves with whether they are already a part of these social groups, or not. In this way, the ad models alternatives for those who may be seeking a sense of socio-cultural belonging that aligns with their personal experience. However, the ad still reinforces aspects of dominant gender discourses and removes practices from their lived social relations. Additionally, despite its challenge to the normative, the dancing functions as form of appropriation and invisibilization because the advertising format offers no explanation of the cultural reference, loosening the dance form's ties to its culture to have it more broadly function as a sign of alternative masculinity, homosexuality, and/or African-American and Latino-American culture. Essentially, in the ad, voguing can be understood as any of these things and still participate effectively in commodity-sign and brand's construction. Thus, despite the appropriation of ball culture, the ad potentially participates in the circulation of new role models and broader identity categories—at least on a surface level—offering them as *styles* of self. Furthermore, the ad promotes these alternative masculinities through consumer culture, suggesting they can be *achieved through consumption* rather than social relations.

As commodity-signs mobilize and circulate an increasing number of social formations, corporeality plays a significant role in the construction of social identity at the national level. Advertising diversifies its potential markets, in part, through dance and its connection to alternative communities of belonging. While my analysis points, on the one hand, to Jean Baudrillard's critique of the political economy of the sign and consumerism's reduction of cultural meanings and social relations to simulacrum, I also have sought to explore advertising's *participation* in popular culture through dance. By looking closely at the web of allusions in each ad, I hope to demonstrate how commodity-signs, and the brands they produce, engage in cultural meaning-making and the construction of national memory. As this chapter draws to a close, I want to consider one more example of dance in advertising—one that I find explicitly demonstrates how dance in advertising responds to changes in social relations and participates in the creation and maintenance of cultural knowledge—a phenomenon recognized in the concept of *convergence* culture, as discussed in Chapter One.[113]

MISTY COPELAND AND DANCE HISTORY
AS CULTURAL CAPITAL

The convergence of media forms, participatory culture, and modes of collective intelligence in the digital age of capitalism has deepened the role of advertising in American culture and social relations. While television has undergone a transformation as more people rely on digital streaming and online content for access to movies and broadcast programming, television has not *yet* entirely left the scene. Taking my experiences as an anecdotal example, I blend my viewing practices, relying on cable, digital subscription services (i.e., Netflix in this case), and online streaming sites (e.g., Youtube, Vimeo) for media content. However, I also know several people in my generation who rely solely on streaming services. While studies show that younger generations rely more on online content, recent studies not only hesitate to claim the death of television but also provide evidence that online media sites will continue to provide new avenues for advertising.[114]

The current trend seems to be more one of overlap and the development of new marketing strategies—including experimentation with advertising length and format—as broadcasters and ad agencies attempt capture both audiences. The prevalence of commercials on Youtube, as content and advertisement, as well as the number of sites that post commercials and facilitate dialogue about them attests to advertising being a ubiquitous mass media form. If anything, Rosemary J. Coombe's (1998) argument that the consumption of commodity forms is a "productive activity in which people engage in meaning-making to adapt signs, texts, and images to their own agendas" not only continues to be true but is increasing as digital media continue to embrace participatory models.[115] Coombe refers to consumer's appropriation of media as "recoding," arguing that it "provide[s] important cultural resources for the articulation of identity and community in Western societies where many traditional ethnic, class, and cultural indicia are fading and minority groups organize along alternative lines."[116] In the final section of this chapter, I favor this (re)appropriation by consumers as I turn to an example that highlights dance in advertising as a participatory, meaning-making form.

A shot of a city street and a tire store on the far side of it frame the blurry, out of focus image of a woman in the foreground. She faces the left side of the screen and turns her head to look toward the tire store as a white truck passes her. Immediately afterward, an off-screen female voice and soft music soundtrack interject. As the woman says, "Millions of girls dream of being a ballerina," the image cuts to a medium shot of the woman seen in the first shot (now in focus along the left edge of the frame) as she walks down an alley, wearing a grey sweatshirt and carrying a bag on her left shoulder. To her right, at shoulder level, the following text appears: "/8,861,674."

Cut to a wide shot of a wooden-floored room as the woman, now wearing only a black leotard, boy shorts and ballet slippers, stands in a narrow second position and folds over to place her hands on the floor in front of her. Her knees and shoulders hyper-extend, maximizing the lines of the body. The female voiceover continues, saying, "But not many get their start at the local boys and girls club," her tone lilting upwards positively toward the end of the sentence. As she speaks, a series of images pass by: the woman (Misty Copeland) now sitting as she puts on pointe shoes, a young girl who resembles her performing en pointe, and the same young girl as she bourrées away from the camera in a dance studio. The female voice continues, "Even fewer go on to perform for American Ballet Theater," as the text "/528,041" appears beside the girl. A new series of shots flow by: Copeland dancing en pointe in her black practice clothes, the girl performing pirouettes and chaînés en pointe, Copeland in a dance studio as she chaînés in a tourqoise leotard and white classical tutu, and finally a close up of Copeland's feet in relevé as "/6" appears next to them.

A series of shots of Copeland in various ballet practice attire as she performs saut de chats and grand jetés streams past. When the image lands once again on the pedestrian version of Copeland as she crosses a street, the female voice continues: "And help open the doors of ballet to everyone." Ballet-attire Copeland rapidly pique turns across a studio, while pedestrian Copeland opens a door to enter a building. The darkness of the doorway dissolves to the view from on stage. The camera follows Copeland as she steps forward, red curtains parting to reveal the stage lights focused on her and the darkness of the audience beyond that. The voice over begins a new line, "I'm Misty Copeland," finishing with "and I'm one of a kind" as the camera cuts to a shot from the audience that captures her in a pose and costume reminiscent of *La Sylphide* or the Wili in *Giselle*. The text "/1" appears next to her, taking up the right side of the screen and veering toward dominating the image. A final shot of Copeland drinking a Diet Dr. Pepper dissolves into the image of the cola in a glass next to "/1," equating the image of Copeland in performance with Diet Dr. Pepper. The image animates, transforming the glass into a can of Diet Dr. Pepper and a sequence of ad copy ("Zero Calories," "Great Taste," and "Always one of a Kind") before cutting to black (see video 4.4 ▶).

This Diet Dr. Pepper commercial (2013)[117] was not Copeland's first promotional venture—she was featured in T-Mobile ads for the Blackberry in 2010—nor her last. She represented Coach, Inc. in 2013 as well, and in 2014, Under Armour featured Misty Copeland in a commercial highlighting her achievement of being an African-American "Ballerina Soloist" with American Ballet Theater (ABT) (see video 4.5 ▶).[118] The company hired Copeland as part of a campaign featuring athletes; her commercial for the "I will what I want" campaign promoted their line of underwear and sports bras.

The Under Armour commercial implicitly highlights Copeland's overcoming of ballet's history of racial segregation in the United States by accompanying her dancing with a voiceover of a young girl reading a rejection letter stating that she lacks the proper body for ballet and is too old to begin training. While the ad and its voiceover do not explicitly state that race or skin color is an obstacle, Copeland's fame as the first African-American soloist in ABT was already a national story.[119] Thus, the rhizomatic nature of mass media ensures that for some viewers the ad implicitly supports the desegregation of ballet and challenges ideologies that view ballet as white. Her appearance in the music video for Prince's "Crimson and Clover" (2009), her 2010 tour with Prince, and her duet to his "Beautiful Ones" on *Lopez Tonight* in 2011 introduced her to popular culture in a way that most ballerinas never see.[120] Much of her media coverage details not only the struggles she faced when she first began training but also her struggle within the company to overcome perceptions of ballet as inherently white.

The Dr. Pepper and Under Armour ads described above are hardly the first advertisements to feature ballet in their construction of commodity-sign and brand image. Ballet has a history of being featured in advertising, though more so in print advertising than television. Judith Lynn Hanna analyzes print advertising's use of ballet images in the 1980s, identifying ideologies informing the choice of ballet as a signifying image.[121] Two aspects of advertising's representation of ballet stand out in her analysis: the gendered notion of the ballerina and the cultural status of the dance form. Lincoln Kirstein, and others, worked to establish ballet as an American art form (as opposed to a European one) in the first half of the twentieth century, building an audience and financial support for the form.[122] The New York City Ballet's home at the Lincoln Center aligned the company, George Balanchine, and ballet with opera and classical music, establishing ballet as an art form frequented by the social elite who supported the development of "culture." Thus, ballet's affiliation with high art, rather than popular culture, became solidified, and it is this affiliation that Hanna's analysis highlights. In addition, the images often depict Classical and Romantic ballet's predilection for presenting ballerinas as the epitome of cultured *white* femininity: ethereal, delicate, expressive, beautiful, sensitive creatures of motion and form guided by their male partners.[123] The promotion of Copeland two decades later suggests things have shifted.

In August 2015 Misty Copeland became the first African-American female principal dancer in ABT, and over the course of her career, she has detailed the kinds of struggles that black dancers still face in the ballet world through her various interviews, her autobiography, and a documentary.[124] In addition to being the first black principal ballerina in ABT, she was the only African-American woman in the company in 2016, though there were three African-American men in the corps de ballet. In contrast, in 2016 The New York City Ballet employed a few black men at the levels of soloist and corps de ballet, but only one black woman at the level of the corps. In a *New Yorker* article, author Rivka Galchen names African-American ballerina Lauren Anderson as the first to reach principal status with a major American ballet company (Houston Ballet) other than the Dance Theater of Harlem.[125]

While the work of choreographers, dancers, and artistic directors such as Josephine Baker, Arthur Mitchell, Talley Beatty, Katherine Dunham, Pearl Primus, and Alvin Ailey created space in the field for artists such as Desmond Richardson, Alonzo King, and Bill T. Jones, black dancers continue to face resistance in the realm of classical ballet. Ballet history includes a long-established tradition of racial segregation explicitly based on differences in white and black body types but implicitly grounded in political and social ideologies. While Balanchine's fascination with African-American culture led him to *imagine* the high-*affect* juxtaposition of a racially integrated corps de ballet, his most prominent act toward breaking down ballet's racial segregation was to feature African-American danseur Arthur Mitchell and white ballerina Diana Adams in a duet.[126] The first substantial rupture in ballet's segregation came from the success of the Dance Theater of Harlem, a ballet company composed predominately of African-American dancers established by Mitchell in 1969.[127] Brenda Dixon Gottschild, Gay Morris, and other dance scholars have detailed the ongoing struggle of black dancers in their study of ballet, as well as the criticism directed at them.[128]

Despite this history, the Diet Dr. Pepper and Under Armour commercials echo Misty Copeland's personal publicity campaign's explicit effort to promote Copeland as singular in her achievement while exposing and countering dominant discourses of ballet.[129] Arguably, Copeland is the only female black ballerina to achieve this level of recognition within a traditional American national ballet company. She is also, arguably, the first black female ballerina to achieve this level of renown within popular culture in the United States. However, the commercials featuring Copeland essentially ignore the details of the larger history, implying Copeland is the first dancer of color to achieve broad recognition while also reinforcing the discursive positioning of ballet as high art and a pinnacle of cultural achievement. Advertising's *affective* narrative of Copeland's achievements threatens to invisiblize the struggles and accomplishments of her predecessors in ways that construct authenticity for both Copeland and the product. Her struggle against ballet's segregation forms the foundation and context for the Diet Dr. Pepper commercial, which is then taken further by Under Armour.

The commercial's ad copy and the Under Armour campaign slogan, "I will what I want," value sheer force of will, determination, and commitment to a goal, holding Misty Copeland up as an example of a successful and powerful female athlete. To emphasize this point, the ad opens on shot looking through a doorway to where Copeland stands in fifth position, arms en bas, in a white room, a ballet barre on the wall behind her. As the voiceover of a young girl reading a rejection letter begins, the ad cuts to a medium shot of Copeland's legs as she slowly élevés in fifth to bourrée leisurely as she rotates in place. A slow boom of the camera upwards along her body is intercut with close ups of her feet and calf muscles. Since she wears pointe shoes without tights, an Under Armour sports bra, and Under Armour underwear ("Pure Stretch Cheeky"),[130] her highly developed leg muscles are amply visible and evident, aligning her movement with athleticism and muscular strength.

Following a close up of her face as she seemingly hovers en pointe, eyes downcast and arms about to unfurl to either side, the ad cuts to a moving shot that reveals stage lights and then a fabricated proscenium stage. Gradually, over the course of the next few shots, the ad reveals the stage to be set in what looks like an airplane hangar, as though a very box-like proscenium stage was deposited inside the larger structure. A mixture of continuous and discontinuous shots (e.g., a series of close-up, medium, and extreme wide shots) capture her dancing as she chainé turns, developés, poses on pointe with one leg extended à la seconde, and saut de chats back and forth across the stage. The camera catches the most spectacular moments in enough detail to give even untrained viewers evidence of her physical strength and flexibility (see figure 4.5). The ad ends with a close up of her face as she looks at the camera, eyes bright and friendly but face determined, followed by a shot with the brand name/logo, the ad copy, and the company URL.

While the Under Armour ad challenges ideological preconceptions about ballet-as-white, dance-as-athletic, and women-as-weak, it reinforces other ideologies of gender. She is, after all, dancing in underwear. The camera plays off long established tropes of the long, slow look that lingers even as it glides smoothly up the woman's body.[131] The ad furthers notions of the female body as erotic by featuring the company's "super cheeky" underwear that bisects each butt cheek, exposing her well-rounded and quite muscular gluteus maximus to the viewer as she turns across the stage. While her ample breasts remain fully covered, the form-fitting sports bra allows the viewer to appreciate them and her exposed, perfectly flat, muscular abdomen. Granted, this female body is visibly strong, but the goal here seems to be to reinforce the idea that this female body is also sexy, feminine, and available. The ad ultimately

Figure 4.5 Misty Copeland in Under Armour sports bra and "Pure Stretch Cheeky" underwear leaps across the "stage" space. Choreography by Marcello Gomes. Commercial. Screen shot.

promotes an image of women as strong athletes who are *still* erotic, *feminine* objects.[132]

Thus, Copeland's Under Armour commercial contributes to shifting gender roles, but it also reproduces a cultural emphasis on women as sexual objects. This tie between Copeland's athletic prowess and her femininity-as-erotic-object appears both in her self-promotional forms and in her advertising for other products. It summons up history's ballerina-as-feminine-ideal and the positioning of Romantic and Classical ballerinas as objects of the male gaze.[133] As a nationally-recognized black ballerina adopting a more explicit sexuality, these images also call to mind early twentieth-century cabaret performer Josephine Baker.[134] Considering this history, the ad participates in American cultural discourses linking female agency and sexuality. In addition, it continues trends found in the positioning of woman-as-erotic object within mass media.[135]

Under Armour is by no means the first corporation to launch an advertising campaign featuring athletic, sexualized female bodies. Nike began actively marketing to women in the 1990s, responding to social changes that made diversifying its market profitable. In the 2000s Nike began a steady campaign to link the display of the female body to images of power and athleticism. The Nike Women "Keep Up" ad (2005) featuring Algerian hip hop/break dancer Sofia Boutella is one example (see video 4.6 ▶).[136] In this Nike ad, Boutella engages in a challenge dance with first one very large and then two smaller speakers suspended from the ceiling. The challenge takes place in what looks like an old military bunker or weapons storage facility. The challenge is designed to call to mind breakdance cyphers where breakers battle each other by exchanging movement sequences (see figure 4.6).[137]

In the commercial, Boutella's attire aligns her with break dancing culture and sports (e.g., baseball cap, sneakers, athletic pants that are loosely fitted though not baggy, elbow pads and arm bands), while also aligning her with women's fashions (e.g., tight-fitted turquoise tank top with narrow straps, a v-neck, and a cut-out in the back that exposes her mid-back). She wears her hair down. The tank's form-fitting fabric accents her breasts, and it tends to ride up so that as she moves she exposes her muscular abdomen. Boutella's solo features several athletic, virtuoso steps: handspins, inverted freezes, the worm, et cetera. Close-up shots between dance sequences reveal glistening skin as evidence of her hard work. Clearly, she demonstrates the power and athleticism of female dancers. However, I suggest that the clothing choices are designed to subtly emphasize her feminine nature and to support viewing her through a heteronormative lens of female sexuality. While the emphasis on her sexuality may be relatively subtle here, this ad led to a series of other promotional and film gigs in which she is featured in more revealing clothing and sexualized poses. This shift in visual representation is paired with written and

Figure 4.6 Sofia Boutella challenges the music. Choreography by Jamie King. Nike Women commercial. Screen shot.

verbal discussions of her as "sexy" and "beautiful," as though there's a need to balance her (masculine) athleticism with her (feminine) sexuality.[138]

The promotion of dance as athletic is tied to the desire to both respond to and continue to build a market for women's athletic wear. Nike and Under Armour promote their clothing to female dancers/athletes *and* consumers who desire what Sofia and/or Copeland represent. While consumer interpretations will vary, the ads highlight several attributes, including athleticism, sexual appeal, "femininity," recognition, determination, ambition, and success. A second Under Armour ad, "Rule Yourself" (2015),[139] featuring Copeland, offers a slightly different balance of the strong, erotic, feminine subject, though some of ballet's traditional gendering remains (see video 4.7 ▶). She still wears form-fitting active wear, which fits current trends; however, in this ad she exposes less of her body, wearing tight shorts that reach her mid-thigh or long yoga tights with a sports bra. The second to last shot of Copeland captures her physical exertion and will with a close up of her face that conveys a combination of yearning, struggle, and hope (see figure 4.7). It is a face of determination but one that expresses struggle and uncertainty more than the male basketball player and golfer portray in their close ups.

I find traces of the ballerina's expressiveness and delicacy in the facial expression, but I also recognize it from footage and photos of Copeland dancing, and the look matches the overall demeanor of her public persona. Copeland's

Figure 4.7 Wearing Under Armour, Misty Copeland expresses struggle and determination. Commercial. Screen shot.

marketing strategy for herself-as-product seems to merge with that of the other products she promotes—Diet Dr. Pepper, Oikos Yogurt—while also reproducing gender roles.[140] The slogan "rule yourself" offers multiple readings. Copeland and the other athletes demonstrate will power and the idea of the subjective "I" bringing the body under control, but she also demonstrates emotional restraint—the performance of barely contained emotion visible in her facial expressions—and sexual restraint—the more modest physical display of her body. Most importantly, Copeland's use of corporate advertising as a form of self-promotion and activism demonstrates the complexity of dance's role in mass media.

Her strategic marketing campaign has gained her recognition well beyond the ballet world. At the time of writing this book, Copeland had her own website, as well as Instagram and Twitter accounts. In October 2015, a new documentary about her life was released, *A Ballerina's Tale*, and in May 2016 Mattel released a Misty Copeland Barbie Doll (in a version of her *Firebird* costume), which was on backorder by June 2016.[141] As of 2016 she is a national figure who is held up as a positive role model for young girls and women both black and white. She has effectively employed ballet in advertising as a means to mobilize social identity and define herself.

Her rise to fame demonstrates the effects of convergence culture and how social media and the participatory aesthetic of the digital age facilitate consumer culture's contributions to cultural knowledge and social identity. Misty Copeland's creative use of mass and social media, and her cross-media collaborations with popular artist Prince, helped catapult her to national mainstream recognition as one of few black ballerinas performing with a major American ballet company.[142] Through self and product promotion, Copeland has built a community of followers joined by their investment in her representation of a strong, black woman achieving success in a white-dominated profession. In recent years, she may be the single most influential person in ballet at the national level, inspiring a love of dance in her fans as well as serving as role model for women both in dance and popular culture contexts.

Misty Copeland's achievements also point to how convergence culture amplifies the importance of self-promotion and the literal marketing of self. For example, selfies function like self-manufactured ads, as do Youtube videos, which not only function as a way of defining self socially but also as a potential means of gaining broader recognition that might lead to a career and/or financial gain. Dance plays a vital role in this economy in the form of postings of choreography for popular music, independently produced screendance, videos of dance competitions, and so on.

By tapping into the cultural logic of neoliberal capitalism, Copeland brought herself and ballet into the forefront of mass media and popular culture. The success of her campaign for recognition seems tied to the proliferation of dance in advertising and music videos, the renewal of the narrative dance film genre, and the development of a televised concert dance aesthetic achieved through *So You Think You Can Dance* (SYTYCD) (and to a degree *Dancing with the Stars*). One might argue that through her self-promotion strategies Copeland models the neoliberal capitalist subject.

CONCLUDING THOUGHTS

Advertising appropriates dance as part of its effort to diversify its market. This effort to diversify serves under-represented communities and subject positions in that it broadens the social identities represented in mass media and creates a space for these voices. However, this appropriation also liberates social categories from lived experience and social relations to market static ideological subject positions as opportunities to change social identity through consumption. Thus, advertising facilitates and provides evidence of changes in ideology (cultural discourses about race, gender, class, etc.) through performances of discursive choreography.

However, dance-in-advertising also serves as a means of transforming lived, emergent, social formations and their meaningful socio-cultural practices into signs (image, appearance) that neoliberal capitalism alters (potentially) by mixing them with other signs and (re)presenting them. Thus, consumers often invest in the appearance of change, finding progress in tokens of difference, rather than making in-roads into actual change. Difference becomes a marketing ploy, not just for products but for people.

The danger here seems to lie in two places: the misrepresentation of communities and their socio-cultural values and the equivalence of social relations with products. Thus, dance in advertising potentially participates in maintaining reductive social categories that limit our understanding of difference, social identity, and subjectivity. Brian Massumi's critique of capitalism as system that subjects all of culture to monetary exchange resonates here and calls to mind recent critical re-thinkings of aesthetics that point to the value of relational, or participatory modes.[143] However, I see this relational aesthetic also at work in advertising as consumers respond and engage with promotional forms. In its own odd way, advertising points to capitalism's mechanism for allowing for the emergence of difference—it's just that difference, like everything else in twenty-first-century America, is subject to a neoliberal capitalist logic. This logic opens up the possibility for everything, or anything, to end up functioning as a sign for something else, a conscious misplacing, or deferral, of socio-cultural meaning in order to make new meanings.

CHAPTER 5

Subjectivity and Performative Consumption

Two men, one black and one white, stand in a beach hut bar looking out at the viewer through the open fourth wall. "Jamaica" is printed on metal sheeting along one side of the bar. As reggae music plays, the black man, who wears an English-style suit with a cravat, easefully dances to the music, performing—it seems—his racial and national identity. To his left, the white man, taller and broader in stature, stands with fisted hands held at chest level, legs planted firmly apart and slightly wider than his hips as he frowns at the dancing man. The white man looks slightly perplexed. In contrast to the black, presumably Jamaican, dancing man, he wears a blue t-shirt and brown knee-length shorts with white tennis shoes. His clothing performs the stereotype of the "American"[1] on holiday (see figure 5.1).

The dancing "Jamaican" gently grooves to the reggae music. Stepping in place with a little grounded bounce, he shifts from one side to the next, arms pushing forward in opposition to legs as he smiles contentedly. After about 13 seconds, still dancing, he hands the Red Stripe beer bottle he has been holding to the immobile, white "American."[2] As he does so, the camera moves into a medium shot to focus on the exchange and the black man's encouraging grin. When the ad cuts back to the wide shot, it reveals two things: the black man's dancing has changed, and the white man has joined him.

Now, the black man shifts his weight from one bent leg to the next, without picking up his feet up, sinking his weight into his heels as he leans and rotates his body away from the standing leg. Bent in a 90-degree angle his arms hover loosely at his sides, framing his torso. In a much less grounded manner, the white man shifts his weight side to side as his bent arms gesture forward slightly with the music. His weight remains lifted out of the floor,

Figure 5.1 Red Stripe's depiction of the "white man's" encounter with Jamaica and reggae via beer. Commercial. Screen shot.

and his movement seems related but detached, as though his energy flow is unmoored and adrift in his body. I understand this change in his behavior to indicate that his consumption of the beer actualizes his potential ability, enabling him to dance. The fact that his dancing assumes the form of the stereotypical "white man's overbite," never quite reaching the same level of ease seen in the spokesman, raises questions about subjectivity, social identity, and performance.

As the white "American" dances, he continues to frown slightly, though the frown has assumed a more appraising look, as though he is reevaluating the situation. This change is highlighted by his being featured in a medium shot. During the shot, his "Jamaican" companion begins to speak and continues his lines as the camera cuts back to a close-up that captures him speaking: "Red Stripe and reggae, helping our white friends dance for over seventy years. Red Stripe, it's beer, hooray beer!" The camera then cuts back to a wide shot of the two as they continue dancing. The final shot, accompanied by the "Jamaican's" parting words, "hooray beer!," is a wide shot of a Red Stripe bottle resting on a table or counter with the ad copy, "Hooray beer!," superimposed below it.

I read this Red Stripe commercial, "White Man Dancing" (2002), as a humorous depiction of Red Stripe beer's power, one that plays on cultural ideologies of race and dance (see video 5.0 ▶).[3] The commercial links Red Stripe to Jamaica and its culture through devices such as the reggae music, the Jamaica sign in the hut, the spokesman's accent and black body, and the ad copy.[4] The rustic shack, laid-back, no-worries attitude of the "Jamaican" man, and the rhythmically challenged, impassive "American" suggest particular notions of difference between black and white cultures: for example, a poor, black working class who began as slaves versus a white middle-upper class grounded in a history of plantation owners; the differing economies of the United States and Jamaica; the stereotype of the carefree, lazy "darkie" who sings and dances his way through adversity; or the white Protestant work ethic's disdain for dancing.[5]

While the commercial grounds the ideological linking of black bodies and an inherent ability to dance in Jamaican nationality, for its United States market this association speaks to long-standing stereotypes and racially-inflected views of dance within US culture.[6] The ad reinforces cultural discourses that mark black bodies as good dancers with inherent ability and white bodies, particularly men, as inherently lacking rhythm, naturalizing stereotypes that link dance and race. Visually, the ad displays this difference through the movement styles of the two men, as their dancing contains similar vocabulary but ultimately differs significantly in its performance. Thus, on the one hand, the ad seems to reproduce ideologies and social identities as stable, static categories of self.

However, while the ad's content points to the differences identified by dance studies scholars between Africanist and Europeanist movement aesthetics and a history of cultural appropriation and assimilation in the United States context, I acknowledge them here to look more closely at what the ad teaches viewers about consumption and subjectivity. More importantly, I ask what it might mean for Red Stripe beer to offer the white man access to dance in this context. In a situation where dancing implicitly stands in for blackness, what does the ad teach us about the relationship between dance, subjectivity, and consumption?

Red Stripe's "White Man Dancing" demonstrates how advertising uses dance to posit the consumer-as-subject as simultaneously a transcendental, psychologically coherent "I" and as a malleable, performative self.[7] Red Stripe offers the white, American male access to blackness, pleasure, and national identity through consumption. However, the ad also demonstrates the importance of performance. The commercial reveals how dance in advertising intentionally shapes movement to establish identity, defining personality while aligning its characters with ideologically sanctioned notions of ethnicity, race, gender, sexuality, nationality, and/or class. The ad's use of dance suggests that the self consists of a collection of attributes (interests, actions, ways of relating, effort/movement quality, physical characteristics, organization of the body, etc.). In this chapter, I attempt to capture these details through descriptive analysis, strategically employing terminology from Laban/Bartenieff conceptual models for reading movement.[8]

On one level, advertising uses dance and performance conventions to ground subjectivity in the concept of an interior "I" that expresses itself through movement and consumption. However, looking at dance-in-advertising in terms of postmodern discussions of subjectivity and their relation to concepts of consumption-as-labor, performance, choreography, and performativity reveals inherent contradictions in advertising's model of the consumer-as-subject. As sociological studies have shown, advertising invites viewers to identify with characters in ads based on socio-cultural markers, encouraging consumption based on maintaining or achieving their desired lifestyle and social status.[9] This identification process entails viewing the characters in ads as coherent selves that are similar and/or dissimilar to oneself. Furthermore, commercials typically rely on performance styles that reinforce Romantic and Enlightenment concepts of subjectivity to produce the sense of a consistent "I" with the freedom to make choices.

However, advertising also promotes a concept of the social self as malleable, offering the possibility of changing one's social standing by changing one's lifestyle through consumption and thus changing how one is perceived.[10] I argue that dance in advertising amplifies and alters this concept of self so that identity in advertising resonates with postmodern theories of subjectivity. Dance amplifies capitalism's positioning of branding as a cultural performance,[11] aligning consumption with the performance of self-identity, by grounding the transformation of identity in the corporeality of the self. Locating change in the body, dance in advertising illustrates how consumption participates in the construction of subjectivity and locates agency in one's ability to bodily assimilate ways of being.[12] Thus, advertising's use of dance points to the possibility that subjectivity is not grounded in a transcendental "I" and that the expressive self is not a stable, psychologically coherent whole. Advertising teaches consumers that they do not need to be genetically *or* genealogically Jamaican to *become* "Jamaican."

Thus, I recognize a contradiction inherent within dance's relationship to consumer culture in the era of neoliberal capitalism. Dance in advertising models a subjectivity that is at once both the rational Cartesian expressive "I" and the *rhizomatic*, ongoing, serial creation of self—an emergent "I," produced through intersecting relational flows of interests and actions.[13] Through the consumption of not only products but practices, consumers can define and redefine their relationship to ideological categories of social identity and their presentation of self in order to evolve as subjects and *become* who they wish to be.[14] Thus, I offer the possibility that dance-in-advertising reveals the expressive "I" to be a performance of subject-hood, as it posits the "I" as a fluid construct, isolated out from the flow and ongoing process of self.

Dance-in-advertising models subjectivity as emergent and relational.[15] Furthermore, advertising's promotion of the ability to mold the body, as a means of altering the self, facilitates capitalism's equivalence of consumers and objects, grounding social relations in consumption.[16] This perspective on advertising's relation to subjectivity emerges from the flow of advertising's dance-based visual texts. Thus, to demonstrate the cumulative nature of how dance-in-advertising theorizes subjectivity and its relationship to concepts of performance, theatricality, choreography and the performative, I offer close readings of a series of commercials over the course of this chapter.

"WORK IT" (CIRCA 2000): I DANCE, THEREFORE I AM

The images described below form the beginning shots of "Work It," a 30-second cotton commercial produced as part of the Fabric of Our Lives campaign by Cotton Inc. (see video 5.1 ▶).[17] The ad copy, "America's Cotton Producers and Importers," is superimposed on the bottom right of the screen in shots two to four. In total, the ad contains 32 distinct shots of 12 soloists, each of whom appears two to three times over the course of the ad. The soloists include a broad range of ages and work positions (e.g., entry-level, mid-career managers, and executives), representing a spectrum of American office workers. The dancers wear a wide range of office work attire, presumably all made with cotton fabric, and each dancer performs a unique solo using distinctive movement vocabulary and style. The combined differences in movement and clothing, along with other physical differences (gender, age, race/ethnicity, hair and skin color), encourage viewers to see them as individuals. These differences are then personalized through the camera's framing of the dancers in one of two ways: either by presenting the soloist in private, positioning camera and consumers as voyeurs, or by showing him/her within the context of a shared office space. The impression of unique individuals is heightened by the fact that their movement vocabularies consist largely of distinctive, freestyle movement. Only two or three perform recognizable dance genres, which has the effect of filtering their individuality through social identities.

A wide shot captures an office elevator and a black woman standing in its brightly lit interior, centered within the frame of the open doors, as the "ping" announces their closing. She wears straight-legged tailored pants, cropped at the ankle, with low heels and a narrow belt. Her outfit is completed by a rust-brown form-fitting top worn under a white jacket. As the doors begin to close, she settles back into the elevator, as though just stepping away from pressing the button for her floor. At the sound of the doors closing, off-screen music begins to play and the camera cuts to another scene: an open office space with desks arranged in pairs and a glass-walled office in the background. Several workers in suits without ties cross the space, as though returning to their desks. Their supervisor, a white man wearing slacks and a button-down shirt, stands in the glass office; he appears to stop and watch them. The next cut reveals him in the general office space, standing hands on hips with his body partially turned to his left and his head turned to his right to face the camera as he smiles. Another cut reveals a white woman in mid-stride as she crosses a hallway to set her portfolio case down on a modern, minimalist leather couch.

The portfolio case suggests she might be an artist or designer. She has short brunette hair and wears a straight calf-length green corduroy skirt with a wide brown belt, a white, red and black sweater, and a pair of high-heeled calf-high boots. The image cuts again to a new scene: an office copy room. In a series of three quick cuts, a blonde woman stands with feet together and arms either at her sides or with her hands clasped in front of her pelvis, as she faces the right side of the screen, then the left, and finally the camera. She wears a white-collared shirt under a blue v-neck sweater with a broach, a white A-line skirt sparsely decorated with flowers, and dark Mary-Jane styled flats.

The camera cuts back to the woman in the green corduroy skirt in a parallel plié, her left foot slightly behind the right in a forced arch. Hinged forward at the hips with her pelvis back in opposition, her torso creates a long diagonal to her forward-high as it spirals to her left. Her left arm extends toward back-high and her right arm forward-high. The camera captures her in mid-action. As she continues and hits the bottom of her plié, she sways slightly, pivoting on the ball of her foot as her lower back arches and her arms collapse slightly, elbows sinking (see figure 5.2).

Once again, the camera cuts to a new scene, this time revealing a darker-skinned woman with her face turned away from the camera. She stands next to a reception desk that appears to be in another part of the same hallway. She wears a long denim skirt with a lavender long-sleeved blouse. The camera seems to catch her in the middle of circling her hips as she extends her arms out to the sides. Quickly cutting to the next location, the camera captures an Indian woman framed in the open doorway of her office and facing the camera in a Bharatanatyam pose—arms extended out to the sides and slightly forward with her right reaching down and her left up, her hands formed into mudras. She wears a light brown A-line skirt and light-colored button-down blouse with elbow-length sleeves.

The commercial continues in this manner, intercutting between soloists and occasionally introducing a new "character." As my description demonstrates, the ad stresses a business casual dress code, which favors clothing made from cotton—a natural fabric. The dancers in "Work It" are filmed in business office settings and staged to appear as though the camera literally captures real people in their real workspace—though the average office is unlikely to include this many spontaneously dancing employees. To facilitate this impression of spontaneity, the commercial adopts film aesthetics, combining a *natural/realist* performance style with a kind of documentary presentation of

Figure 5.2 A "modern" dancer expresses herself in cotton clothing. Cotton Inc. commercial. Screen shot.

the dancers, as part of its *not-ad* strategy. This presentation of dancing-as-self is in part due to the realist cinematic performance style employed by the cast.

Realist film has developed acting methodologies, such as Konstantin Stanislavsky's, designed to present characters as people we observe, as opposed to people who perform for us.[18] Theater scholar Debby Thompson describes his approach as arising out of a liberal humanist perspective that "views human nature as transcultural and transhistorical, and views a character's identity as having an essential core of interior objectives and the character's (or actor's) bodily acts as the outward manifestation of the character's interior identity."[19] In his analysis of performance theories in relationship to logocentrism and différance, Philip Auslander describes Stanislavsky's approach as one that "implicitly designate[s] the actor's self as the *logos* of performance . . . [and] assume[s] that the actor's self precedes and grounds her performance. . . ."[20] Stanislavsky's approach works to achieve the appearance of the character's identity as a truth and a self that the audience can understand and find believable. To achieve this effect, the actor must minimize or eliminate distinctions between him or herself and the role played.

By eliminating this distinction, the actor presents the character as having an essential, coherent, consistent identity that arises out of a psychological interiority. Thus, the performance works to hide the constructed nature of the fictional identity and the social and cultural ideologies that inform its construction. In doing so, the performance naturalizes the "I" and reinforces categories such as race, gender, sexuality, and class as stable, coherent, natural, truths.[21] In realist cinema this acting style eschews theatrical modes of projection, as well as the artifice and exaggeration of melodrama, in favor of a more pedestrian, vernacular presentation of self.

This performance style is one way in which the commercial draws on the visual style of cinematic realism. In addition, as caught in the earlier shot descriptions, several soloists are introduced with a shot of her/him standing and looking at the camera prior to shots that capture the dancing. In this way, the ad creates the impression of a series of documentary portraits.[22] However, most of the dancing shots capture the soloists in moments when they are *not* looking at the camera, creating the impression that they are *not* performing but rather being themselves. The sense of portraiture and the impression of realism (i.e., the natural performance style) are reinforced via the frame-within-a-frame strategy of filming through doorways and windows. This strategy positions the viewer as a witness and/or voyeur as though viewers are being allowed to sneak a peek at the soloists in moments of uninhibited dancing that reveal aspects of their unique, individual personalities.

Correspondingly, given the setting, acting style, and filming strategies, the commercial invites viewers to see the actor-dancers as real people. Physical attributes, clothing, and dance unite with socio-cultural markers to present the dancers as individuals, relying on Romantic and Enlightenment concepts of individualism and subjectivity that ground expression in the psychologically-coherent interiority of a transcendent "I."[23] The combination of realist aesthetics and humanist acting style works in conjunction with variations in movement vocabulary and style to define each soloist as an individual subject by illustrating agency. Philosopher Judith Butler describes the notion of agency prior to postmodernism: "The question of locating 'agency' is usually associated with the viability of the 'subject', where the 'subject' is understood to have some stable existence prior to the cultural field that it negotiates."[24] The presentation of dance as uninhibited, self-expression creates a sense of agency because it attributes movement to subjective interiority.

The Cotton ad adopts this realist approach to performance to present its soloists as "real" people. Two executives, an older white man and woman, concretize this sense of dance as self-expression. The older, gray-haired male wears a casual suit of dark slacks, a light-colored Oxford shirt, a white suit jacket, black shoes, and glasses. The camera cuts to him as he lands from a little foot-switching jump, and then it tracks to follow alongside him as he wiggle-walks across a conference room—his head jutting forward, while his torso and hips twist in opposition. The conference room is empty, and his dance is shot from the hallway with the camera first catching him in the doorway and then filming him through the glass wall as he travels. His dance reminds me a bit of Jerry Lewis in goofy mode, playful and intentionally caricature in nature. He seems to almost purse his lips as he wiggles, as though the energy of the hips needs an additional outlet. The walk appears focused but light and quick overall, and he plays with restricting motion in parts of his torso and head to allow the movement to bounce freely in his legs, hips, and left arm. The personalized style of movement combined with the camera filming from outside of the space conveys the idea that the dance expresses interior feeling and that it is unique to him.

The older female executive's choreography is similar, except that the commercial first briefly introduces her as she stands in her office and looks at the camera. Her short, white hair, brown pants suit, and glasses are more conservative than some of the other women's clothing and hair. They suggest a woman who has minimized the outward show of femininity, but they align with traditional notions of age-appropriate clothing. The only other time the viewer sees her is near the end of the ad, as she dances across the office (and screen). She travels from the doorway toward the far wall in a kind of staccato, shuffling step as her arms and shoulders alternately push and pull on the space, as though helping propel her body forward. As with the man, her head strains forward, creating the appearance that it pulls the movement along.

Overall, the movement feels free and indirect, sending energy out through the body in a kind of release. The dance performs the expression of inner vitality and feeling, an opportunity to allow the body to express what is normally held in reserve. Both she and the man perform quirky choreographies that seem specific to them; their movement does not demonstrate codified dance techniques, per se, but rather personalized movement styles. In doing so, the solos participate in the ad's *naturalizing* of dancing, encouraging viewers to read the choreography as moments of expressive display. While the soloists' clothing and hair conform to expectations of the workplace and their age, their dancing is excessive, constituting a form of spectacle and *affective* embodiment.

These two examples of the older executives dancing demonstrate the ad's strategies for presenting movement as a sign of personal identity. First, they both demonstrate the ad's tendency to introduce dancers via "portraits" or in pedestrian moments before capturing them dancing. Second, both examples demonstrate the tendency to frame the dance as occurring in "private" moments. The impression of perceived privacy creates a sense of seeing movement that is personal and encourages the viewer's perception that the dancing is an expression of internal feelings because it suggests that the dances are not theatrical performances. Rather, the ad encourages viewers to view the dances as moments of indulgence where movement exceeds appropriate social behavior. Finally, the progression of shots produces a sense of gradually getting to know each soloist, as though their real self emerges out of the shot sequence.

The ad's montage provides both a sense of related difference and depth, minimizing the emphasis on linear, narrative progression. For example, the young blonde woman, initially seen standing still in the copy room, is seen later in the commercial slowly pivoting in place as she pulls shredded paper from a box and scatters it around the copy room like confetti. Shortly after, she is seen once more, this time in a medium-wide shot, as she once again stands in the copy room. However, this time she holds a small stack of paper in her hands and smiles contentedly at the camera. The camera seems to capture her in the middle of mischief, as decorating the copy room with shredded paper is not typically appropriate work behavior, and her smile in the third shot suggests she found pleasure and satisfaction in her moment of "excessive," "disorderly" movement. The stillness and containment of her standing postures present her as disciplined and quiet, while the gentle gliding arc of her arm as she swirls strips of paper around herself suggests that a suppressed, though still gentle, reservoir of energy flows through her. Over the course of the shot sequence, she emerges as a self whose outward demeanor hides a vitality and creativity that longs for release—a vibrating stillness waiting to unfold (see figure 5.3).

As seen in the above examples, shot progressions convey a sense of development focused more on revealing character than on narrative action, as

Figure 5.3 The "quiet" girl's creative expression disrupts the order of the office copy room. Cotton Inc. commercial. Screen shot.

evident in the soloists who perform quirky, eccentric movement that conveys distinct personal style and choice. Film and dance conventions suggest that these dances express personality through movement style and convey the embodiment of feeling. Their movement and how it is filmed presents the dancing as spontaneous expression, as though the ad captures unexpected bursts of feeling surfacing in private moments. In this sense, the ad relies on the ideological underpinnings of early twentieth-century movement systems.

Dance historian Nancy Lee Chalfa Ruyter offered one of the first scholarly accounts of Francois Delsarte's nineteenth-century "methodology for developing vocal and dramatic expression," arguing his system "demonstrates a keen interest in movement as an expressive means."[25] Ruyter traces Delsarte's influence on American modern dance through the lineage of his students and their efforts to teach and perform his work in the United States. She identifies Genevieve Stebbins, the student of Steele Mackaye (who was a student of Delsarte), as the practitioner that brought American Delsartism directly into relation with dance and other movement-based genres of physical culture and performance.[26] As Carrie J. Preston details in her work on gender and performance in the early twentieth century, Delsarte's methodology rested on the correspondence between "an inner 'soul' and its tangible manifestations in the body of the individual."[27] Delsarte's system of dramatic expression was built on the notion that physical gestures were indications of inner ones (thoughts, feelings, etc.). In turn, he thought that producing the appropriate physical forms or poses would produce the corresponding emotion or feeling.[28]

Both Ruyter and Preston identify points of transmission between Delsarte's system and early American modern dance practitioners, particularly Ruth St. Denis and Ted Shawn. The number of early modern dancers trained at Denishawn (e.g., Martha Graham, Doris Humphrey, Charles Weidman) and their roles as founding choreographers and teachers helped to instill Delsarte's concept of the body's gesture as the-manifestation-of-inner-being into American culture and concert dance. While direct ties between Delsarte and modern dancer Isadora Duncan are not evident, both Ruyter and Preston point to similarities between Duncan's work and Delsarte's. This connection was strengthened and sustained, in part, by the influence of Rudolf Laban's theories of movement and the work of his student, Imgard Bartenieff.[29] Laban and Bartenieff saw connections between the body's movement and the mover's inner life, between movement and expression. This notion of movement as the visible sign of inner life, as the expression of emotion and feeling informed not only American physical culture in the early twentieth century but also theories of acting in early cinema.[30]

These theories of movement are particularly salient to an analysis of subjectivity conveyed through dance in advertising because of the relationship they established between the body, expression, and performance, and their continued pervasiveness. They offer a historical context for contemporary popular understandings of the relationship between the body and expression in American dance and culture more generally. In fact, early psychological theories of *affect* seek to support this correspondence.[31] However, Delsarte's theory rests on an inherent contradiction in that it posits an innate correspondence between physical action and inner feeling but offers to teach students *how* to achieve a harmonious and efficient relation between the two. Delsarte's movement system employed codified postures, gestures, and facial *affects* to express emotion, thereby creating a shared system of socially defined signs by which to convey subjective feeling.

The Cotton commercial's presentation of human individuality and self-expression grounds notions of originality and personal identity in the interiority of a coherent, stable self/subject. However, the ad complicates this notion by grounding these subjectivities in ideologically-saturated sociocultural identities. A few of the soloists perform movement seen in specific dance genres. Two of the ad's more prominent solos fall into this category: the white female in the green corduroy skirt first seen in the hallway with the portfolio case and the Indian female first seen holding a Bharatanatyam pose.

Seen in five distinct shots interspersed throughout the commercial, the woman in the green skirt performs movement suggestive of modern concert dance. In addition to the shot of her sinking into a parallel plié, the camera captures her in a non-traditional medium-wide shot that frames her body from chest to ankles, catching her in mid-motion as she pivots on her right leg, spiraling to reach her right arm toward her raised, extended left leg. The camera cuts away before she finishes the action. In a fourth shot, the video cuts to her in a medium shot, catching her entire upper body in the frame but cutting off her lower legs. Head and elbows lead her, as she spirals to the left in a low wide plié. The commercial ends with one last shot of her as she walks backward circling extended arms back to front two times before wrapping them across her body.

Despite the fragmentation of the shots, the framing of her body works in combination with the shape and direction of her movement to create a sense of choreographic wholeness and continuity, as well as to align the solo with the compositional values of modern dance. The abstract movement and its motifs of diagonal facings, spirals, and lingering moments suggest a trained, facile body establishing and then developing a movement idea. Throughout, she never gazes directly at the camera and her focus appears internal, which calls to mind alternative approaches to focus in performance that are more common in modern dance than other genres. Additionally, match-cutting emphasizes continuity; she is never seen in a static posture but rather is always caught mid-action. This ongoingness reinforces the flow and internal focus of her movement, aligning the solo with somatic-based practices such as Bartenieff Fundamentals and release technique.[32]

In contrast, the Bharatnatyam dancer is seen in three distinct shots interspersed throughout the commercial. After her initial introduction, she is seen twice more as she dances. The shots provide just enough detail to associate her movement with the South Indian dance form. Both times, the camera catches her in mid-motion as she arcs and carves her hands and arms through a sequence of gestures consisting of hastas or mudras.[33] Each time, she remains framed within the doorway, emphasizing the verticality of her movement and suggesting the form does not travel in space. Thus, while the traditional dance form does at times travel in space, the ad's framing of it emphasizes containment and formal shape. This framing and emphasis on position aligns the classical Indian dance with static form in contrast to that of the modern dancer, whose solo's vocabulary and location emphasize motion and freedom to move. Her arms glide through the space around her body as she follows their paths with her gaze. While her feet move, the camera shots prevent the footwork from being visible. Her face, though directed toward her moving arms while dancing, is expressive.

Like the modern dancer in green, the Bharatanatyam dancer's movement aligns her with a codified dance technique and its cultural ideologies and context (see figure 5.4). While Bharatanatyam's history, unlike that of American modern dance, includes ritual and social contexts in addition to theatrical

Figure 5.4 An office worker expresses herself through Bharatanatyam. Cotton Inc. commercial. Screen shot.

ones,[34] both solos portray individual subjectivity within a framework of ethnic and national identity. In this context, and given the overall emphasis on individual style, the ad's appropriation of Bharatanatyam threatens to submerge subjectivity in cultural tokenism.

However, the genre-based solos by the two women also reveal the cultural specificity of movement practices. The full-bodied spiraling lines of the dancer-in-green and her averted neutral gaze link her movement to the complex interweaving of ballet and modern technique, as well as postmodern compositional practices and the historical role of female dancers in developing theatrical modern dance in the United States. The expressive face, vertical sitting posture, and mudras link the Indian dancer to Bharatanatyam, the history of the Devadasi, and the dance's twentieth-century revival by Brahmin women as a means of preserving cultural heritage.[35]

While many viewers may not have ready knowledge of histories and cultural values inherent in the dance forms, some viewers will and those who do not may still grasp the underlying message of commonality inside of difference—that is, natural cotton fabric and its suitability to a variety of activities and identities. Thus, while the Cotton ad relies on an understanding of dance as the outward expression of an interior "I"—movement as emotions and feelings written on the surface of the body—it also points to how we consume culture, reshaping it into personal expression. By employing dance-as-self-expression the Cotton commercial creates authenticity through the performance of subjectivity and self.[36]

CHOREOGRAPHIES OF SUBJECTIVITY AND THE PERFORMANCE OF IDENTITY

Drawing on post-structuralist theories that challenged the concept of absolute and foundational truths,[37] in 1990 philosopher Judith Butler argued:

> [g]ender ought not to be construed as a stable identity or locus of agency from which various acts follow; rather, gender is an identity tenuously constituted in time, instituted in an exterior space through a *stylized repetition of acts*. The effect of gender is produced through the stylization of the body and, hence, must be understood as the mundane way in which bodily gestures, movements, and styles of various kinds constitute the illusion of an abiding gendered self.[38]

Butler argued that outward signs of gender are not "expressive" but "performative" and thus the signs themselves "constitute the identity they are said to express or reveal."[39] Butler's theory of gender de-naturalizes gender as a concept and suggests that gender identity, and by extension the subject, is culturally constructed. She argues that through the repetition of acts ideology establishes and maintains social categories of identity (e.g., gender).

In response to Butler's theory of performativity, dance studies scholar Susan Foster applies the terms choreography and performance to the concept of identity. Foster argues that while Butler's concept of performativity articulates how individuals are interpellated into discourse and subjectivity through the repetition of acts, Butler's theory does not address the relationality of acts and fails to fully account for the role of corporeality. Foster challenges Butler's unexamined use of the terms "performance" and "performativity," questioning their efficacy in her theorizing of identity.[40]

According to Foster, Western concert dance's concept of choreography is better able than Butler's concept of performativity to account for "cultural values" and how they are established and maintained. Key to Foster's argument is dance theory's ability to distinguish between the *choreography* and the *performance* of identity:

> Choreography resonates with cultural values concerning bodily, individual, and social identities, whereas performance focuses on the skill necessary to represent those identities. Choreography presents a structuring of deep and enduring cultural values that replicates similar sets of values elaborated in other cultural practices, whereas performance emphasizes the idiosyncratic interpretation of those values.[41]

Foster's approach enables a distinction between the discursive system (i.e., choreography) that creates shared meaning and the individual performance (i.e., the way in which subjects put the system into action). Her work also emphasizes and demonstrates how the body and corporeality participate in the construction of gender identity. While both Butler and Foster address subjectivity through the lens of gender identity specifically, I extend their analysis to other categories of social identity. The following analysis draws on Foster's theory to look at the role of corporeality in the construction of social identity and subjectivity in advertising.

A Boost Mobile commercial, "Party" (2002),[42] paradoxically offers an example of how advertising, like television and cinema, composes fictional subjects through the corporeal embodiment of "static" social relations and cultural values (see video 5.2 ▶). Through the performance of social choreographies, actors generate recognizable ideological subject positions. As seen in the Cotton commercial above, advertising typically employs performance styles that naturalize the constructed (or choreographed) nature of these identities and reinforce Romantic notions of the authentic individual. However, advertising agencies occasionally employ tactics that call attention to the performance of these choreographies in ways that bring normative ideologies of bodily, social, and cultural identities into high relief. In these moments, advertising also positions identity as a performance, highlighting consumers' ability to interpret norms and conventions in new ways. One way that advertisers accomplish this effect is by drawing attention to performances that demonstrate a lack of skill, or a failure to correctly and skillfully embody the conventions, while still retaining the codes that signal the intended identity. In these moments, identity resides between the body, its visible attributes, and the relation it enacts to other subjects. Dance is key in that it draws attention to performance and the role of movement and relationality in identity.

The Boost Mobile ad draws on ideologically racialized and gendered sociocultural practices to mobilize bodily, social, and cultural identities. Souped-up cars, couches, chairs, a huge boom box, and a "raging" party occupy what looks like an entrance to the Los Angeles riverbed. A woman stands in the foreground of the shot facing the camera. While holding a mobile phone, she begins to speak to the viewer, as rap/hip hop music plays in the background: "So, I was like at home having like a really lame time, so I used by Boost mobile phone to two-way my friend. And she's like wanna go to a banging party, yo? And I'm like, yeah! And she's like should we two-way Alicia, and I'm like, hells yeah. And we're all at this banging party and getting ten kinds of nasty."

As she talks, she gestures with the phone. At one point, she flips it open, and the camera cuts to a close-up of the phone as she discusses two-waying Alicia. The woman speaking, as well as everyone else at the party, appears elderly—upward of 70 years old. The women wear knee-length or longer dresses, or skirts and blouses. Most of them wear long-sleeved sweaters and jackets, too. The men wear slacks paired with everything from only a wife-beater tank top to button-down shirts and suit jackets. A few wear hats. One man rides around on a bicycle with tricked out handlebars, a live rooster perched in front of him on the bike. Toward the end of the ad, an IV bag and oxygen tank are visible in the background.

All the dancers the camera highlights (i.e., they are positioned in the foreground or isolated in a shot) are white, except for one black man, holding what looks like a beer can as he dances. Most of the cast dances, and most of the dancing consists of stepping and pulsing, or gesturing with their arms, to the beat of the music. There is one man who "gets down"[43] more than the others. Bouncing and swaying, he drops his body into the rhythm as he polishes his car.

The one more prominent display of choreography is a male-female-male threesome, featured in a medium-wide shot toward the end of the ad. The man positioned behind the woman is freaking her, standing close to her with his hands on her hips as he thrusts his pelvis forward against her ass. The man in front of her alternates between facing toward and away from her as he gingerly (and somewhat playfully) grinds his hips at hers. The woman shifts her weight side to side and stands still for the most part, not articulating her pelvis in the sagittal plane, and holds her hands up to keep the man in front from pressing too closely against her body. She smiles but looks somewhat ill at ease, possibly slightly embarrassed, or possibly just a little giddy, turning her head away from the camera at one moment. The man in front smiles slightly, while the man in back makes faces that seem more reminiscent of what one might expect to see in a cheesy sex scene (see figure 5.5).

After a moment of the trio dancing, the ad copy, "Boost Mobile. Designed for young people," appears over the image. The last shot of the party scene is a medium-wide shot of the spokeswoman seen at the start. The once diegetic music dominates the image now, having transformed into extra-diegetic (i.e., off-screen) sound. As a male voice sings, "woo hoo, holler back young'un," the spokeswoman, Boost mobile phone in hand, opens her mouth as if saying "woo hoo," while she weakly (i.e., light and free veering from indirect to direct) pushes her hands up and forward in the air in a pale imitation of the 1990s "raise the roof" gesture.[44] The ad copy, "But it's just more fun showing old people," appears over her image.

As the ad copy confirms, the commercial juxtaposes the elderly (and white) bodies with popular culture associated with youth, lower socio-economic populations, and a mix of racial and ethnic social identities. The choreography contributes by reproducing normative gender roles (i.e., the freaking threesome) and mediated representations of African-American and Latinx expressive

Figure 5.5 An elderly threesome getting freaky at the party. Boost Mobile commercial. Screen shot.

culture on elderly white bodies.[45] MTV taught mainstream US culture to expect this behavior from young women, especially black women, wearing tiny outfits (e.g., booty shaking shorts and skirts, tight cleavage exposing tops, and bare midriffs and legs) as they dance at rap parties or in clubs.[46] The age and race demographic suggest this choreography is inappropriate, being either too sexually charged and, therefore, the purview of younger adults or a poor imitation of African-American and/or Latinx expressive culture.[47]

The inappropriateness of their dancing is signaled by the quality of their performance and the distance between this performance and a "successful" one.[48] The elderly cast falls short, overall, in their embodiment of the get-down stance, rhythm, and flow that convention dictates should accompany Fabolous's "Young'n (Holla Back)."[49] I find this distance to lie in the failure to fully inhabit the movement qualities; their performance gestures toward the movement aesthetic but never fully arrives. This inability to accurately perform the movement is capped off by the spokeswoman's flimsy "raise the roof," which looks more like shooing something away, or flapping her hands, than a demonstration of support or rallying a crowd.[50]

The Boost Mobile ad suggests several contradictory things about the choreography of identity. One, these social choreographies appear to be fixed and available as pre-existing subject positions. Two, anyone can attempt them but that not all people achieve the same level of performance—in this case, age is explicitly identified as a stable social choreography that is difficult to overcome. Thus, the ad suggests the possibility of a failure to fully realize the conceptual body through consumption, seemingly supporting the notion of social identity and its corporeality as foundational. In this sense, the ad suggests that simply performing the requisite choreography is not always sufficient. In other words, if you don't *really* belong, you won't be able to *authentically* perform the actions.

This notion of authenticity is supported by the humorous juxtapositions, which encourage viewers to see the performance as "wrong." Thus, paradoxically, the ad works to naturalize social identities, while promoting the consumption of Boost Mobile phones as a way of performing identity. While the performance seems to gesture toward the idea that social choreographies are linked to stable raced and classed social identities, their performance also suggests that these choreographies are learned behaviors. After all, the elderly cast is performing them, though poorly. Their ability to do so puts these social choreographies into motion, creating relationality and movement between ideologically-defined subject positions. In turn, this proposed movement potential opens the door to the possibility that one *can* assume different subject positions through performance. The consumption of corporeality as identity-in-motion is supported by the odd mish mash of cultural references conveyed through location, set, and music—all of which confuse and conflate classed and raced identities.

The settings evocation of the Los Angeles riverbed calls to mind specific Los Angeles communities, as the riverbed runs from downtown to the ocean passing along/through East Los Angeles, Compton, and Long Beach. Thus, the location also associates the ad with rap culture, Long Beach and Compton being home to rap artists like N.W.A. and Snoop Dogg. At the same time, the association with East Los Angeles links the ad to Latinx culture. In the latter half of the twentieth-century these communities have included largely lower economic Latinx and African-American populations and gang culture.[51] While the hip hop/rap music and "raise the roof" gesture link the choreography to African-American expressive culture, the souped-up parked cars initially call to mind Chicano low-rider culture. However, since its origins in the late 1950s, low-rider culture has expanded to include African-American communities.[52] Further confusing things, the cars also evoke the illegal Los Angeles drag race subculture represented in the film *The Fast and the Furious* (2001).[53]

These cultural associations are furthered by props and clothing: the giant boom box summons images of rap and b-boy culture, and the rooster and inside-furniture in an outdoor space evoke stereotypes of lower socio-economic classes. The overall blending of cultural references creates a composite stereotype designed to evoke non-white, LA youth culture. While setting, props, and music work to associate Boost Mobile with ideological positons and cultural values, it is the bodily performances that point to consumption as an act of agency and a definer of identity.

In his sociological analysis and history of consumer culture, Don Slater surveys theories that address consumption as the performance of identity. Drawing on sociologist Richard Sennett's work, Slater traces concepts of a "performative self" dating back to the eighteenth century; however, in this context the performative self is a conscious performance achieved through one's consumption of goods and seen as distinct from one's true self.[54] This historical notion of a "performative self" is essentially that of Thorstein Veblen, the nineteenth-century sociologist who coined the term "conspicuous consumption" in his *The Theory of the Leisure Class*.[55] His theory of conspicuous consumption points to consumer practices made possible by the industrial revolution, initially within the rising middle class, that are fueled by a desire for increased social status rather than the need or function of products. However, Slater also cites contemporary theories of consumer culture from the 1980s and 1990s that point to advertising's promotion of the notion of self as something constructed through consumption and individual choices.[56]

Slater argues that late-twentieth-century theories of modernity and social identity moved from notions of the "other-directed" self to a "cult of the self" that veers toward what has been described in its extreme forms as a kind of narcissism.[57] He connects these theories to consumer culture, arguing that this other-directed self views "other people and social relations . . . only in terms of their implications for maintaining a coherent self-identity."[58]

Consumption becomes a way of defining and maintaining oneself to the point that "advertising and the media routinely offer aspirational narratives of the self—images of lifestyles, goods, advice—with which the viewer can identify . . . they offer up the very idea of the self as a narrative form, something to be constructed through individual choice and effort."[59] However, because Romanticism's notions of authenticity and individualism have continued to inform cultural notions of identity, consumerism "vaunts promises of a coherent, authentic and valued self"[60] while simultaneously promoting the construction and performance of identity via consumption. Slater's analysis of consumer culture aptly sums up the inherent contradiction I find at work in advertising's concept of subjectivity and its relation to social identities. Dance amplifies this ambiguity through its associations with self-expression and learned behaviors, encouraging a sense of self-as-performance while also locating self in an identifiable "I."

The Boost Mobile ad demonstrates this contradiction, encouraging consumption as a way to both willfully shape one's identity and demonstrate one's authenticity. While the ad models a lifestyle cobbled together from cultural stereotypes and available via consumption, it legitimates and authenticates the social identities conveyed in the stereotypes. In this way, the ad practices what Douglas Holt has termed "cultural branding," as it "spin[s] a charismatic myth" and offers consumers the Boost Mobile brand as a pre-made form of self-expression.[61] Holt, writing more from the perspective of marketing than cultural analysis, argues that branding grants agency to consumers and allows them to transform themselves. David Savran summarizes this theory of branding in the following way: "A brand, then, . . . represents a cultural performance, or, further, the imprint left on a commodity by a series of cultural performances that 'casts a halo' over the brand, allowing it to 'resonate [. . .] with authenticity."[62] From a marketing perspective, consumption then places consumers in relation to this authenticity. Tapping into movement's potential, advertising employs dance as a means of heightening authenticity and agency, promoting a philosophy of consumption-as-becoming and a fluid, dynamic subjectivity.

LOCATING IDENTITY IN DANCE: SOCIAL CHOREOGRAPHIES, STYLE, AND THE GAP

The Cotton commercial discussed earlier demonstrated an approach to performance that worked to naturalize the choreography of identity, predominately reinforcing the idea that movement arises *naturally* out of individuals and encouraging viewers to read bodily identities as signs of interior subjectivity. Thus, instead of presenting the solos as performances of identity dictated by social and cultural conventions—as choreographies constructed largely of reiterated prescribed behaviors—the commercial conveyed the idea that the choreographies were authentic performances of individual expression that captured soloists' unique personalities. The Cotton ad asks consumers to believe that cotton fabric will let them be themselves and that it can accommodate a wide range of identities through modifications in style.

However, both the Boost Mobile and Cotton ads introduce how dance in advertising links commodity-signs (i.e., brand image) to social and cultural identities as sources of authenticity, while simultaneously offering consumers the opportunity to (re)define themselves through consumption-as-performance. The reliance on dance to produce authenticity draws not only on its association with self-expression but on the *affective* resonance generated by dance's relation to existing culture and social relations. Dance represents socio-cultural positions through the choreography of mannerisms, gestures, and actions; the energy or quality of movement; the form of the body; and the organization of bodies in space. In doing so, dance associates performers with social and cultural values, constructing identities that are then transferred to the product. Thus, the use of dance allows advertising to simultaneously point to and disavow the concept of identity as constructed through discursive repetition. On the one hand, ads present dancers as "live" or "real" bodies whose movement speaks the truth of their realities as individuals in the process of occupying ideologically saturated socio-cultural positions. On the other hand, ads offer the "real" of the body and its movement as transformation, putting identity in motion by treating identity as just another set of signs to be consumed.

By looking at a series of ads from a single campaign, I demonstrate how dance in advertising employs a concept of style-as-identity that posits identity as relational. The campaign demonstrates how advertising promotes the notion of individual choice in the performance of identity, offering consumers a range of options selected from previously established ideologically saturated, socio-cultural choreographies. In doing so, it offers consumers the opportunity to challenge, reshape, or otherwise alter ideology through their idiosyncratic performances. The campaign promotes the idea that subjectivity and identity are relational and process-based by showing the products ability to assume a range of choreographies and styles. Style and the ability to combine (and recombine) proliferating signs situates agency within the act of consumption.[63] I refer here to the 1998–99 Gap Khaki campaign, which marks the moment I first began to question how and why advertising employs dance.[64] This campaign also corresponds to a cultural shift, as instances of dance in advertising began to increase.[65] The Gap Khaki campaign consists of six distinct commercials, each highlighting a different genre of music and dance but sharing similar visual aesthetics, positioning strategies, and product lines.[66] To begin, I look at the Gap's "Khaki Country" (1999).

A brilliantly white space greets the viewer. The camera looks down on the action from the downstage right corner of the performance space. The dancers wear beige and stone white khaki pants and skirts paired with gray or dark blue t-shirts and tank tops, jean shirts, jean jackets and cowboy boots. The men wear brown cowboy hats. A white corral fence runs along both sides and the back of the space with a large marquee sign that reads "COUNTRY" suspended above it *upstage*.[67] A line of dancers stands shoulder to shoulder in a diagonal that runs across the space from downstage right to upstage left. The dancers bounce their right leg in time to the sound of a guitar striking the opening chords of Dwight Yoakam's cover of "Crazy Little Thing Called Love" (1999).[68] As Yoakam begins to sing, the line of dancers splits in two as the men side step to retreat upstage and the women mirror them, traveling downstage.

The entire commercial consists of one choreographed country and western line dance performed primarily in unison. This unity is inflected with normative gender and sexuality through compositional structure and movement vocabulary. The movement vocabulary consists largely of unisex movement: shuffling heel-first steps, hands slapping heels, chainé turns, heel taps, grapevines, and hip rolls. The bodies remain vertical with a slight flexion at the hips, and the dancers allow their torsos and hips to respond to and accent the rhythm and actions of the legs, though the movement is controlled (see figure 5.6). However, the women's hips and torsos are slightly more expressive than the men's. This subtle difference works with other variations to produce gender roles that support other heteronormative choreographic choices. The choreography and camera work reinforces the group's organization into heterosexual couples, including the occasional partnered do-si-do. The choreographic form consists of dancers arranged in a grid pattern that alternates man-woman-man-woman; it includes group formations that move the dancers through partnered steps as heterosexual couples or split the space in half, so that men dance in rows on one side and women on the other. The shot sequencing furthers this impression of normative heterosexuality by alternating between close-ups of male and female dancers, which sometimes produces the effect of one dancer smiling at another and organizes shots into heterosexual exchanges.

While unison vocabulary is the emphasis, the men perform movement that the women do not. At one point, the camera catches a row of men kneeling on their right legs as they extend their left legs and right arms out to the either side, tapping their hats and heels on the ground. At another point, as their female partners circle around them, the men touch the tips of their hats in a slight nod to the women. In the partnered sections, the men turn the women and contain them, standing slightly behind and to the side as they hold their hands. Finally, just before the end of the ad, two men traveling across the downstage area perform barrel turns, while three couples perform a partnered side-by-side step with the men's right arms wrapped around

Figure 5.6 Gap's "Khaki Country." Choreography by Jerry Grans. Commercial. Screen shot.

the shoulders of the women. The choreography's staging adopts theatrical strategies, establishing and maintaining a clear front, so that dancers rarely and only briefly turn their backs to an imagined audience. This sense of theatricality is further reinforced by parsing the choreography into sections in which the group formation changes, individuals are singled out, and duets are highlighted.

As the above description demonstrates the ad combines theatrical composition with social dance vocabulary, embodying socio-cultural values. Dance scholar Susan Foster articulates the role of the choreographer as a shaper of cultural norms and conventions. Describing the role of choreography, Foster argues that: "The choreographer . . . engages the body's semiotic field—the connotations that head, hand, pelvis, or heels carry with them, the meanings evoked by tension, undulation, collapse—and situates the body within the symbolic features of the performance space—the center, side, high, and low that the architectural context designates."[69] The use of the term "choreography" allows one to speak not only about movement (bodily lexicon, effort, organization, etc.) but also about the relationship between bodies and space, as well as strategies for organizing these elements. As seen in my description, viewing corporeality through concert dance compositional strategies highlights how ideologically defined subject positions inform both dance and everyday movement. Foster's approach explains how ideology and social relations inform one's sense of self, as well as how social identities are visibly present in movement.

For example, the dancing in Gap's "Khaki Country" reveals the blending of cultures unique to America and their influence on US dance practices. The emphasis on linearity (e.g., both the lines of bodies and the body's verticality), the organization of the group into heterosexual pairs, unison movement, codified steps, their dancing squarely on the 4/4 meter of the music, and the compositional design of the bodies (e.g., interweaving lines, grid patterns, rows of dancers etc.) reflect cultural values passed along from Western European culture (e.g., classical notions of harmony/order/balance, bodily control/containment/discipline), and traditional gender roles (e.g., distinct roles for men and women, patriarchy, chivalry). At the same time, though more hidden, the choreography reveals the Africanist influence and presence within American dance history through the subtle use of torso articulation, hip and shoulder isolations, and room for improvised individual expression in the performance of the choreography.[70] The dancing embodies group identity through the values it expresses; to identify with its conventions is, at least on a non-conscious level, to recognize and/or embrace the associated cultural and social values.

At the same time, the ad offers the opportunity to analyze the concepts of performance Foster addresses. Linking individual embodiment to the act and concept of performance, she argues that: ". . . performance concentrates on the individual execution of such codes . . . [,] focuses on the skill necessary to represent those identities . . . [and] emphasizes the idiosyncratic interpretation of those values."[71] She posits performance as being about both an individual's choice to embody normative behaviors (i.e., codes and conventions of sociocultural identity) and the skill with which individuals does so. Seen through the lens of Foster's model, the performance of identity in "Khaki Country" is located in the subtle variations of the choreography: how individuals move their hips and shoulders or incorporate facial expressions; how long a hand lingers as a man tips his hat or touches his female partner; how much energy dancers exert; how a woman angles her head as she looks at her partner; and the ease with which they perform the steps using the correct facings, timings, and shapes of the body.

Of course, The Gap makes a point of extending performance to include how the dancers wear Gap clothing. They don't wear identical outfits. As discussed above, there is a color and clothing palette, and dancers employ these elements in various ways. For example, one woman wears a long, straight khaki skirt, while another wears a knee-length version. One woman wears a gray tank with a brown scarf knotted around her neck, while another wears a button-down jean shirt with the front tied in a knot, exposing her stomach. These variations create different relationships between the women and cultural ideas of femininity and sexuality, linking each one in different ways to expressions of gender. These differences, as well as the differences in their performances point to the concept of style and its role in identity and consumption.

I want to return to for a moment to a reconsideration of theatricality, dance, and genre conventions to consider how they inform the choreography and performance of identity in advertising. The Gap khakis campaign further illustrates this concept in two ways. Each ad employs an all-white sound stage—sometimes, as in "Khaki Country," with minimal set design or textured lighting—that looks like an inversion of a black box theater and creates a liminal space of performance rather than a specific social context for the dance. The choreography's staging, the camera placement, and the dancers' performance all work together to produce a clear sense of downstage and frontal focus, directing the performance toward the television audience. Thus, the ad hails viewers by positioning them as audience members. The use of popular music by well-known artists enhances the commercials' association with music videos and thus furthers this sense of performance. The Gap campaign consistently employs not-ad positioning strategies by presenting theatrically staged choreography framed by supporting production elements. By refraining from any form of ad copy or logo until the end of the commercials they present themselves as performances, rather than ads. Unlike the Cotton commercial, the Gap ads position the dancing as a theatrical performance, linking the performance of identity with the conventions of theatrical presentation.

While the Cotton and Boost Mobile ads differ in that they situate the dancing in social contexts and on the surface present dance as personal and social expression, rather than theatrical performance, I argue that staging and camera work, as well as television's historical ties to theatrical performance forms, associate dance in advertising both with social practice and theatrical presentation.[72] As discussed in Chapter Two, the tendency of film musicals to transition from realist, vernacular gesture into elaborate choreography uses conventions to code dance as both self-expression and theatrical performance. The history of film musicals, and later developments such as music videos, allows the use of theatrical conventions in commercials to allude to performance modes and self-expression simultaneously. By equating performance with the individual embodiment of social and cultural conventions, it is possible to see capitalism modeling consumption and subjectivity as theatrical performance. This equation allows dance in advertising to link everyday performances of identity, which on some level are unintentional/non-conscious and learned behaviors, with the glamour and spectacle of theatrical performance (i.e., intentional, skilled manipulations of social and cultural behaviors), blurring distinctions between the everyday and the theatrical.

Performance scholar Janelle Reinelt represents Erika Fischer-Lichte's analysis of theatricality as developing the notion that theatricality results from the rupturing of everyday perception and spectators' recognition of the transformation of "material (bodies and objects) into signs of signs" that then "prevails over their customary semiotic function."[73] Furthermore, Fischer-Lichte theorizes that "theater, unlike everyday life, deliberately provides an experience of the 'very process of construction and the conditions underlying it . . . theater turns out to be a field of experimentation where we can test our capacity for and the possibilities of constructing reality.'"[74] Extending these ideas, I argue that advertising's production of theatricality through dance "foreground[s] the capacity of different spectators to create reality and to model the process of constructing reality."[75] Thus, dance in advertising promotes both the concept of dance as the self-expression of an interior stable "I" *and* dance as the performance of a constructed subjectivity arrived at through consumption. Advertising, through dance, locates subjectivity within the conscious and habituated performance of socio-cultural choreographies and associates agency with the consumer's mixing and remixing of these choreographies along with his/her performance style.

Viewing Gap's "Khaki Country" spot in relation to the whole campaign demonstrates the importance of style as a metaphor for identity and the construction of self through consumption. The six commercials that comprise the 1998 khakis campaign use differences in dance genres to highlight the stylistic possibilities of Gap clothing. The ads included the following genres: "Khakis Swing" (lindy hop), "Khakis Groove" (b-boy, poppin'), "Khaki Soul" (freestyle), "Khaki a-go-go" (1960s go go), "Khaki Country" (country line dancing), and "Khakis Rock" (in-line skating/skateboard choreography) (see videos 5.5, 5.6, 5.7, and 5.8 ▶). Airing the ads as a series over the course of a year allowed The Gap to claim a brand identity based on versatility and the ability to meet the needs of American popular culture's diversity. Difference became a matter of style and variation, and the commercials emphasized the products potential through the demonstration of possibilities.

Half the ads feature group choreography with an emphasis on unison.[76] However, the movement vocabulary and staging differ dramatically from one ad to the next. The two ads that differ the most are "Khakis Groove" and "Khaki Soul," which consist predominately of solos, duets, and trios performing individualized choreography, and they include a higher proportion of black performers (see videos 5.4 and 5.8 ▶). The style of their Gap clothing varies, too. For example, in "Khakis Groove" the dancers wear khaki pants (no skirts) paired with everything from tank tops to open button-down Oxfords worn over t-shirts to baggy sweatshirts and polo shirts. One dancer wears a baseball cap. Several of the performers wear their khakis baggy. Instead of cowboy boots, the male dancers wear sneakers, and the only female dancer wears chunky-heeled black shoes. While the choreography is set in an empty white space, the filming emphasizes high and low angle shots—including shots filmed from below the dancers through a Perspex floor—while still retaining a sense of performing for the camera and the at-home audience.[77] However, it is the choreography that reveals the versatility and potential of Gap clothing; "Khakis Groove" opens with a shot of its only female dancer.

The black female dancer grooves to Bill Mason's jazz/funk sound in an empty white-gray space. The camera looks up at her through the floor, catching her in a low angle wide shot from the front. The soles of her shoes are visible, making her appear to dance in mid-air. She performs a quick leg sequence, sliding along the floor as she heel-toes her legs open and closed to end with her feet about hip's width apart in a shallow bent-legged stance. Her legs mark the rhythmic accents in the music.

The camera cuts to a young, white man as he rolls a wave through his upper body from the fingertips of his right hand to his arm, across his shoulders, and down his left arm. Just as the movement is ending, the image cuts to catch a black male dancer as he jumps into the now empty space. As he lands on the beat, he looks at the camera, immediately springing up into a b-boy footwork sequence. Almost as soon as he starts, the camera cuts, replacing him with a Latino man in mid top rock, who drops into a down rock step only to be replaced by the white dancer as he does his own version of opening/closing leg work.

The commercial continues in this manner, cutting from one dancer to the next mid-action and traveling across bodies. The choreography is an eclectic combination of disconnected actions connected by a mixture of corresponding energy, rhythms, and shapes. Two shots capture a duet of tall black men. The first time they relate by creating an illusion as one forms a circle with his arms that the other seems to walk through (head first), and the second time they dance side by side in a jumping/bouncing unison choreography. The ad ends with the b-boy in a hand spin pose, left leg crossed over the right above his head; he balances on his left arm as he frames his face with his right hand and looks forward and down at the camera, grinning (see figure 5.7). His pose is almost invisible, as the camera immediately cuts to a screen with the ad copy "Khakis Groove" in the center, which is replaced in the final shot with the blue-and-white Gap logo.

The "Khakis Groove" choreography and its dancers' performances present consumers with a distinctly different sense of identity than "Khaki Country." The collection of solos stresses the value of individuality in a way that the unison of "Khaki Country" does not. However, the performances still demonstrate Foster's theory of performance as the individual embodiment of sociocultural choreographies.

First, gender roles are still evident to a degree: only men perform b-boy and strength moves; there is only one woman but seven men; the female dancer wears heeled boots instead of sneakers; and she performs a little hip jutting sequence (like a girly version of top rock) that emphasizes the display of her body. The differences between her movement and the men's makes a brief but noticeable allusion to female sexuality and distinguishes between male and female movement styles. Second, the use of solos and the eclectic array of movement with its nod to hip hop culture links the dancing to Africanist

Figure 5.7 In Gap's "Khakis Groove" a b-boy grins at the camera as he freezes in an inversion. Choreography by Tony Basil. Commercial. Screen shot.

movement aesthetics. The staging and diversity of movement suggests the possibility that the dancing may all be improvised, despite Tony Basil's choreography credit. Given the range of movement vocabulary, it seems likely that Basil staged and directed the dancers' original contributions. Conceptually, dance improvisation places more value on process and individual contributions in relation to the whole versus the symmetry, balance, and harmony of group form so often emphasized in Euro-American social dance and theatrical choreography.[78] The ad's movement vocabularies reinforce this contrast.

Overall, these bodies are less contained than those of "khaki country," performing a wider range of movements, shapes, and energies. The use of isolations is more varied and extensive. The movement is more grounded, and often there is more than one center of action in the body. While much of the movement is still vertical, the b-boy floorwork counters this verticality. The vocabulary embraces syncopation, establishing a relationship to the music that embraces multiplicity. Thus, the movement links the ad to dance genres arising out of African-American and Latinx cultural practices, which is supported to a degree in the styling of the performer's Gap clothing.

The variations in choreography, music genres, and styles of Gap clothing across the body of ads suggests that the performance of identity lies in what you do, how you do it, what you wear, and how you wear it. While the ads reinforce the association with cultural practices and values through casting (i.e., performers' gender, race, and age), they incorporate enough diversity to open up to the possibility that biology is *not* identity. The Gap ads posit that at least some social and cultural categories are *performed* rather than innate and that *who* you are is subject to change. Identity is in motion. However, the social identities (i.e., ideological subject positions) that seem to remain as stable truths, gender and age, allow for some variation but are not emphasized. Thus, to a degree, The Gap argues that identity is a matter of style—executed through individual performance and tied to consumption.

The links between choreography, performance, identity, style, and consumption are furthered through an important aspect of the campaign's not-ad strategy. At no point in the ads is there a mortise (i.e., a picture inset separated from the main signifying image) of the product. Instead, the product is visible on the dancers throughout the ad. This condensation means that the clothing, in a sense, performs. The Gap's not-ad strategy successfully collapses the distinction between product and signifying image, subtly reinforcing the abstraction and transfer of human attributes to the product, equating dancing bodies with Gap clothing. However, sometimes the processes of abstraction, reification, and equivalence are taken to even further extremes within dance-in-advertising.

CONSUMPTION AS PERFORMATIVE AND FLUID SUBJECTIVITIES

A woman in a pale pink sleeveless dress and ballroom heels walks down the driveway of a house to approach a man in all black, who stands posed in a neutral stance in the driveway. Walking behind him, she places her left, then right arm firmly over each of his shoulders. The next shot captures them from the side as she straddles him from behind, arms and legs extended forward on either side of his body. He begins walking backward down the driveway, looks over his shoulder once, and then suddenly tosses her right leg around his back to slide her to the ground. As he descends into a runner's stance, she smoothly pivots around his body, leaning forward, to come to stillness with her elbow on his back and her chin resting on her hand as she watches a boy on a skateboard ride down the sidewalk. As the woman watches the boy, the announcer states, "moving object detection."

The ad then cuts to the couple side by side as they travel down streets in a walking choreography—wide second plié, slouched pirouette, a series of walks and suspensions accompanied by a gestural arm sequence. On the highway, she is once again on his back; he glances over his shoulder; she slides off him to chaîné to a parallel stance in front of him, leaning forward as he briefly suspends her in a counter-balance just as a motorcycle speeds past.

The voiceover announces "blind spot warning." In the next shot sequence, a speeding semi truck is barely avoided as he lifts her from behind to move her out of the lane: she sits back into his arms, resting her hands on him and pikes her body, extending both legs toward the sky, as he pivots her to safety (see figure 5.8). The off-screen voice says, "Lane departure warning. Safety, down to an art." The ad cuts to the couple on a parking structure rooftop; she stands beside him and trails one hand down his chest, while he stands in neutral looking straight ahead. She lingers briefly, turns, and walks away. The final wide shot reveals her walking away from a black Nissan Altima that stands in his place.[79] The announcer states, "The Nissan Altima with safety shield technologies; Nissan, innovation that excites."

The above 2013 Nissan Altima commercial[80] uses the male-female duet to transfer the choreography and performance of identity to the product (see video 5.9 ⓟ). The ad begins in a middle-class suburban housing development, idyllic in its serenity and apparent economic security.[81] Over the course of their journey, they create abstract representations of the car's capabilities as the voiceover narrative describes each one. The ad uses modern dance compositional principles: abstraction to convey concepts and common experiences, pedestrian movement, and partnering sequences to embody the driver–car relationship. In doing so, the ad associates the car with concert and social dance codes and conventions associated with white, Euro-American culture.

Avoiding the high-affect juxtaposition, groundedness, and polycentrism found in Africanist movement aesthetics, the ad draws on English style ballroom in its aesthetic more than other forms of social dance. Their partnering

Figure 5.8 Personifying the Nissan Altima, Robert Prescott Lee pulls Emily Williams to safety. Choreography by Fatima Robinson. Commercial. Screen shot.

follows traditional gender roles as he manipulates and supports her, extending the notion of the man as the active, decision-maker and the woman as passive by incorporating his role as protector (i.e., a performance of chivalry). In a "fitting" embodiment of Nissan's Safety Shield Technologies, his lifts and manipulations of her body ensure her safety literally, as he prevents her from running into or being hit by other people and cars. The differences in their clothing both support their embodiment of traditional heterosexual gender roles and their "characters" in the ad. Her pale pink dress is made of a light, supple material that ripples and billows throughout the choreography, adding to her femininity with its delicacy. Being clothed entirely in black neutralizes his presence—a tactic seen, for example, in theater crews and Bunraku puppetry—and unites him via color with the car at the end of the commercial.

This Nissan Altima commercial demonstrates what sociologist and consumer culture theorist Celia Lury describes as a shift in the ontology of objects. This shift is the result of changes in advertising. As marketing moved from promoting a product's function to producing brand identity, the commodity-sign's process of abstraction, equivalence, and reification focused on transferring style and social relations to the product.[82] This process produces advertising that markets objects/products based on human qualitative attributes and performative potential. Advertising effects a shift in being.

Lury argues that consumerism has produced a cultural system in which, "Objects are no longer understood in terms of the quality of . . . a product but rather as a system of relations, a set of performances."[83] Within the industry, literature on branding posits it as a cultural performance that instills authenticity in the product and enables objects to function as vehicles of self-expression and signifiers of consumer identity.[84] The advent of the phenomenon of "convergence culture" extends this aspect of branding as products come together in advertising and mass media, creating relationships that produce pre-fabricated identities and relations-of-belonging from which consumers assemble identity.[85] The neoliberal capitalist and media-driven proliferation of spectacle and sign production supports this shift, and this change aligns with concepts found in post-structuralism and deconstruction.[86] In the hands of consumer culture, the unmooring of the sign, the death of truth, and the endless deferral of meaning support the circulation of social relations as signs to be tried on and discarded as consumers relentlessly construct and reconstruct themselves.

I argue that dance-in-advertising as made explicit in this Nissan Altima ad, enacts the "stylistic autonomy of objects" and locates subjectivity in movement by engaging products in choreographies that perform cultural identity and social relations. Like dance, the concept of mass, as discussed by sociologist Robert Cooper, posits movement and its choreographies of relations and space as central to understanding consumerism and reproduction in late twentieth-century capitalism. Drawing on Pablo Picasso's collage art as a model, Cooper argues that Picasso's work makes relations visible, rather than "self-contained, substantive things."[87] Picasso's collages model the accumulation of mass as sites of convergence where various elements meet and meaningful relations emerge. I argue that Cooper's description of mass as the "ceaseless movement of collection and dispersion, production and consumption"[88] highlights the roles of motion and emergence in consumer culture. In this world of endless change and motion, at first, dance appears to instill human agency.

However, Cooper links the concept of mass to questions of agency, arguing that: "Instead of voluntary human agency expressing its conscious desires, we see human action as the interactions between body parts and external objects in . . . [a] *materialization of acts* in which, for example, the spoon as object materializes the act of eating . . ."[89] Cooper describes the process by which human actions (and thus also agency and *affect*) become associated with physical objects, which in turn come to stand in for those actions. Within neoliberal culture, people and objects have become interchangeable.[90] Dance-in-advertising facilitates this transfer of human agency to objects through its abstract embodiment of human attributes and social relations.

Consumer culture conceptualizes agency as grounded in mass production-consumption by understanding agency as an assemblage of incomplete parts that are in a constant state of flux. In turn, advertising models the construction and development of agency as a form of assemblage. Dance furthers this dynamic by depicting agency, along with identity, as a literal performance, as the performance of a choreography of ready-made attributes, skills, values, and social relations that can be assimilated into and onto the body, modified through stylistic variations, and discarded at will in an endless series of combinations.[91] Thus, identity becomes a matter of style and the performance of identity occurs through one's consumption of signs. In advertising, dance embodies *change*, putting bodies into motion and revealing agency as a process in which static ideological subject positions are inhabited as consumers move between and inside of them.

Dance produces the virtual through excess, embodying possibilities. In this way, dance-in-advertising contributes to the production of a Deleuzian multiplicity (i.e., a body without organs) in the guise of the expressive Cartesian subject.[92] Consumerism echoes Deleuze and Guattari's call for the body without organs, encouraging a sense of self as a shifting mass of signs that functions as a site of expression that expresses the self at the moment of expression, the self as a plane of relations that performs singularity but is not singular. The self-in-motion whose stylistic variations shift the rules of the game even as it enacts them.

I offer one final example of dance in advertising that draws advertising's concept of subjectivity to the surface, exposing the dynamics at play in its construction. A high-angle "extreme" wide shot of a science classroom, as initially evident by the skeleton in the foreground, greets the viewer. The prevalence of wood furniture establishes a sense of tradition and heritage, giving the impression of a New England prep school, rather than the fabricated materials found in California elementary schools in the twenty-first century. A close-up shot of the classroom clock striking 9 am cuts to a close-up of the floor as rapidly firing feet tap dance into view. The camera quickly cuts back to a wide shot to reveal internationally renowned Savion Glover tap dancing his way down an aisle past studious children. In classic Savion Glover style, his whole body inhabits the energy and rhythm of his percussive steps. Dreads shroud his bowed head and engage in their own responsive dance. He crosses one end of the classroom and then suddenly ascends from floor, to chair, to desk and makes another pass down the classroom—this time tapping his way across desktops. Notebooks, chemistry flasks, and a frog become instruments that sound in time to his danced percussion. As he taps past students, they continue their work without disruption. Reaching the far end of the room, he grabs the skeleton and spins back down the center aisle with it in his embrace.

Immediately, the camera cuts to a shot of him jumping onto a wooden rolling chair and pushing himself backward with enough force to send him sailing back down that center aisle (see figure 5.9). A wide shot reveals Glover

Figure 5.9 Savion Glover hops onto a rolling chair near the end of his V8-fueled tap solo. Campbell's V-8 Juice commercial. Screen shot.

seated, feet lifted off the floor, as the chair glides backward, only to have the ad cut to a medium shot in which the edge of a desk is visible in the foreground. As the chair sails into view, the hand that rests on the arm is white now, not black. When the ad cuts to a wide shot, it reveals a middle-aged, white man wearing clothing identical to that of Glover's, drinking the last of a V-8 as he sits in the chair. A close-up reveals graying hair at his temples and a satisfied smile as a sing-song voiceover announces, "drink it. feel it," which then appears as ad copy imposed on the image of a desktop where a V-8 Juice bottle sits (see video 5.10 ▶).[93]

While the teacher appears to be the picture of traditional educational values and white male patriarchal culture, clearly, on the inside, he is the epitome of youthful African-American culture and the aesthetic of the cool. Tap dancing Glover stands in for the virtual vitality of V-8 and the potential ephebism and polyrhythmic cool of the teacher. The teacher's reverse transformation suggests that this potential resides within him and that V-8 is the cause of his transformation. Even as he functions as a visible sign of white patriarchy, the teacher embodies a fluid subjectivity that reifies inequalities in discursive and ideological subject positions. The ease with which he assimilates the African-American body calls forth the history of racial inequality in the United States and neoliberal capitalism's emptying out of corporeal oratures.[94]

The commercial enacts its own consumer culture form of magical realism, depicting the magical transformation of self within a cinematic realist context. The potential for transformation becomes a possibility, the commercial argues, through the consumption of V-8. Thus, the consumer product provides access to ways of being and feeling that appear to fall outside of personal experience and established social relations. The commercial teaches consumers that the power to define one's self-identity and to change one's sense of belonging and *affective* experience of the world lies in the act of consumption. Perhaps the essential "I" of advertising's subjects exists because it consumes; its foundational truth not being individual essence, or soul, but rather its ability to choose and the choices it makes.

Does subjectivity emerge, or emerge in part, from consumption? Massumi draws on complexity theory and the concept of self-organization to rethink the nature of subjectivity, the body-mind, and self. His philosophy draws on science to reorient these concepts. Continuing the work of Deleuze and Guattari, he argues that "sensation is never simple. It is always doubled by the feeling of having a feeling. It is self-referential."[95] He distinguishes this self-reference from self-reflexivity, because what he is referring to here is simply the fact that to experience sensation one must have a certain awareness of the feeling that one is experiencing. Here, he is not referring to emotions, per se. So, without going so far as to turn back and reflect on sensation, the sensation is already a doubling without the distancing inherent in self-reflexivity. Based on this concept of sensation, he argues that experience is "intensity" and in turn that this intensity is the "conversion of the materiality of the body into an *event*."[96] He claims that the *event* "may well be the conditions of emergence of a subject: an incipient subjectivity" that points to the self as a "relation" (intangible) rather than a "substantive" (tangible).[97] Thus, subjectivity requires relationality.[98] The perception of self occurs in relation to others.[99]

Is it possible to look at examples of dance in advertising as the "manifestation of a concept"?[100] If so, what I have attempted over the course of this chapter is to examine the concepts of self and subjectivity as manifested through dance in advertising. Relation and movement (rather than static positions) are inherent in dance. The variations that become possible in performance speak to the potential of the body-mind and the ability to change. Choreographies, be they social behaviors or danced ones, themselves are emergent rather than static structures placed on subjects. Dance teaches us about subjectivity because it is in motion, because dance relies on self-organization at the level of the body-mind but also at the level of the relations between bodies, bodies and the space, and subjects and objects. Dance understands the subject-object relation as a two-way fluctuating relation.

While dance-in-advertising participates in consumer culture's appropriation of social identities and the reduction of subjects to ideologically saturated selves defined by consumption, dancing bodies bring with them not only ideologies but also challenges to those ideologies. Dance locates agency in action and potential. While the white middle-aged teacher in the V-8 commercial cannot, perhaps, literally become Savion Glover, a [then] younger African-American tap dancer, the ad taps into the *affective* power of dance, the potential of the thinking-body, and the emergent nature of self. While locating subjectivity and agency solely within consumerism confines and subjects the self and social identity to discursive and economic powers, dance reminds us that agency resides in motion and social relations. Movement has the power to affect change, in the self and in the social.

However, dance also serves as *affective* spectacle that plays off ideological subject positions to produce feeling and engagement in viewing consumers. And in this way, dance serves as a vehicle for both enhancing and eliding the destructive power of advertising's portrayal of the post-structuralist subject. The "deconstructed subject, fluid, fragmented and decentered"[101] that manifests via dance in advertising consumes identities and social relations as objects. Advertising encourages this deconstructed subject to navigate culture monetarily, creating equivalences that deny lived realities by instilling the belief that relations are reducible to the *affect* and socio-cultural status of the products one consumes. Or, perhaps, it is important to remember that consumption, like dance, puts bodies into motion and that agency lies in action, and action is relational and emergent.

Conclusion

Material Bodies and Advertising

In conclusion, I offer some additional tentative thoughts regarding advertising's appropriations of dancers' bodily labor. In commercials, advertising strategies position the dancers first as a medium of transmission and second as subjects with agency. However, the goal of advertising is to disguise the mechanism by which people become objects and objects agents. This transformation of live bodies intersects with questions about property, labor, ownership, and copyright in ways that I have not discussed in this book.

However, the nature of advertising's "borrowing" of dance differs in each circumstance. In the case of ads using stock footage, say Gap's Audrey Hepburn "Keep it Simple" spot, the use of her likenesses becomes, in a legal sense, a question of who holds the copyright to the archival footage. The use of stock footage in ads elides ontological differences between archived images of absent bodies and live performing bodies—as the mediated form of the dance lives on beyond the moment of performance. Once, they were both live; they are just once removed from each other—generations of simulacra. Scholars working within dance, philosophy, and law have addressed concepts of labor and ownership in relation to identity in ways that are productive for examining dance in advertising.[1] While I haven't tackled these questions in my research, I want to end by offering some industry data and my thoughts on the positioning of dancers in advertising as "possessive individuals and rights-bearing subjects rather than as commodities and objects of exchange."[2] I largely raise questions here, rather than supply answers, in acknowledgment that this line of questioning deserves further attention.

In twenty-first-century advertising, copyright and licenses vary depending on content, context, and contract.[3] Furthermore, print advertising differs from on-air and online commercials. For example, in 2016 *Ad Week* echoed a *New York Post* piece that "outs" one of the dancers from the initial Apple iPod silhouette print campaign, revealing contract practices. Mandy Coulton, the striped bikini silhouette, told the paper that she received a flat $1500 fee for the photo shoot and use of her image but did not receive any residuals.[4] Apple bought out the image of Coulton's silhouette, which is a standard contract practice in print advertising that results in performers signing away copyright to their image. Her compensation speaks to the realities of dancers and performers within America's capital-driven economy, but it also differs from that of performers working in on-air or online commercials.

In commercials differences also exist between dancers who appear as extras and those who are featured as an on-camera principal (OCP). Extras appear primarily in the background and receive direction from the First Assistant Director. However, OCPs are easily identifiable, engage directly with the ad's action/meaning, and receive instructions from the Director. The details of each contract vary depending on the time needed and the requirements of the client; typically, performers must sign contracts with both the agency and the production company. These distinctions then affect compensation. The agency negotiates with all performers and choreographers to establish their talent sessions fees, which may consist of either a daily or hourly rate paid on the day of filming. As with composers, choreographers license their choreography to the client/product by medium and for set periods of time (television vs. online). However, when it comes to performers, it isn't uncommon for only the OCP contracts to include residuals. The typical cycle for cable and network TV residuals is three weeks versus one year for internet and industrials. After 23 months, the residual license expires, and extending the run requires that the client further compensate performers.

In advertising, many choreographers and performers are not celebrities. Consequently, they typically remain nameless, hired bodies whose creative contributions go largely unrecognized outside of the industry. While advertising agencies house contracts and detailed production credits, information regarding performers and choreographers is often not released to the public. Press releases, news stories, and archives do not typically record the names of performers—this practice is true for both dancers and actors—and they only sometimes identify choreographers. Credits go to production and celebrities. Thus, advertising primarily promotes the authorial presence and recognition of film directors, ad agencies, and production companies.

Choreographers and dancers rarely receive recognition. The exceptions are noteworthy, and most often these exceptions are due to cross-promotional strategies, pre-existing celebrity status, or self-promotion on the part of the artist. This difference is evident in the ease with which information about the choreographer and dancers in each commercial is or is not readily available online. Thus, the notion of appropriation as a borrowing grounded in unequal distributions of power is here grounded in relations of neoliberal capitalism where choreographers and dancers are often denied recognition and retain limited control of their moving image or choreographic labor.

However, celebrities, even when appearing in stock footage, typically receive recognition as performers and creators because industry articles identify them and/or because viewers either track down the reference or already possess knowledge of their performance history. Celebrities retain their value, even when reduced to an image.[5] Even in the case of deceased performers, the monetary value of established publicity personas provides insurance that whoever holds the copyright retains legal ownership, which helps ensure that the body's labor continues to be recognized and compensated.

Three contemporary examples of dance in advertising demonstrate a range of approaches to valuing the labor of dancing bodies. All three premiered between 2014 and 2016. These examples are all longer than the now standard 15- to 60-second television spot, running between 1:43 to 3:48 minutes in length. While the full-length versions are designed to run as viral videos online, the campaigns include shorter versions of the ads, making it possible to run them in different contexts, such as network or cable television. All three ads promote brands (Kenzo World, Diesel, and H&M) linked to the fashion industry.

Kenzo World's "My Mutant Brain" advertises their new perfume line and features actor Margaret Qualley in a performance that mixes improvisation and set material under the direction of choreographer Ryan Heffington (see figure C.1 and video C.0 ▶).[6] The nearly four-minute commercial is an example of

Figure C.1 Ballet-trained Margaret Qualley imitates a gorilla for Kenzo World's new fragrance. Choreography by Ryan Heffington. Commercial. Screen shot.

a work where cross-promotion and strategic self-promotion ensured that the choreographer, dancer, director, and brand all received equal attention. In this instance, the brand explicitly benefits from cross-promotion that highlights choreographer, director, and dancer.[7]

The celebrity status of all three directly informs the intended meaning of the ad. Qualley, daughter of actor Andie MacDowell, began by studying ballet—earning an apprenticeship at the American Ballet Theater—before moving into modeling and acting. The commercial is directed by Spike Jonze, and in style it quite resembles his music video featuring actor Christopher Walken for Fatboy Slim's "Weapon of Choice."[8] Jonze is well known as a director, having worked in commercials, music videos, and film since the early 1990s, and he has garnered considerable recognition for films such as *Being John Malkovich* (1999). Heffington, a contemporary Los Angeles choreographer, recently choreographed Sia's music videos, creating an idiogest for the featured female dancer, Maddie Ziegler. Given global flows of capital and the ubiquity of American mass media, his work with Sia has garnered him national, perhaps international, recognition.

Qualley's body acts as transducer[9] for the styles of Heffington and Jonze, seamlessly joining conceptual and compositional eccentricity with traditional notions of elegance and beauty. Combining these three artists, both in terms of product and reputation, facilitates the brand's image construction, merging high fashion aesthetics with brazen individuality. My reading aligns with the brand's goals; on their website, Kenzo World describes the perfume as a "bold, spontaneous and surprising world." Thus, the marketing strategy directly relies on this combination of artists *and* ad concept to produce the desired brand image for the product. This strategy strengthens the position of the artists and ensures they receive recognition for their work in addition to compensation for their labor and intellectual property.

However, most commercials do not operate based on this dynamic of cross-promotion between performers and product. An example that employs a different strategy is Diesel's "The A to Z of Dance" (see video C.1 ▶).[10] This promotional video was created by *i-D* magazine for Diesel and consists of a series of clips featuring one or more dancers performing different genres and styles of dance—one dance sequence per letter of the alphabet (see figure C.2). This promotional video's duration is 3:30, which is long enough to indicate it was not made for television commercial breaks, marking it, like Kenzo World's, as designed for online and industrial venues. Significantly, it is one of very few commercials to include full credits for both performers and production, furthering its not-ad agenda and disguise as a short film. Unlike "My Mutant Brain," this ad features numerous performers, only some of whom would be easily recognizable at the national or international level to the general public.

For example, choreographer Ryan Heffington "X-presses" himself and dancer Lil' Buck performs Memphis jookin'. However, at the end of the film,

Figure C.2 Nick Lanzisera performs "D" for "Death Drop" in "The A to Z of Dance." Diesel promotional. Screen shot.

all the dancers are credited by name for their work in the ad, and articles on-line reference working with the dancers' managers, suggesting that many, if not all, are connected to the commercial dance industry. Thus, in this ad, the dancers' labor grants them access to compensation, self-promotion, and authorial presence, even though ad agency, film director, brand, and any celebrities outweigh the average performer as authorial voices for the work as a whole.[11]

Arguably, both the Diesel and Kenzo ads veer into the world of music video and experimental film shorts. The ads draw on the promotional aspects of those genres but also on their positioning as entertainment forms—a part of capitalist consumer culture that may be more easily accepted as innocent of intentionally furthering capitalism's agenda.[12] Drawing on this strategy but aligning, perhaps, more with a traditional commercial format, the H&M's "School is Back—Dance-off" demonstrates the standard attitude toward performers (see video C.2 ▶).[13] The ad is 1:43 in length (a 30-second version exists too) and features a school yard dance battle between two crews of elementary school children to advertise grade-school fashions for Fall 2016 (see figure C.3). The ad provoked a colleague of mine to casually query the political economy of the commercial dance world—in response, perhaps, to how young the dancers are.

The commercial's cast of children features talented dancers who are spotlighted throughout the battle sequences (see figure C.4), evoking the challenge dance format made popular in films such as *You Got Served* (2004) and the *Step Up* franchise (2006–2014). Unlike the other two ads, the H&M spot does not directly or indirectly (through other media outlets) promote the

Figure C.3 H&M's "School Yard Dance-off" features elementary school street dancers. Choreography by Tricia Miranda. Commercial. Screen shot.

Figure C.4 As the H&M battle continues, the dancers form a cypher. Choreography by Tricia Miranda. Commercial. Screen shot.

dancers as individuals by providing easily locatable credits. While it is usually possible to find at least minimal credits (i.e., ad agency, director, production company) for commercials airing in the 1990s or after, they still do not typically credit performers or choreographers. Thus, the H&M ad is a typical ad in this sense. The lack of credit for individuals whose labor is essential to the work in an industry based, no less, on promotion is striking. When considered in light of mass media's use of stock footage, it suggests that unlike celebrities, the dancers in most ads are effectively reduced to objects of light and sound.

This failure to directly credit dancers and choreographers as subjects of their own labor effectively reduces them to spectacle, conveyors of *affect*, and objects of exchange—images to be bought and sold for use in promoting other commodities.[14] Advertising's disenfranchisement of dancers and choreographers is not unprecedented within American capitalism. For example, over the course of the twentieth century practices for crediting choreographers and dancers in cinema have varied.

The Academy Awards included a category for Best Dance Direction, awarded for three years 1935 to 1937 before being discontinued, and four Special Awards were given to choreographers between 1949 and 1968. However, IMDB's online archive of films often includes dancers in the full cast listing—sometimes indicating when dancers have gone uncredited—though advertising is not typically archived here. In contrast, television's Emmy Awards do include a category for Best Choreography, though this award goes to choreography for television programming rather than advertising. The largest form of recognition comes from the commercial dance industry working together to generate their own awards system, The American Choreography Awards,[15] just as the concert dance world has done with its regional awards (e.g., Los Angeles's Horton Awards, San Francisco's Isadora Duncan Dance Awards, or nationally recognized New York City's Bessie Awards). To my knowledge, the only awards ceremony to acknowledge dance in advertising were the American Choreography Awards. While advertising has its own awards system, the Clio Awards being a prominent one, awards for choreography would most likely be encompassed in the categories for best Innovation or Events/Experiential.

Awards are not necessarily the most important form of recognition, but I address them here because in a capitalist economy where success is, essentially, grounded in promotion, this kind of recognition indicates forms of investment and the valuing of some forms of labor over others. The larger issue that deserves greater attention is the dancer's and choreographer's labor within America's economic system. As I indicated at the start, this research is labor that I have not done—a remainder that awaits further investigation.

While working in the commercial industry guarantees dancers and choreographers are paid for their labor—in comparison to the concert dance world where smaller companies are not always able to financially compensate dancers, or have limited means for doing so—commercial work remains piecemeal and evidence suggests their bargaining power is limited. A comprehensive examination of dancers' and choreographers' bodily labor in relation to capitalism remains to be done.

Thus, I end my examination of how dance fuels advertising and its engagement in cultural meaning-making by introducing a new avenue of research. I realize I have merely nudged the doors open here, gesturing toward lines of inquiry without delving into their complexities or details. The dearth of *detailed, organized, comprehensive* public advertising archives makes this work difficult, as does the lingering tendency to view television and advertising as transitory, trivial, or tenuous in their relationship to culture. Further research calls for more archival work in collaboration with advertising agencies and the choreographers and performers who work for them. The era of neoliberal capitalism demands a more tangible examination of the political economy of advertising's engagement with dance.

NOTES

INTRODUCTION

1. In an earlier article, I describe each campaign in detail, addressing positioning strategies and framing devices as forms of hooking within and across ads. Colleen Dunagan, "Performing the Commodity Sign: Dancing in the Gap," *Dance Research Journal* 39, no.2 (2007): 3–22. Gap, "America," "Cool," and "Dance at the Gym," directed by Mike Mills, featuring choreography by Al Johnson after Jerome Robbins, commercials aired 2001, 30 seconds, accessed June 15, 2017, https://youtu.be/PwMzn25Iqs0, Gap https://youtu.be/BjyOpiNuLBw, and https://youtu.be/3zsJcMJ08d0.

2. Award for Best Directing went to Jerome Robbins and Robert Wise. Oscars.org, accessed January 16, 2017, https://www.oscars.org/ceremonies/1962 and Larry Billman, *Film Choreographers and Dance Directors: An Illustrated Biographical Encyclopedia, with a History and Filmographies, 1893 through 1995* (Jefferson, NC: McFarland & Company, Inc., Publishers, 1997), 9.

3. James Monaco, *How to Read a Film: Movies, Media, Multimedia*, 3rd edition (New York: Oxford University Press, 2000), 184.

4. *West Side Story* was Al Johnson's first Broadway show. At the time of the Gap ad's production, Johnson was one of few dancers authorized by the Jerome Robbins Trust to restage Robbins's choreography. He also restaged choreography for the "Cool" and "Dance at the Gym" spots.

5. Gap also uses this strategy in their 1989–1999 khaki campaign. Robert Goldman describes not-ads as ads that disguise their agenda by assuming the guise of other media. Robert Goldman, *Reading Ads Socially* (New York: Routledge, 1992), 155–172.

6. Through the recognition of the hail, and all that this recognition implies in terms of the mantle of identity, the addressee assumes his/her social position and becomes a subject. Louis Althusser, "Ideology and Ideological State Apparatuses (Notes Towards an Investigation)," in *Essays on Ideology* (London: Verso Editions, 1984), 1–60.

7. One might think of affect as sensation and intensity. Brian Massumi, *Parables of the Virtual: Movement, Affect, Sensation* (Durham, NC: Duke University Press, 2002); Lawrence Grossberg, *Dancing in Spite of Myself: Essays on Popular Culture* (Durham, NC: Duke University Press, 1997).

8. These ads originally aired on television prior to the ubiquity of digital online media, though it is still possible to watch them on Youtube in 2017.

9. Lawrence Grossberg, *We Gotta Get Out of this Place: Popular Conservatism and Postmodern Culture* (New York: Routledge, 1992), 70.

10. Grossberg, *We Gotta Get Out*, 70.

11. Grossberg, *We Gotta Get Out*, 79.

12. Grossberg, *We Gotta Get Out*, 80–82.

13. Philip Auslander, *Liveness: Performance in a Mediatized Culture* (New York: Routledge, 1999), 197; Misha Kavka, *Reality TV* (Edinburgh: Edinburgh University Press, 2012).

14. Gilles Deleuze and Félix Guattari, *A Thousand Plateaus: Capitalism and Schizophrenia* (Minneapolis, MN: University of Minnesota Press, 1987).

15. Guy Debord, *La Société du Spectacle* (Paris: Gallimard, 1992).

16. Debord, *La Société*, Sections 1 and 4.

17. Debord, *La Société*, Section 10.

18. "Trees" and "Mountains" each feature a chorus of dancers and ice skaters who magically multiple and disappear through kaleidoscopic editing effects. They are set to music that samples Vanilla Ice's "Ice Ice Baby" (1990) and Leroy Anderson's "Sleigh Ride" (1949). Gap, "Mountains" and "Trees," directed by Michel Gondry, featuring choreography by Blanca Li, commercials aired 1999, 30 seconds, accessed June 15, 2017, https://youtu.be/6k0Kv78evKI and https://youtu.be/NjTuexVS1ug.

19. The ads feature expansive Berkeleyesque musical numbers with a female chorus costumed as Whopper ingredients (i.e., tomatoes, lettuce, hamburger patties, pickles, etc.) that promenades and poses before plummeting from a raised platform to the "staging area" below where, as they fall one by one, they form a Whopper. The campaign was imagined by Crispin Porter + Bogusky [Miami] in collaboration with production company Hungry Man [NY and Rio de Janeiro] and features Brooke Burke as the "Top Bun" and as "Queen" to the BK King. The ads premiered during Super Bowl XL. Burger King, "America's Favorite," "Extra Cheese," and "More Mayo," directed by Brian Buckley, featuring choreography by Michael Rooney, commercials aired 2006, 1 minute, accessed June 15, 2017, https://youtu.be/OGheRqgD3fw, https://youtu.be/35um_-pJa40, and King https://youtu.be/Cv4nuT1yNGY.

20. Jean Baudrillard, *Simulacra and Simulation*, trans. Sheila Faria Glaser (Ann Arbor, MI: University of Michigan Press, 1999), 6.

21. Jean Baudrillard, *The Consumer Society: Myths and Structures* (Los Angeles, CA: Sage Publications, Ltd., 1998), 124.

22. Jean Baudrillard, *For a Critique of the Political Economy of the Sign*, trans. Charles Levin (Candor, NY: Telos Press, Ltd., 1981).

23. Baudrillard, *The Consumer Society*, 122.

24. Baudrillard, *The Consumer Society*; Baudrillard, *Simulacra*.

25. Jacques Derrida, *Writing and Difference*, trans. Alan Bass (Chicago: University of Chicago Press, 1978).

26. Baudrillard, *Simulacra*, 3.

27. Here I connect Maya Deren's concept of vertical film form as discussed by Erin Brannigan with Brian Massumi's theorization of intensity and/as affect. Massumi, *Parables of the Virtual*, 27; Erin Brannigan, *Dancefilm: Choreography and the Moving Image* (New York: Oxford University Press, 2011), 101.

28. I draw on Massumi's analysis of how emotions and meaning emerge from the undifferentiated flow of affect. Massumi, *Parables of the Virtual*, 27–28.

29. Grossberg, *Dancing in Spite*, 147–148.

30. When I say television I mean television and a range of stations, including both local and cable, that feature both content programming and commercial

breaks. While I use the Internet and streaming options (e.g., Netflix), I typically encountered ads online for the first time on occasions when I was searching specifically for commercials featuring dance.

31. Agencies sometimes claim an inability to access the information and/or stress the importance of maintaining confidentiality and intellectual property rights in relation to concept and execution. In addition, brands sometimes have received substantial criticism of their advertising practices. For example, see Naomi Klein, *No Logo: Taking Aim at the Brand Bullies*, 1st edition (New York: Picador, 2000).

32. The Federal Communications Commission (FCC) began taking steps to remove cigarette advertising from television in 1969, which came to fruition in 1971 with the Public Health Cigarettes Smoking Act. Prior to the Act, cigarette commercials were a notable presence in television advertising. In 1969 the tobacco industry invested $273 million in broadcast advertising, which made up 8 percent of all network/station revenues. Lincoln Diamant, *Television's Classic Commercials: The Golden Years 1948–1958* (New York: Hastings House, Publishers, 1971), 104.

33. In cases where television spots are easily accessible online, I have incorporated particularly salient examples even though they were made originally for a foreign market.

CHAPTER 1

1. Samsung, "Use Your Influence," produced by The Viral Factory, featuring choreography by Michael Thomas Voss, commercial for Samsung Galaxy 580 aired 2010, 1 minute 45 seconds, accessed May 20, 2017, https://youtu.be/VQ3d3KigPQM; Duncan Macleod, "Samsung Use Your Influence with Cute Dance," The Inspiration Room, September 18, 2010, accessed January 15, 2017, http://www.theinspirationroom.com/daily/2010/samsung-use-your-influence; Kara Swisher, "Viral Video: Adorable Tyke Dancing with Less Adorable Adults," *Wall Street Journal*, September 16, 2010, accessed January 15, 2017, http://www.allthings.com/20100916/viral-video-adorable-tyke-dancing-with-less-adorable-adults.

2. This definition is somewhat problematic because its wording maintains a distinction between mental and physical cognition—a notion that runs counter to current theories of *affect* and cognition that inform my analysis. Despite this contradiction, I offer the definition as way of initially grounding the reader before moving into a more theoretical discussion.

3. Erin Brannigan, *Dancefilm: Choreography and the Moving Image* (New York: Oxford University Press, 2011), 141.

4. Brannigan, *Dancefilm*, 160.

5. Brannigan, *Dancefilm*, 100–124.

6. For example, see Barry C. Stillman, "Making Sense of Proprioception: The Meaning of Proprioception Kineasthesia and Related Terms," *Physiotherapy* 88, no. 11 (2002): 667–676; Glenna Batson with Margaret Wilson, *Body and Mind in Motion: Dance and Neuroscience in Conversation* (Chicago: Intellect, University of Chicago Press, 2014).

7. Batson with Wilson, *Body and Mind*, 91. A more detailed discussion of the term within scientific studies may be found in Mark Paterson, "On 'Inner Touch' and the Moving Body: Aesthesis, Kinaesthesis, and Aesthetics," in *Touching and Being Touched: Kinesthesia and Empathy in Dance and Movement*, eds. Gabriele

Brandstetter, Gerko Egert, and Sabine Zubarik (Berlin, Germany: Walter de Gruyter Gmbh, 2013), 122–124.

8. Batson with Wilson, *Body and Mind*, 91; Gabriele Brandstetter, "'Listening': Kinesthetic Awareness in Contemporary Dance," in *Touching and Being Touched: Kinesthesia and Empathy in Dance and Movement*, eds. Gabriele Brandstetter, Gerko Egert, and Sabine Zubarik (Berlin, Germany: Walter de Gruyter Gmbh, 2013), 166.

9. Batson with Wilson, *Body and Mind*, 91.

10. Batson and Wilson cite several texts I have read, linking them to particular ideas about the role of kinesthesia in moving and perceiving movement. I list those that inform my use of the following terms: for movement dynamics, empathy, and action observation see Susan Leigh Foster, *Choreographing Empathy: Kinesthesia in Performance* (New York: Routledge, 2010) and Dee Reynolds and Matthew Reason, *Kinesthetic Empathy in Creative and Cultural Contexts* (Chicago, IL: University of Chicago Press, 2012); for body-based consciousness see Maxine Sheets-Johnstone, *The Corporeal Turn: An Interdisciplinary Reader* (Charlottesville, VA: Imprint Academic, 2009) and Sheets-Johnstone, *The Primacy of Movement*, expanded 2nd edition (Philadelphia, PA: John Benjamin's Publishing Company, 2011), and for agency see Carrie Noland, *Agency and Embodiment: Performing Gestures/Producing Culture* (Cambridge, MA: Harvard University Press, 2009). In addition, these concepts are taken up by various scholars looking at a range of practices in *Touching and Being Touched: Kinesthesia and Empathy in Dance and Movement*, eds. Gabriele Brandstetter, Gerko Egert, and Sabine Zubarik (Berlin, Germany: Walter de Gruyter Gmbh, 2013).

11. Batson with Wilson, *Body and Mind*, 41.

12. Batson with Wilson, *Body and Mind*, 90.

13. Francisco J. Varela, Evan Thompson, and Eleanor Rosch, *The Embodied Mind: Cognitive Science and Human Experience* (Cambridge, MA: MIT Press, 1991), 173.

14. Mark Johnson and George Lakoff, *Metaphors We Live By* (Chicago, IL: University of Chicago Press, 1980); Johnson and Lakoff, *Philosophy in the Flesh: The Embodied Mind and Its Challenge to Western Thought* (New York: Basic Books, 1999) and Johnson and Lakoff, *Women, Fire, and Dangerous Things: What Categories Reveal About the Mind* (Chicago, IL: University of Chicago Press, 1987).

15. Varela, Thompson, and Rosch, *The Embodied Mind*, 178.

16. Batson with Wilson, *Body and Mind*, 93.

17. Shaun Gallagher, *How the Body Shapes the Mind* (Oxford, UK: Clarendon Press, 2005), 24.

18. Gallagher, *How the Body*, 24.

19. While Gallagher sees the two concepts as related, he argues that case studies show one can have a dysfunctional *body image* but still have a functional *body schema*. He further clarifies these concepts by breaking body image down into a *body percept* (perceptions of one's body), *body concept* (conceptual knowledge of), and *body affect* (emotional attitude toward). These categories of body image work in tandem with the *body schema*: a "system of sensory-motor functions that operate below the level of self-referential intentionality" and "involves a set of tacit performances—preconscious, subpersonal processes that play a dynamic role in governing posture and movement." See Gallagher, *How the Body*, 25–26.

20. Gallagher, *How the Body*, 26.

21. Batson with Wilson, *Body and Mind*, 94. The authors quote Varela, Thompson, and Rosch, *The Embodied Mind*, 9.
22. Erin Manning and Brian Massumi, "Just Like That: William Forsythe—Between Movement and Language," in *Touching and Being Touched: Kinesthesia and Empathy in Dance and Movement*, eds. Gabriele Brandstetter, Gerko Egert, and Sabine Zubarik (Berlin, Germany: Walter de Gruyter Gmbh, 2013), 43–44.
23. Manning and Massumi, "Just Like That," 43–44.
24. Maxine Sheets-Johnstone, *The Corporeal Turn: An Interdisciplinary Reader* (Exeter, UK: Imprint Academic, 2009), 221.
25. Manning and Massumi, "Just Like That," 50.
26. Manning and Massumi, "Just Like That," 40.
27. Batson with Wilson, *Body and Mind*, 93. Gallagher, *How the Body*, 220–223.
28. Dee Reynolds, "Empathy, Contagion and Affect: The Role of Kinesthesia in Watching Dance," in *Touching and Being Touched: Kinesthesia and Empathy in Dance and Movement*, eds. Gabriele Brandstetter, Gerko Egert, and Sabine Zubarik (Berlin, Germany: Walter de Gruyter Gmbh, 2013), 212.
29. Reynolds, "Empathy, Contagion," 212.
30. Reynolds, "Empathy, Contagion," 215.
31. For example, see Brandstetter et al., *Touching and Being Touched*.
32. Dee Reynolds, "Kinesthetic Empathy and the Dance's Body: From Emotion to Affect," in *Kinesthetic Empathy in Creative and Cultural Practices*, eds. Dee Reynolds and Matthew Reason (Chicago, IL: Intellect, University of Chicago Press, 2012), 124.
33. Paterson, "On 'Inner Touch'," 117.
34. Reynolds, "Kinesthetic Empathy," 129. Her description of how *affective* empathy operates resonates with Mark Franko's analysis of expression in the work of Isadora Duncan: "Motion was Duncan's solution to the problem . . . of subduing expressive outwardness while maintaining sensate inwardness. Duncan stages herself as a subject of expression, not an expressive subject." Here Franko notes a distinction between the dancer's facilitation of expression, or *affect*, and the dancer as emotive subject. Mark Franko, *Dancing Modernism/Performing Politics* (Bloomington, IN: Indiana University Press, 1995), 11.
35. Susanne Langer, *Feeling and Form: A Theory of Art Developed from Philosophy in a New Key* (New York: Charles Scribner's Sons, 1953), 174.
36. Langer, *Feeling and Form*, 175.
37. Langer, *Feeling and Form*, 176–177.
38. Langer, *Feeling and Form*, 178.
39. Brian Massumi, *Parables of the Virtual: Movement, Affect, Sensation* (Durham, NC: Duke University Press, 2002), 133.
40. Massumi, *Parables of the Virtual*, 134.
41. Massumi, *Parables of the Virtual*, 136.
42. Langer, *Feeling and Form*, 175.
43. Massumi, *Parables of the Virtual*, 104.
44. Massumi, *Parables of the Virtual*, 104.
45. Mark Franko analyzes how Martha Graham's choreography reveals her intentional effort to distance her work from pervasive ideologies linking women and the expression of personal emotions: "Reducing flow is tantamount to removing the link that renders weight, tension, and angularity organic, emotional, and conventionally human for many spectators. The creation of a new aesthetic adequate to the modern age thus risked alienating segments of the audience unwilling to

receive affect through geometry, the impersonality of forms." Franko, *Dancing Modernism*, 45.

46. Massumi, *Parables of the Virtual*, 139.

47. Bill Medley and Jennifer Warnes, "The Time of My Life," recorded 1987, on *Dirty Dancing*, RCA Records. I note the original recording here. In an email, a representative from the company indicated that the song was re-recorded for the commercial; but she did not supply the musicians' names. Stacy A. Schultz, email message to author, June 30, 2017.

48. I use descriptive language from Laban/Bartenieff Movement Analysis, in this case from the category of Shape, which describes a mover's inner attitude about the body's changing form. Peggy Hackney, *Making Connections: Total Body Integration through Bartenieff Fundamentals* (New York: Gordon Breach Science Publishers, 1998); Irmgard Bartenieff, *Body Movement: Coping with the Environment* (New York: Gordon and Breach Science Publishers, 1980).

49. *Dirty Dancing*, directed by Emile Ardolino, featuring choreography by Kenny Ortega (Great American Films Limited Partnership, 1987), DVD (Artisan Entertainment, 1997).

50. Created by ad agency Leo Burnett, Chicago. United Healthcare, "Our Song," directed by Josh Gordon and Will Speck, featuring Emily Berry and Tom G. McMahon and choreography after Kenny Ortega, commercial aired 2015, 1 minute, accessed November 5, 2016, https://youtu.be/v9YiTIYO-2A.

51. Massumi, *Parables of the Virtual*; Gilles Deleuze and Felix Guattari, *A Thousand Plateaus: Capitalism and Schizophrenia* (Minneapolis, MN: University of Minnesota Press, 1987).

52. Colleen Dunagan and Roxane Fenton, "*Dirty Dancing*: Dance, Class, and Race in the Pursuit of Womanhood," in *The Oxford Handbook of Dance and the Popular Screen*, ed. Melissa Blanco Borelli (New York: Oxford University Press, 2014), 135–154.

53. Lawrence Grossberg, *We Gotta Get Out of this Place: Popular Conservatism and Postmodern Culture* (New York: Routledge, 1992), 85.

54. Grossberg, *We Gotta Get Out*, 86.

55. Grossberg, *We Gotta Get Out*, 86.

56. Grossberg, *We Gotta Get Out* and *Dancing in Spite*.

57. see note 3 Massumi, *Parables of the Virtual*, 260.

58. see note 3 Massumi, *Parables of the Virtual*, 260.

59. The choreography references commercial forms of hip hop, and the dancers reflect racial diversity to a degree. The first mother/child duet appears to be white, while the second and third appear to be black. I have chosen not to address race here given the focus of this section, but this decision is not meant to indicate a lack of significance.

60. Created by ad agency Bromley, Saatchi & Saatchi. Cheerios, "Be Heart Healthy," directed by unknown, featuring choreography by Tianne King and performances by Charlene Chi-Chi Smith and Tianne and Heaven King, commercial aired 2016, 30 seconds, accessed June 10, 2016, https://youtu.be/klDDHU8HZp4.

61. Sara Ahmed, "Happy Objects," in *The Affect Theory Reader*, eds. Melissa Gregg and Gregory J. Seigworth (Durham, NC: Duke University Press, 2010), Kindle.

62. Ahmed, "Happy Objects," loc. 390.

63. Ahmed, "Happy Objects."

64. Ahmed, "Happy Objects," loc. 480.

65. The spot promoted Mt. Dew Kickstart and was produced and created by Golin Harris and BBDO New York for Super Bowl XLIX. PepsiCo, Inc., "Come Alive,"

directed by Keith Schofield, featuring choreography by Bijoya BJ Das and dancers Evan Moody, Jonathan Ebeling, and Joshua Hoover, commercial aired 2015, 1 minute 30 seconds, accessed May 5, 2016, https://youtu.be/X4ITRA72i1w. Post-game, the ad ran online (Twitter, Youtube, Snapchat, and Vine). When viewing the interactive digital version, you could put the cursor over objects to see them dance; see Katie Richards, "Mountain Dew's Kickstart Turns Dudes into the Craziest Dancers: Along with Almost Everything Else in the House," *AdWeek*, January 29, 2015, accessed May 2, 2016, http://www.adweek.com/news/advertising-branding/ ad-day-mountain-dews-energy-drinks-turn-dudes-craziest-dancers-162631.

66. A-Trak with Milo & Otis, "Out the Speakers," featuring Rich Kidz, recorded 2015, Green Label Sound; see Gordon Murray, "Mt. Dew Ad Lifts," *Billboard*, February 13, 2015, accessed April 29, 2015, http://www.billboard.com/articles/columns/ chart-beat/6472725/a-trak-giorgio-moroder.

67. Katie Richards, "Mountain Dew's."

68. Created ad agency BBDO New York and set to Kid Cudi's "Bus Ride" (2015). PepsiCo, Inc., "Neighborhood," directed by Cary Murnion and Jonathan Milott, featuring performances by Evan Moody, Jonathan Ebeling, and Joshua Hoover, commercial aired 2015, 1 minute 17 seconds, accessed June 10, 2017, https:// youtu.be/utZojCbNmdk. Mt. Dew.

69. I've chosen to describe only the figures that the camera highlights in individual shots.

70. Grossberg, *Dancing in Spite*, 43.

71. For example, see Barbara Browning, *Infectious Rhythms: Metaphors of Contagion and the Spread of African Culture* (New York: Routledge, 1998).

72. Reynolds, "Empathy, Contagion," 213.

73. Reynolds, "Empathy, Contagion," 213–214.

74. Reynolds, "Empathy, Contagion," 215, 219–220.

75. Grossberg, *We Gotta Get Out*, 80

76. Grossberg, *We Gotta Get Out*, 82

77. Miriam Felton-Dansky, "Viral Performance: Contagious Hoaxes in the Digital Public Sphere," *Theater* 42, no. 2 (2012): 120.

78. Felton-Dansky, "Viral Performance," 119–121.

79. Felton-Dansky, Viral Performance," 119.

80. Felton-Dansky, "Viral Performance," 120.

81. Jonah Berger, *Contagious: Why Things Catch On* (New York: Simon & Schuster, Inc., 2013).

82. Margarita Alexmanolski, "Music as First Order and Second Order Conditioning in TV Commercials," *Music and the Moving Image* 3 (Summer 2010): 39–50.

83. Avant-garde artists have tackled the idea of mimicking, subverting, and/or commenting on this aspect of mass media and Felton-Dansky analyzes it as well; see Miriam Felton-Dansky, "Artistic Epidemiology," *PAJ: A Journal of Performance and Art*, 33 no. 2 (May 2011): 117 and Felton-Dansky, "Viral Performance."

84. Ishmael Reed, *Mumbo Jumbo* (New York: Atheneum, 1989).

85. Thomas F. DeFrantz, "Unchecked Popularity: Neoliberal Circulations of Black Social Dance," in *Neoliberalism and Global Theaters: Performance Permutations* (New York: Palgrave Macmillan, 2012), 130.

86. Silvan S. Tomkins, "What and Where are the Primary Affects? Some Evidence for a Theory," *Perceptual and Motor Skills* 18 (1964): 119–158 and Eve Kosofsky Sedgwick, *Touching Feeling: Affect, Pedagogy, Performativity* (Durham, NC: Duke University Press, 2004).

87. Felton-Dansky, "Viral Performance," 125.

88. Nicolas Bourriaud, *Relational Aesthetics* (France: Les Presses du Réel, 1998, 2002), 112.

89. Bourriaud, *Relational*, 21–23.

90. Bourriaud, *Relational*, 9–13.

91. Bourriaud, *Relational*, 43.

92. Henry Jenkins, *Convergence Culture: Where Old and New Media Collide* (New York: New York University Press, 2006), 2.

93. Jenkins, *Convergence Culture*, 2. Jenkins traces the development of convergence culture back to MIT political scientist Ithiel de Sola Pool's 1983 *Technologies of Freedom* in which Pool claims that "the 'convergence of modes' is blurring the lines between media . . . [and that] . . . the one-to-one relationship that used to exist between a medium and its use is eroding." Jenkins, *Convergence Culture*, 10.

94. Jenkins, *Convergence Culture*, 3.

95. He cites Pierre Lévy as the originator of the term "collective intelligence." Jenkins, *Convergence Culture*, 4.

96. Due to the interactive ad copy, my first encounter with "Come Alive" was confusing. While I use varying levels of digital technology daily, I choose not to fully integrate it into my life. I have never used apps like Twitter or Snapchat. While I have looked at Facebook pages, I have never made an account. For me, digital technology is a convenience. I can shop without dealing with crowds and have access to a greater selection of products. I can find digital videos of dance (social, concert, advertising, movies, etc.) that I need for my teaching and research. The point of this self-revelation is to say that, at first, the ad copy had me flummoxed. It was a colleague who suggested the digital interactive component, which I confirmed by reading about the ad online. At the time of writing, Mt. Dew Kickstart's webpage offered consumers the opportunity to create their own version of another of their commercial characters, the PuppyMonkeyBaby, and then watch it dance.

97. Jason T. Jacque, Mark Perry, and Per Ola Kristensson, "Differentiation of Online Text-based Advertising and the Effect on Users' Click Behavior," *Computers in Human Behavior* 50 (2015): 535–543.

98. Here I use terminology from Laban Movement Analysis; the "diagonal" gesture refers to movement that is three-dimensional in the sense of being to the side, forward, and low and thus points to a corner of an imaginary cube; see Bartenieff, *Coping with the Environment.*

99. Created by ad agency Saatchi & Saatchi, London. T-Mobile, "Dance," directed by Michael Grazey, featuring choreography by Ashley Wallace, commercial aired 2009, 2 minutes 35 seconds, accessed October 15, 2015, https://youtu.be/VQ3d3KigPQM.

100. Duncan Macleod, "T-Mobile Dance Flashmob in London," The Inspiration Room, accessed August 23, 2016, http://theinspirationroom.com/daily/2009/t-mobile-dance-flashmob-in-london/.

101. Recent examples of this scholarship include Susan Leigh Foster, "Why Not Improv Everywhere?" in *The Oxford Handbook of Dance and Theater*, ed. Nadine Georges-Graves (New York: Oxford University Press, 2015), 196–210 and John H. Muse, "Flash Mobs and the Diffusion of Audience," *Theater* 40, no. 3 (2010): 8–23.

102. Thomas Marchbank, "Intense Flows: Flashmobbing, Rush Capital, and the Swarming of Space," *Philament: An Online Journal of the Arts and Culture* 4 (2004),

accessed July 28, 2017, http://www.philamentjournal.com/issue4/marchbank-intense/.

103. Georgiana Gore, "Flash Mob Dance and the Territorialisation of Urban Movement," *Anthropological Notebooks* 16, no. 3 (2010): 125 and Thea Brejzek, "From Social Network to Urban Intervention: On the Scenographies of Flash Mobs and Urban Swarms," *International Journal of Performance Arts and Digital Media* 6, no. 1 (2010): 111, doi:10.1386.

104. Gore, "Flash Mob Dance," 125; Brejzek, "From Social Network," 111; Marchbank, "Intense Flows."

105. Foster, "Why Not Improv."

106. Brejzek, "From Social Network," 111.

107. Gore, "Flash Mob Dance," 126.

108. Marchbank, "Intense Flows."

109. Marchbank, "Intense Flows."

110. For tactic versus strategy, see Michel de Certeau, *The Practice of Everyday Life* (Berkeley, CA: University of California Press, 1984).

CHAPTER 2

1. For historical developments in advertising, see Lincoln Diamant, *Television's Classic Commercials: The Golden Years 1948–1958* (New York: Hastings House Publishers, 1971), xi–25, 105. For a semiotic reading of standard print conventions, see Judith Williamson, *Decoding Advertisements: Ideology and Meaning in Advertising* (New York: Marion Boyars Publishers, Ltd., 1978).

2. I address some aspects of these historical intersections throughout the book, but a quick summary of some these intersections can be found in Larry Billman, *Film Choreographers and Dance Directors: An Illustrated Biographical Encyclopedia with a History and Filmographies 1893 through 1995* (Jefferson, NC: McFarland & Co., 1997), 17–195; Colleen Dunagan, "Consuming Dance: A Brief History of the Dance Commercial," in *Proceedings of the Thirty-first Annual Conference*, Society of Dance History Scholars, Skidmore College, June 12–15, 2008 (Riverside: Dance History Scholars, 2008), 118–121; and Judy Mitoma, ed. *Envisioning Dance on Film and Video* (New York: Routledge, 2002).

3. Gilles Deleuze and Felix Guattari, *A Thousand Plateaus: Capitalism and Schizophrenia* (Minneapolis: University of Minnesota Press, 1987) and *Anti-Oedipus: Capitalism and Schizophrenia* (Minneapolis: University of Minnesota Press, 1983).

4. L&M Cigarettes, "Today's Best Taste," commercial aired 1966, 12 seconds, accessed February 15, 2007, https://www.youtube.com/watch?v=HxMeHxdxmgk. My source for the date came from another online posting of the spot: "I Want Moore Retro Youtube Channel," Youtube, accessed February 10, 2013, https://www.youtube.com/user/MiscVideos78rpm/search?query=L%26M+cigarettes.

5. My assessment draws on physical experience with basic step patterns and descriptions of the dances; see Julie Malnig, ed., *Ballroom, Boogie, Shimmy Sham, Shake: A Social and Popular Dance Reader* (Chicago, IL: University of Illinois Press, 2009), 146–181.

6. See Roland Barthes, *Image Music Text* (New York: The Noonday Press, 1977), 32–51; Judith Williamson, *Decoding Advertisements: Ideology and Meaning in Advertising* (New York: Marion Boyars Publishers, Ltd., 1978), and Robert Goldman, *Reading Ads Socially* (New York: Routledge, 1992).

7. Robert Goldman, *Reading Ads*, 18.

8. Goldman, *Reading Ads*, 18. For similar analyses and examples with dance, see Sherrill Dodds, *Dance on Screen: Genres and Media from Hollywood to Experimental Art* (London: Palgrave Macmillan: 2001, 2004), 44–45 and Colleen Dunagan, "Performing the Commodity-Sign: Dancing in the Gap," *Dance Research Journal* 39, no. 2 (Winter 2007): 3–22.

9. The term commodity-form arises out of Marxist theories of capitalism and alludes to the economic relations of the product as a commodity; see Karl Marx, Edward B. Aveling, Friedrich Engels and Samuel Moore, *Capital Vol. I, Book One, The Process of Production of Capital: A Critique of Political Economy* (London: Electric Book Co., 2001).

10. Simply put, the use value equals the functional value of the product (and symbolically the labor used to produce it); surplus value is equivalent to the net profit earned by selling the product; and exchange value describes the monetary value of the commodity within the capitalist system as well as its cultural and social value. My use of the terms and their relationship to sign structures draws primarily on Jean Baudrillard, *For a Critique of the Political Economy of the Sign* (New York: Telos Press Ltd., 1981).

11. For more on the relationship between the commodity-form and sign structures, see Barthes, *Image Music Text*, 32–51; Williamson, *Decoding Advertisements*; Goldman, *Reading Ads*; and Guy Cook, *The Discourse of Advertising* (New York: Routledge, 1992).

12. Baudrillard, *For a Critique*, 130–163.

13. See Barthes, *Image, Music, Text*; Cook, *Discourse of Advertising*; Goldman, *Reading Ads*, and Williamson, *Decoding Advertisements*.

14. The mortise is an image of the product that is set off from the rest of the ad's signifying image because it is a separate photograph laid over or into the main image.

15. "Two shot" is a film term that refers to shots where two subjects are captured in the frame and share the focus of the shot.

16. The success of his studio franchise is demonstrated by his ability to produce a successful television show, *The Arthur Murray Dance Party*, which aired from 1950 to 1962 on all four networks of the time (ABC, Dumont, CBS, and NBC); see "TV. com," CBS Interactive, Inc., last modified 2017, accessed July 31, 2017, http:// www.tv.com/arthur-murray-party/show/2186/summary.html. For a history of Arthur Murray and his ballroom instruction industry see "Arthur Murray Dance Studios: Celebrating 105 Years," Arthur Murray International, last modified 2017, accessed July 31, 2017, http://arthurmurray.com/history/.

17. For example, "best in show" is used in dog shows to name the dog chosen as best across breeds and categories. See "The Westminster Kennel Club Home Page," The Westminster Kennel Club, accessed July 31, 2017, http://www. westminsterkennelclub.org/.

18. Pierre Bourdieu, *Distinction: A Social Critique of the Judgement of Taste* (Cambridge, MA: Harvard University Press, 1984) and Robert Dixon, *The Baumgarten Corruption: From Sense to Nonsense in Art and Philosophy* (East Haven, CT: Pluto Press, 1995).

19. In a previous article, I demonstrate this phenomenon through an analysis of a series of TV spots created for the 1998 Gap khaki campaign; see Dunagan, "Performing the Commodity-Sign," 6. In these spots the product is worn by the dancers featured in the main signifying image but never actually shown in a separate mortise shot.

20. In contemporary culture, most commercials aired on television last between 30 and 60 seconds; however, the history of commercials includes both shorter and longer examples, and the development of online commercials allows for longer run times, often anywhere from one to three minutes.

21. Goldman, *Reading Ads*, 63–65.

22. Goldman, *Reading Ads*, 38–40 and Dodds, *Dance on Screen*, 44–45.

23. Althusser describes the concept of *hailing* as the process by which political ideology constitutes the subject as individual: ". . . all ideology hails or interpellates concrete individuals as concrete subjects [in other words, ideology] 'transforms' the individuals into subjects . . . by that very precise operation which I have called *interpellation* or hailing, and which can be imagined along the lines of most commonplace everyday police (or other) hailing: 'Hey, you there!'" Through the recognition of the hail, and all that this recognition implies in terms of the mantle of identity, the addressee assumes his/her social position and becomes a subject. Louis Althusser, "Ideology and Ideological State Apparatuses (Notes Towards an Investigation)," in *Essays on Ideology*, (London: Verso Editions, 1984), 48.

24. The mechanism of direct address in song lyrics and musical performances is a familiar one. Many songs position the listener opposite the "I" of the singer through pronouns, imperatives, questions, and lyric content. The singer addresses an unseen Other for which the listener stands in. This aspect is then paired with the physical performance of direct address. For example, in the music video for "Lady Marmalade" the lyrics tell the story of Marmalade to an imagined listener and include the pronoun "you" within the question asked in the chorus, "Voulez-vous coucher avec moi?" In the music video, the body reinforces the intent of the lyrics as the four singers (Pink, Christina Aguilera, Maya, and Lil' Kim) tend to face and physically present themselves to the camera, often literally gesturing toward the camera as though physically directing their words and actions to the audience. In addition, the singers are seen both backstage in their dressing rooms and on stage, filmed either from behind so that they are seen singing to rows of seats or from the front so as to capture the audience perspective. These elements work together to directly address the listener, positioning the listener as the intended receiver of the message. The music video explicitly cites traditional theatrical performance and its conventions, in effect reminding the viewer that the music videos is a performance and encouraging the viewer to, on some level, view the video as equivalent to seeing the performance live. See Pink, Christina Aguilera, Maya, and Lil' Kim, "Lady Marmalade" (music video), directed by Paul Hunter (2002, Interscope Records), posted December 24, 2009, accessed July 31, 2017, https://youtu.be/RQa7SvVCdZk.

25. Guillemette Bolens, "Kinesthetic Empathy in Charlie Chaplin's Silent Films," in *Kinesthetic Empathy in Creative and Cultural Practices* (Chicago, IL: Intellect Ltd., 2012), 143–156 and Lucy Fife Donaldson, "Effort and Empathy: Engaging with Film Performance," in *Kinesthetic Empathy in Creative and Cultural Practices* (Chicago, IL: Intellect Ltd., 2012), 157–174.

26. Diamant details how in the initial years, before the development of videotape, the only way to prerecord content was on film that was then "'rolled in' on cue by motion picture projectors shining into modified TV cameras" (6); see Diamant, *Television's Classic Commercials*, 6–11. Television's relationship to radio is discussed in Barbara Moore, Marvin R. Bensman, and Jim Van Dyke, *Prime-Time Television: A Concise History* (Westport, CT: Praeger, 2006), 1–25.

27. Colleen Dunagan, "Dance and Theater: Looking at Television's Deployment of Theatricality Through Dance," in *The Oxford Handbook of Dance and Theater* (New York: Oxford University Press, 2015), 169–195; Diamant, *Television's Classic Commercials*; Jason Mittell, *Television and American Culture* (New York: Oxford University Press, 2010); Moore, Bensman, and Van Dyke, *Prime-Time Television*.

28. Dunagan, "Dance and Theater," 169–195.

29. Moore, Bensman, and Van Dyke, *Prime-Time Television*, 1–80.

30. Television broadcasts aired for the first time as early as 1928; however, the first regular seven-day per week schedule wasn't broadcast until 1931 by W2XAB (CBS). In these early years, live broadcasts were for experimental purposes only, not for commercial audiences. However, the broadcast technology (though it shifts during this time from "mechanical" to electronic) and content during this period aligned with practices seen in the onset of commercial television in 1940. TV sets were not being manufactured at this point; commercial broadcasting was still in the early stages in 1941, when WWII disrupted production. Shortly after the war's end, the commercial industry began to produce television sets, which quickly became a coveted commodity. For more information on the early ears of experimental television and its content, see Moore, Bensman, and Van Dyke, *Prime-Time Television*, 28–33.

31. Moore, Bensman, and Van Dyke, *Prime-Time Television*, 44.

32. Moore, Bensman, and Van Dyke, *Prime-Time Television*, 44.

33. Moore, Bensman, and Van Dyke, *Prime-Time Television*, 37.

34. Moore, Bensman, and Van Dyke, *Prime-Time Television*, 45–79.

35. For example, the first televised variety show, "Hour Glass," premiered May 9, 1946 and included a chorus line; see "Hour Glass (1946–1947)," IMDb, accessed July 31, 2017, http://www.imdb.com/title/tt0128878/plotsummary and Moore, Bensman, and Van Dyke, *Prime-Time Television*, 35.

36. The commercial spot I describe here is one example of Old Gold's "Dancing Butts" advertising campaign that aired in 1950; other versions exist. The ad agency is Lennen & Newell, Inc. and the creative directors for the ad are Nicholas Keenly and Peter Keverson. See Diamant, *Television's Classic Commercials*, 108–110 and Old Gold/P. Lorillard Co., "Dancing Butts," CBS-TV Network (NY), commercial aired 1950, 57 seconds, accessed July 31, 2017, https://youtu.be/Z023OAz4fkI.

37. Born in 1917, James started out in radio at WNEW in 1936. He was involved in television from the beginning, taking on a role in 1938 at the experimental station owned by Alfred B. Dumont, which was licensed after WWII as WABD-TV as part of the Dumont Television Network. He first became popular as a wrestling announcer and was known as the voice of Old Gold cigarettes. He died in 1997 from lung cancer. See Robert McG. Thomas Jr., "Dennis James, 79, TV Game Show Host and Announcer, Dies," *New York Times*, June 6, 1997, accessed July 31, 2017, http://www.nytimes.com/1997/06/06/arts/dennis-james-79-tv-game-show-host-and-announcer-dies.html; "Dennis James," IMDb.com, Inc., last modified 2017, accessed July 31, 2017, http://www.imdb.com/name/nm0416424/; and Moore, Bensman, and Van Dyke, *Prime-Time Television*, 34.

38. I believe the music consists of an up-tempo version of Harry Dacre, "A Bicycle Built for Two," recorded in 1892, Hal Leonard Music Publishing, Music Notes.com, accessed February 3, 2015, http://www.musicnotes.com/sheetmusic/mtdFPE.asp?ppn=MN0109113&ref=google. The song is referenced in a description of

another version of the "Dancing Butts" commercial spot found in Diamant, *Television's Classic Commercials*, 108–110.

39. For more on the development of proscenium theaters, the framing of dance performances, and the staging of choreography in relation to the audience, see Susan Foster, *Reading Dancing: Bodies and Subjects in Contemporary Performance* (Berkeley, CA: University of California Press, 1986).

40. Auslander argues that "Television's essence was seen in its ability to transmit events as they occur, not in a filmic capacity to record events for later viewing. Originally, of course, all television broadcasts were live transmissions. Jane Feuer (1983) argues that the definition of television as an ontologically live medium remains part of our fundamental conception of the medium—even though television ceased to be live in an ontological sense, it remains so in an ideological sense." Philip Auslander, *Liveness: Performance in a Mediatized Culture* (New York: Routledge,1999), 12 and 22.

41. Thorton Caldwell, *Televisuality: Style, Crisis, and Authority in American Television* (New Brunswick, NJ: Rutgers University Press, 1995), 367.

42. Colleen Dunagan, "Dance and Theater," 171.

43. Lenox R. Lohr, *Television Broadcasting: Product, Economics, Technique* (New York: McGraw-Hill, 1940), 52, original emphasis. The concept of *liveness* as a result of the incorporation of live performance practices in television has been documented and conceptualized by a number of scholars, including: Auslander, *Liveness*; Moore, Bensman, Van Dyke, *Prime-Time Television*; Misha Kavka, *Reality Television, Affect and Intimacy: Reality Matters* (New York: Palgrave Macmillan, 2008); Jane Feuer, "The Concept of Live Television: Ontology as Ideology," in *Regarding Television: Critical Approaches—An Anthology*, ed. Ann Kaplan (Frederick, MD: University Publications of America, 1983); Stephen Heath and Gillian Skirrow, "Television: A World in Action," *Screen* 18, no. 2 (1977): 7–59; and Elizabeth Burns, *Theatricality: A Study of Convention in Theater and in Social Life* (London: Longman Group, 1972).

44. Misha Kavka and Amy West, "Temporalities of the Real: Conceptualising time in Reality TV," in *Understanding Reality Television*, ed. Su Holmes and Deborah Jermyn (New York: Routledge, 2004), 136–153; Auslander, *Liveness*; Burns, *Theatricality*.

45. For more on Phelan's theory of performance as "un(re)productive" and therefore beyond the realm of "regulation and control," see Peggy Phelan, *Unmarked: The Politics of Performance* (New York: Routledge, 1993), 148.

46. Caldwell, *Televisuality*, 27–31 and 310–311.

47. Caldwell, *Televisuality*, 367.

48. Guillemette Bolens, "Kinesthetic Empathy in Charlie Chaplin's" and Lucy Fife Donaldson, "Effort and Empathy."

49. Auslander, *Liveness*, 23.

50. André Gaudreault and Tom Gunning, "Introduction: American Cinema Emerges (1890–1909)" in *American Cinema, 1890–1909: Themes and Variations*, ed. André Gaudreault (New Brunswick, NJ: Rutgers University Press, 2009), 1–21.

51. At this time, I have not yet been able to confirm the production details; however, I believe they were created by the ad agency Lintas. My titles are descriptive. Coca-Cola, "Coke is It—Rehearsal," director unknown, commercial aired in 1982, 1 minute, accessed June 3, 2016, https://youtu.be/3rArYMm4DHs and Coca-Cola, "Coke is It—Saxophone," director unknown, commercial aired in 1985, 30 seconds, accessed June 3, 2016, https://youtu.be/weAZn3VdH_c.

52. Erin Brannigan describes the gestural anacrusis as the moment in which the moving body transitions between modes of performance: " . . . the gestural anacrusis as the pre-movement zone refers to Masson's degree zero. It is the moment between one mode of performance and another—a space where the shift occurs between walking and dancing, utilitarian movements and choreography, between recognizable behavior and dance-like deviations." Erin Brannigan, *Dancefilm: Choreography and the Moving Image* (New York: Oxford University Press, 2011), 141.

53. See Rick Altman, *The American Film Musical* (Bloomington, IN: Indiana University Press, 1989).

54. See Altman, *The American Film Musical*; Jane Feuer, *The Hollywood Musical*, 2nd edition (Bloomington, IN: Indiana University Press, 1993); Martin Rubin, *Showstoppers: Busby Berkeley and the Tradition of Spectacle* (New York: Columbia University Press, 1993), 34–36.

55. Rubin, *Showstoppers*, 36.

56. Rubin, *Showstoppers*, 37.

57. See Feuer, *The Hollywood Musical*, 52 and Altman, *The American Film Musical*.

58. Altman, *American Film Musical*, 62–74.

59. Altman, *American Film Musical*, 62–63.

60. Feuer, *The Hollywood Musical*, 52.

61. Rubin, *Showstoppers*, 38.

62. Altman, *American Film Musical*, 62–74.

63. Altman, *American Film Musical*.

64. I am using the term "scene" here to indicate a location identified within the ad by a particular actor/character, activity and time, as one would in shooting narrative film. Some of the scenes within this ad occur more than once and consist of more than one shot; however, some contain only one shot and/or occur only once over the course of the commercial.

65. In discussing these strategies, I am thinking of the standard realist narrative film conventions as developed and employed within the Hollywood film industry. However, these are by no means the only conventions employed in the film industry, either in Hollywood or elsewhere, and films regularly subvert these conventions. The late twentieth and early twenty-first century has seen popular cinema employ a wide range of filming and editing strategies.

66. Sergei Eisenstein, the Russian cinematographer, is known for contributing to the concept of montage within cinema. Montage is often used to edit shots together to condense time, space, and information, and more rapidly depict events and the passage of time. However, the term montage is also understood within Soviet montage theory as editing shots together to create a new (third) meaning that functions more through symbolism than realism. See Jame Monaco, *How to Read a Film: Movies, Media, Multimedia*, 3rd edition (New York: Oxford University Press, 2000), 216–220.

67. Goldman, *Reading Ads*, 159.

68. Misha Kavka, *Reality TV* (Edinburgh: Edinburgh University Press, 2012).

69. Bacardi, Inc., "No Bad Dancing," directed by Traktor through Partizan, commercial aired 2005, 40 seconds, accessed July 3, 2016, https://youtu.be/uJ9Jtdhv6TI. See "No Bad Dancing by Fallon London for Bacardi," Coloribus: Creative Advertising Archive, accessed February 6, 2015, http://www.coloribus.com/adsarchive/tv-commercials/bacardi-no-bad-dancing-7639555/.

70. Goldman, *Reading Ads*, 155-171.

71. Created by ad agency TBWA\Chiat\Day and produced by Anonymous Content. Apple, "The Band," directed by Mark Romanek, commercial aired 2004, 2 minutes, accessed June 28, 2016, https://youtu.be/MhCAPmR68KE.

72. Andrew Goodwin, *Dancing in the Distraction Factory: Music Television and Popular Culture* (Minneapolis, MN: University of Minnesota Press, 1992).

73. Goodwin, *Dancing in the Distraction Factory*, 72–97.

74. The only exception to this being the iPod, as mentioned previously, and one shot where the stripes on a dancer's sweater match the background, as though the background color has bled onto the silhouette.

75. Multiple versions of the commercial exist, which is common as ad agencies often produce more than one, particularly when producing longer versions (more than 30 seconds). The description I provide here is for the 2-minute and 22-second version.

76. He actually says "catorce" (i.e., fourteen) and sings the numbers in half-time.

77. Goodwin might view the relationship between the swoop of the camera and the lyrics' mention of vertigo as an example of *synesthesia*, a conceptual component of the musicology of the image that refers to a condition where sensory input is experienced in an alternate sensory modality. For example, a word or sound might evoke a particular image, movement, or color.

78. Here I employ the concept of parody as a repetition that highlights difference within similarity to create new meaning without using humor to satirize the imitated work. For a fuller discussion see Linda Hutcheon, *A Theory of Parody: The Teachings of Twentieth-Century Art Forms* (Chicago, IL: University of Illinois Press, 2000), 6.

79. Raymond Williams, *The Long Revolution* (New York: Harper & Row, 1966).

80. The music video for the song produces this same *affect* or *structure of feeling* through similar strategies.

81. See Goodwin, *Dancing in the Distraction Factory*, 49–71 and Dodds, *Dance on Screen*, 49–55.

82. The commercial was produced by creative agency Tribal DDB Worldwide, Korea for Levis' Korean market. As noted by creative director, Tim Paradise, the ad is an adaptation commissioned by the creative team for Levi's at Weiden+Kennedy in Portland. It is set to an original composition by Rafael May. Levi Strauss & Co., "Levi's X Korea National Ballet," directed by Lee Jae Cheol, featuring Lee Dong Hoon and Kim Li Hoe in choreography by Sejung Hong, commercial aired 2012, 3 minutes 42 seconds, accessed August 8, 2016, https://youtu.be/CAckx0aPf-k.

83. For a discussion of the larger history of screen dance and the differences that abound between dance on screen and live concert dance, see Dodds, *Dance on Screen*, 1–35. For additional discussion of the categories of mediated dance, including the notion of screen dance as dance made for the camera, see Douglas Rosenberg, *Screendance: Inscribing the Ephemeral Image* (New York: Oxford University Press, 2012).

84. Tim Paradise, Levi's Ballet, accessed January 1, 2015, http://www.timparadise.com and DDB Group Korea, Levis Ballet—Jeans that Stretch, accessed January 1, 2015, http://www.ddbkorea.com/en/portfolio/levis-ballet-2/ 2012.

85. I use a French ballet term here to describe her making a circle with her lower leg. While her action most closely resembles a rond de jambe en l'air, which is commonly performed off the ground with the leg extended to the side of the body in à la seconde, she performs the action while sitting and tracing a circle on the ground with the tip of her toe.

86. I read the choreographic choice of using montage and continuity of action to carry the dancers through several locations in Seoul in relation to Michel de Certeau's distinction between tactics and strategies in city spaces and one's ability to find agency and create space (tactics) within the terrain of institutionalized places (strategies). Of course, the transgressive nature of the act of dancing in city spaces and disrupting the strategies of the institution that govern the flow of bodies in those spaces is countered by the fact that the advertising agency most likely obtained permits, making the dancing a (temporarily) sanctioned activity. However, for the viewer, the ad conveys an act of transgression by using the space in new ways. See Michel de Certeau, *The Practice of Everyday Life* (Berkeley, CA: University of California Press, 1988), 34–40. Site-specific performances and the disruption of place through movement is theorized in more detail in work such as Melanie Kloetzel and Caroline Pavlov, eds., *Site Dance: Choreographers and the Lure of Alternative Spaces* (Gainseville: University of Florida Press, 2009). It has more recently been taking up in relationship to the flash mob phenomenon, for example; see Thea Brejzek, "From Social Network to Urban Intervention: On the Scenographies of Flash Mobs and Urban Swarms," *International Journal of Performance Arts and Digital Media* 6, no. 1 (2010): 109–122; Gretchen Miller and Sara Rubidge, eds., *Choreographic Dwellings: Practicing Place* (London: Palgrave Macmillan, 2014) and Nicolas Whybrow, *Art and the City* (New York: Palgrave Macmillan, 2011).

87. For a brief account of ballet as a dance practice in Korea, see Judy Van Zile, *Perspectives on Korean Dance* (Middletown, CT: Wesleyan University Press, 2001), 25–27, 44–45.

88. For more on the cultural cold wars and their relation to contemporary South Korean culture and economics, see Charles K. Armstrong, "The Cultural Cold War in Korea 1945–1950," *The Journal of Asian Studies* 62, no. 1 (Feb. 2013): 71–99.

CHAPTER 3

1. Black Eyed Peas, "Hey Mama," *Elephunk*, recorded 2003, by will.i.am, A&M Records and Interscope Records, CD.

2. Apple, "Hip Hop," directed by Dave Meyers, featuring choreography by Hi Hat, commercial aired 2004, 45 seconds, accessed January 9, 2017, https://youtu.be/iqxS2hILO8s. Created by TBWA\Chiat\Day, Los Angeles to market iPod + iTunes.

3. A series of iPod + iTunes commercials feature well-known music stars (e.g., U2 and Mary J. Blige) filmed in low lighting, so that they are recognizable but barely visible, and accompanied by one or more silhouette dancers set against colored backdrops/screens. In Chapter Two, I examined U2's "Vertigo" iPod + iTunes ad as an example of this format and how it borrows music video codes and conventions. In this chapter, I do not attempt to address or explicitly name all the commercials. For more about the global reach of the campaign and its success, see Justin D. Burton, "Dancing Silhouettes: The Mobile Freedom of iPod Commercials," in *The Oxford Handbook of Mobile Music Studies*, eds. Sumanth Gopinath and Jason Stanyek (New York: Oxford University Press, 2014), 311–338; David Allan, *This Note's For You: Popular Music + Advertising = Marketing Excellence* (New York: Business Expert Press, LLC., 2015), Kindle.

4. The commercial was created by TBWA\Chiat\Day, Los Angeles, and set to the song "Ride" by The Vines. Apple, "Wild Postings," directed by Dayton/Faris, commercial aired 2004, accessed January 9, 2017, https://youtu.be/qmX1WUddzdY. The date included in the title of the Youtube posting is 2005; however, Youtube

postings are not reliable sources and usually require cross-checking. The above date was sourced from Burton, "Dancing Silhouettes" and "Apple—Wild Postings," Creativity Online, Crain Communications, accessed August 2, 2017, http://creativity-online.com/work/apple-wild-postings/10409.

5. Allan, *This Note's For You*, Chapter 14.

6. The ad was created by TBWA\Chiat\Day Los Angeles and is set to Cut Chemist, "The Audience is Listening Theme Song," recorded 2006, *The Audience is Listening*, Warner Brothers, Records, CD. Apple, "Nano Colors," directed by Mark Romanek, commercial aired 2006, 30 seconds, accessed January 9, 2017, https://youtu.be/0ua-v8COk3s.

7. The ad is set to Miss Li, "Bourgeois Shangri-La," recorded 2009, *Dancing the Whole Way Home*, National Records, CD. The commercial and the official music video employ similar, though not identical, composition and content. Apple, "Capture," directed by Phil Morrison Morano, commercial aired 2009, accessed January 9, 2017, https://youtu.be/l-jNxx-4ubE. Produced by Epoch Films for TBWA\Chiat\Day, Los Angeles.

8. Produced by Green Dot Films for TBWA\Chiat\Day, Los Angeles. The commercial is set to Leslie Feist, "1234," recorded 2007, *The Reminder*, Polydor, France, CD; the ad, essentially, mimics the first 30 seconds of the official music video. Apple, "1234," directed by Mark Coppos and Virginia Lee, commercial aired 2007, accessed January 9, 2017, https://youtu.be/LarZG0l3dPc?list=PLAAoH5WX7G3m-yFItEhM2_RyNeJ9MOmCb.

9. Lawrence Grossberg, *Dancing in Spite of Myself: Essays on Popular Culture* (Durham, NC: Duke University Press, 1997), 179.

10. This collaboration continued into 2007 when, according to a January 9, 2007 Apple press release, Cingular became the exclusive carrier for Apple's iPhone. Through a series of mergers Cingular became AT&T Wireless in 2007. The ads were directed by Dave Meyers and produced by @radical.media for BBDO. To my knowledge, there are three shadow/reflection commercials made to market iTunes + Cingular: "Alter Ego Girl," commercial aired 2005, accessed August 2, 2017, https://youtu.be/XFLkyfl3d4s; "Alter Ego Guy," commercial aired 2005, accessed August 2, 2017, https://youtu.be/vn7oRy5kiqE; and "Shadow," commercial aired 2006, http://adland.tv/commercials/cingular-motorola-slvr-itunes-shadow-2006-30-usa.

11. Andrew Wernick, "Resort to Nostalgia: Mountains, Memories and Myths of Time," in *Buy this Book: Studies in Advertising and Consumption* (London: Routledge, 1997), 207–223.

12. Sherril Dodds, *Dance on Screen: Genres and Media from Hollywood to Experimental Art* (London: Palgrave Macmillan, 2001), 137.

13. In Chapter Two, I explain Robert Goldman's concept of *not-ads*, or ads that attempt to disguise their marketing agenda by assuming the guise of other media. Robert Goldman, *Reading Ads Socially* (New York: Routledge, 1992).

14. In referring to authenticity, I draw on Andrew Goodwin's sense of authenticity in relation to music videos; see Andrew Goodwin, *Dancing in the Distraction Factory: Music Television and Popular Culture* (Minneapolis, MN: University of Minnesota Press, 1992), 121 and 136. While advertising's intertextuality, or appropriation of pre-existing works, inevitably raises the issue of the nature of the author and questions of copyright, I have not tried to tackle that topic here.

15. My use of the term "self-referentiality" refers to mass media's tendency to refer itself, both within and across genres. Serial advertising campaigns would be one example of this dynamic. While this form of reference could be viewed as a kind

of intertextuality, I argue that it differs in that media forms refer to each other not only as a way of building meaning (as one might do in an allusion) but also as a way of collapsing distinctions between mediated forms and reality. Mass media, itself, becomes the "real" and thus a source of authenticity.

16. Paul David Grainge, "Advertising the Archive: Nostalgia and the (Post)national Imaginary," *American Studies* 41, nos. 2–3 (Summer/Fall 2000): 137–158 and Paul David Grainge, "Reclaiming Heritage: Colourization, Culture Wars, and the Politics of Nostalgia," *Cultural Studies* 13, no. 4 (Oct. 1999): 621–638.

17. Rather than referencing reader response theory, I am referring to Brian Massumi's discussion of how *affect* takes on specific meaning by being "actualized" locally. Brian Massumi, *Parables of the Virtual: Movement, Affect, Sensation* (Durham, NC: Duke University Press, 2002), 41.

18. Goldman, *Reading Ads Socially*.

19. Marlboro began using the cowboy image in the 1950s as part of an effort to reposition the brand from being a woman's to a man's cigarette. The initial 1950s' image was created by the Leo Burnett Company. In the early 1960s Marlboro launched the "Come to Marlboro county" campaign, which by 1972 had moved the brand into the number one position in cigarette sales. See John McDonough and Karen Egolf, eds., *The "Advertising Age" Encyclopedia of Advertising Vol. 1 A–E* (New York: Fitzroy Dearborn/Taylor and Francis Group, 2003), 312.

20. P. Lorillard Co., Old Gold Cigarettes, "Dancing Butts," creative directors Nicholas Keesely and Peter Keverson, commercial aired 1950, 1 minute, accessed July 31, 2017, https://youtu.be/Z023OAz4fkI. Created by Lennen & Newell, Inc. for CBS-TV (NY).

21. The American Tobacco Co., Lucky Strike Cigarettes, "Barn Dance," creative directors G. David Gudebrod and John Esau, commercial aired 1948, 1 minute, accessed August 2, 2017, https://youtu.be/eqJ2y8GIUys. Created by N.W. Ayer & Son and John Handy Organization (Detroit).

22. The caller begins, "Places all" and initially continues with standard square dance instructions: "All join hands and circle left. Now circle right and listen to me. . . ." However, in these early lines, the caller inserts references to the brand, "L.S., L.S., M.F.T.," before returning to square dance calls: "Allemand your corner like swinging on a gate. A right to your honey, to your honey, to your right and left mate." The caller gradually transitions to more directly marketing the product: "Promenade, and don't you fall, Promenade around the hall. Lucky Strike is first again, First again with tobacco men. Promenade, straight down the pike, It's time right now for a Lucky Strike." Lincoln Diamant, *Television's Classic Commercials: The Golden Years (1948–1958)* (New York: Hastings House, Publishers, 1971), 105–107.

23. Wernick, "Resort to Nostalgia," 218–220.

24. Fredric Jameson, "Postmodernism and Consumer Society," in *The Continental Aesthetics Reader*, ed. Clive Cazeaux (New York: Routledge, 2000), 284–286.

25. Smoking can in fact build a kind of community; it forms an instantaneous, temporary bond and is an easy form of "sharing" that can cross class, gender, and race divides.

26. The construction of square dancing as white American folk was already in play by the 1940s; square dancing played a role in the "fancy-dress events" at the Savoy Ballroom in Harlem during the annual "Barn Dance on Labor Day": " . . . women were invited to dress in their 'gingham gowns' and the men in their 'best overalls' to do 'folk dances'. Authenticity was not a great concern when attempting square dancing, but complaints were voiced on occasions if real bales of straw were

not used to decorate the ballroom." See Karen Hubbard and Terry Monaghan, "Negotiating Compromise on a Burnished Wooden Floor: Social Dancing at the Savoy," in *Ballroom, Boogie, Shimmy Sham, Shake: A Social and Popular Dance Reader*, ed. Julie Malnig (Chicago, IL: University of Illinois Press, 2009), 137. The above description points to how the construction of American folk was well under way by 1948; the link between square dancing and white, traditional culture was established. Clearly, dance was playing a role in imaging America's cultural history.

27. Martin Rubin, *Showstoppers: Busby Berkeley and the Tradition of Spectacle* (New York: Columbia University Press, 1993), 36–43.

28. I refer to the connections between square dancing's composition and partnering sequences and those of country line dancing, quadrilles, and Renaissance and Baroque dance. There are a number of sources; for examples, see Marion Kant, *The Cambridge Companion to Ballet* (New York: Cambridge University Press, 2007), 19–31; Susan Leigh Foster, *Reading Dancing: Bodies and Subjects in Contemporary American Dance* (Berkeley, CA: University of California Press, 1986), 100–120; Elizabeth Aldrich, "The Civilizing of America's Ballrooms: The Revolutionary War to 1890," in *Ballroom, Boogie, Shimmy Sham, Shake: A Social and Popular Dance Reader*, ed. Julie Malnig (Chicago, IL: University of Illinois Press, 2009), 36–54.

29. Rubin, *Showstoppers*, 43.

30. Rubin, *Showstoppers*, 142.

31. Grainge, "Advertising the Archive"; Jameson, "Postmodernism"; Wernick, "Resort to Nostalgia."

32. Grainge develops this concept to account for a 1990s media trend that sought to "authorize a consensual past, a core memory—what might be called an archival essence—for a stable and unified concept of 'America'." I argue that advertising engages with similar forms of nostalgia without memory earlier in its history. Grainge, "Advertising the Archive," 137.

33. Grainge, "Advertising the Archive."

34. Grainge, "Advertising the Archive," 140.

35. Colleen Dunagan, "Performing the Commodity-Sign: Dancing in the Gap," *Dance Research Journal* 39, no. 2 (2007), 9–10.

36. Linda Hutcheon, *A Theory of Parody: The Teachings of Twentieth-century Art Forms* (Chicago, IL: University of Illinois Press, 2000), 43.

37. Hutcheon, *A Theory of Parody*, 50. She cites Ziva Ben-Porat, "The Poetics of Literary Allusion," *PTL* 1 (1976): 28–105.

38. Hutcheon, *A Theory of Parody*, 43.

39. Massumi, *Parables of the Virtual*, 33.

40. Produced by Moxie Pictures and created by ad agency Goodby, Silverstein & Partners, San Francisco. eBay, "Do You Know the Way to Use eBay?" directed by Sam Mendes, featuring choreography by Michael Rooney (unconfirmed), commercial aired 2003, 42 seconds, accessed March 15, 2016, https://youtu.be/MHCh1zvkbVE.

41. The original song credits are: Dionne Warwick, "Do you know the way to San Jose?" by Burt Bacharach and Hal David, Dionne Warwick in *Valley of the Dolls* album, recorded 1968, Scepter, CD. The Bacharach/David song has been recorded numerous times; however, it was originally written for and recorded by Warwick, who won her first Grammy Award (Best Female Pop Vocal Performance) for her performance.

42. While there are arguably connections between musical theater productions and the musical numbers found in commercials, my analysis focuses on comparisons

to film musicals because the films form part of the mass media world commercials take part in, and both television and film undertake a negotiation between theatrical and filmic performance conventions. *Gentlemen Prefer Blondes*, directed by Howard Hawks, featuring Marilyn Monroe and choreography by Jack Cole (20th Century Fox, 1953); *Grease*, directed by Randal Kleiser, featuring choreography by Patricia Birch (Paramount Pictures, 1978).

43. Arm gestures in the choreography are reminiscent of body builder poses used by Shawn in his 1930s choreography for his all-male company. Examples can be found in *Kinetic Molpai* (1935), *Polonaise* (1923), and to some extent in *The New World* (1936). In the ad, these gestures are performed as actions rather than still poses and are reminiscent of a masculine version of the female choreography in Fosse's "Rich Man's Frug" from *Sweet Charity* (1969), especially the female choreography for "The Aloof" and the boxing references from "The Heavyweight". *Sweet Charity*, directed by Bob Fosse, featuring choreography by Bob Fossse (Universal Pictures, 1969).

44. Carolyn M. Goldstein, *Creating Consumers: Home Economists in Twentieth-century America* (Chapel Hill, NC: University of North Carolina Press, 2012); Shelley Nickles, "More is Better: Mass Consumption, Gender, and Class Identity in Postwar America," *American Quarterly* 54, no. 4 (Dec. 2002): 581–622.

45. Erin Brannigan, *Dancefilm: Choreography and the Moving Image* (New York: Oxford University Press, 2011), 141–163.

46. Dodds, *Dance on Screen*, 35–60 and 135–146.

47. Regrettably, there are several engaging contemporary commercials I do not discuss that highlight media's self-referentiality, celebrities, and cross-promotion. For example, a 2006 Target/Gwen Stefani commercial advertising her album *Sweet Escape* reproduces sections of her "Wind it Up" music video, which contains samples and alludes to the *The Sound of Music*. In 2007 Kia Motors advertised their Kiafest with a commercial featuring Keith Young's restaging of choreography from *Flashdance* (1989) (ad, directed by James Rouse for David & Goliath). In it a car salesman performs his excitement through choreography excerpts from "What a Feeling" and "He's a Dream" set to a jingle version of "Maniac." In 2013 Pepsi and Beyoncé teamed up in "Mirrors," in which Beyoncé dances with mirror images of herself that reproduce choreography and costumes from several of her music videos (choreography by Frank Gatson, directed by Jake Nava, produced by Bellevue Media for 180 Los Angeles).

48. Pepsi-Cola, "Make a Wish," directed by Joe Pytka, featuring choreography by Vincent Paterson, commercial aired 1989, 2 minutes, accessed July 15, 2017, https://youtu.be/rM-0rmUgOnY. Created by BBDO Worldwide. This ad also included a 30-second promotional spot (accessed July 15, 2017, https://youtu.be/ UVdGmmVJdmE) advertising the longer 2-minute ad and her video: Madonna, "Like a Prayer" (music video), directed by Mary Lambert (Sire/Warner Brothers, 1989). The ad originally aired one day before the release of the music video for Madonna's "Like a Prayer," before being pulled in response to complaints about religious imagery in the music video and despite the reported $5 million paid to Madonna. Consumers were apparently confused by the crossover and interpreted the video as part of the commercial. See "Pepsi Cancels Madonna Ad," *New York Times*, April 5, 1989, accessed January 11, 2017, http://www.nytimes.com/1989/ 04/05/business/pepsi-cancels-madonna-ad.html.

49. Correspondences between video and ad would have encouraged consumers' confusion regarding the two; however, press accounts of Pepsi's response to

consumer outrage suggests that Pepsi was unaware of the potentially contro-versial elements of Madonna's music video, despite what seem to be intentional overlaps in content. For example, see the "Pepsi Cancels Madonna" article in note 48.

50. Brannigan, *Dancefilm*, 160.
51. Maureen Needham, *I See America Dancing!: Selected Readings (1865–2000)* (Urbana, IL: University of Illinois Press, 2002); Lindsey Michelle Timmons Summers, *Soul/Forbidden Body: Dancing Christian from Ruth St. Denis to Pole Dancing for Jesus*, PhD diss., University of California, Riverside, 2014: ProQuest Database.
52. This connection is particularly intriguing given Ailey's choreography "challenges the binary of blackness and whiteness . . . through choreographic struc-ture . . . [and] mixed-race casting." See Susan Manning, "Danced Spirituals," in *Of the Presence of the Body: Essays on Dance and Performance Theory*, ed. André Lepecki (Middletown, CT: Wesleyan University Press, 2004), 93.
53. The campaign of 30-second TV spots was created by advertising agency Young & Rubicam for Dr. Pepper, working with director Paul Hunter and H.S.I. (production company). Most of the ads feature choreography by Michael Rooney, but I was unable to confirm this fact for all of them. By the time these ads were produced, Hunter was already well known as a director of music videos and commercials featuring dance.
54. While microphones and sound equipment fall outside my field of expertise, after some research I believe the microphone is a Shure 55 model.
55. The combination of McGrath and the band references Buddy Holly and the Crickets.
56. *Grease*, directed by Randal Kleiser, featuring choreography by Patricia Birch (Paramount Pictures, 1978), film.
57. Larry Starr and Christopher Waterman, *American Popular Music: From Minstrelsy to MTV* (New York: Oxford University Press, 2003), 222–223.
58. According to their website, Dr. Pepper is a unique blend of 23 flavors. Century. "Fact Sheet," Dr. Pepper/Snapple Group, accessed January 12, 2017, http://news.drpeppersnapplegroup.com/brand-fact-sheet.
59. Anne Anlin Cheng, *Second Skin: Josephine Baker and the Modern Surface* (New York: Oxford University Press, 2011); Jayna Brown, *Babylon Girls: Black Women Performers and the Shaping of the Modern* (Durham, NC: Duke University Press, 2008).
60. *America Dances! 1897–1948: A Collector's Edition of Social Dance in Film* (Kentfield, CA: Dancetime Publications, 2003) DVD.
61. Danielle Robinson, *Modern Moves: Dancing Race during the Ragtime and Jazz Eras* (New York: Oxford University Press, 2015); Brian Harker, "Louis Armstrong, Eccentric Dance, and the Evolution of Dance on the Eve of Swing," *Journal of the American Musicological Society* 61, no. 1 (Spring 2008): 67–121; Donald Clark, *Billie Holiday: Wishing on the Moon* (Cambridge, MA: Da Capo Press, 2002); Starr and Waterman, *American Popular Music*, 39–61.
62. Kate Daubney, "Songbird or Subversive?: Instrumental Vocalization Technique in the Songs of Billie Holiday," *Journal of Gender Studies* 11, no. 1 (March 2002): 17–28.
63. I refer here to his dance style. Expanding Brannigan's notion of the "gestural idiogest" and drawing on Susan Leigh Foster's discussion of style in *Reading Dancing* (1986), I refer to tendencies in his movement vocabulary, phrasing,

sequencing, and qualitative inflection. For an example, see The Black Eyed Peas, "The Boogie that Be" (music video), *Elephunk* album, A&M Records, accessed January 12, 2017, 2003 https://youtu.be/hDpnpaaE2vY.

64. Brenda Dixon Gottschild, *Digging the Africanist Presence in American Performance: Dance and other Contexts* (Westport, CT: Praeger, 1996/98).

65. Fredric Jameson, as well as others, has noted this use of pastiche as a characteristic of postmodern culture. Jameson, "Postmodernism and Consumer Society".

66. Linda Hutcheon, *A Theory of Parody: The Teaching of Twentieth-century Art Forms* (Chicago, IL: University of Illinois Press, 2000), 33 and 38–39.

67. I do not have the title or director for this spot, but a *New York Times* article cites the ad agency as Lintas New York. The spot features stock footage of Gene Kelly in *Anchors Aweigh* and *On the Town*, Groucho Marx from *Duck Soup*, and Cary Grant from *The Awful Truth* and *Indiscreet*. A second spot featuring Elton John ran earlier in the same year and included clips of Louis Armstrong, Humphrey Bogart, and James Cagney. See Stuart Elliott "New Spots are Set for Diet Coke, Pepsi," The Media Business: Advertising, Addenda, *The New York Times* July 24, 1992; Robert Goldman and Stephen Papson, *Sign Wars: The Cluttered Landscape of Advertising* (New York: The Guilford Press, 1996), 24.

68. Hutcheon, *A Theory of Parody*, 32.

69. Hutcheon, *A Theory of Parody*, 32.

70. Hutcheon, *A Theory of Parody*, 42–43.

71. Hutcheon turns to Bakhtin and his analysis of the transgressions of Carnival for an explanation of how parody is itself a kind of "authorized transgression" and what this status allows it. She notes that, "This paradox of legalized though unofficial subversion is characteristic of all parodic discourses insofar as parody posits, as a prerequisite to its very existence, a certain aesthetic institutionalization which entails the acknowledgement of recognizable, stable forms and conventions." Hutcheon, *A Theory of Parody*, 74–75.

72. *Royal Wedding*, directed by Stanley Donen, featuring choreography by Fred Astaire with Nick Castle (MGM/UA, 1951) Film.

73. *Easter Parade*, directed by Charles Walters, featuring choreography by Fred Astaire with Robert Alton and Ann Miller (MGM, 1948), film.

74. Dirt Devil, "Dance," "Ceiling," and "Stairs," directed by Greg Strom and Doug Magallon, featuring Fred Astaire, commercial aired 1997, 15 seconds, accessed July 3, 2017, https://youtu.be/q-ix5IYz0cc, https://youtu.be/QASUovFOquw, https://youtu.be/lYfU8qUQ9S8. Produced by Atomic Films SME for Meldrum & Fewsmith Communications, Cleveland, 1997. Kris GoodFellow, "The Fleetest Feet in the Super Bowl were Fred Astaire's," *The New York Times* (January 27, 1997) http://www.nytimes.com/1997/01/27/business/the-fleetest-feet-in-the-super-bowl-were-fred-astaire-s.html (accessed January 13, 2017).

75. James William Smith, "Sinatra's Stamp and Fred Astaire's Vacuum," Buzzle.com, June 20, 2010, accessed December 15, 2016, http://www.buzzle.com/articles/sinatras-stamp-and-fred-astaires-vacuum.html and "Fred Astaire's Last Dance," *Entertainment Weekly Online*, EW.com, June 18, 1999, accessed June 20, 2010, http://www.ew.com/ew/article/0,,273770,00.html.

76. Smith, "Sinatra's Stamp".

77. There are other examples of dance in advertising that remix existing works. In 2006 The Gap announced the return of its skinny black pants with a commercial featuring Audrey Hepburn's bohemian solo dance from *Funny Face* (1957). The ad begins with the original film footage, and as Hepburn dances, digital editing

transports her to an abstract off-white space and creates mirror images of her as she dances (producing a small-scale kaleidoscope effect), before returning her dancing-self back to the world of the film. The commercial updates the dance and reorients it toward how skinny black pants support self-expression, setting her dance to AC/DC's "Back in Black" and including excerpts of her lines from the film ("I rather feel like expressing myself now," "I'm not inhibited," "a girl wants to dance, a girl wants to dance," "it's nothing more than an expression or release"). The Gap, "Keep it Simple," directed by Trey Laird, featuring choreography by Eugene Loring, commercial aired 2006, 1 minute. Produced by Method Studios for Laird + Partners, New York.

78. Other dance studies publications have analyzed this ad; however, I began working with the ad when it first premiered in 2005, and since it serves my analysis, I have chosen to retain it. While my description of the ad is remarkably similar in language, it was written prior to Fogarty's publication. See Mary Fogarty, "The Original, Updated" in *The Oxford Handbook of Dance and the Popular Screen*, ed. Melissa Blanco Borelli (New York: Oxford University Press, 2014), 83–97; "Singin' in the Rain," directed by Jake Knight and Ryoko Tanaka, featuring Gene Kelly, commercial aired 2005, 1 minute, accessed July 17, 2008, http://image. guardian.co.uk/sys-video/Media/video/2005/01/27/golfgti.mov. Created by DDB London Ltd. See "Volkswagen Golf Range—Volkswagen Golf GTI Singing in the Rain," Visit4info-The place for Ads, Visit4 Ltd., accessed July 17, 2008, http://www.visit4info.com/advert/Volkswagen-Golf-GTi-Singing-In-The-Rain-Volkswagen-Golf-Range/2025.

79. Jason Kottke, "Golf GTI commercial and Elsewhere," kottke.org, accessed July 17, 2008, http://www.kottke.org/05/02/golf-gti-commercial-and-elsewhere; "Gene Kelly Singin' and Break Dancin' in the Rain," Press Release, Volkswagen UK, January 27, 2005, accessed July 17, 2008, http://www.volkswagen.co.uk/ company/press/GTI_advert.

80. The big beat remix of "Singing in the Rain" featured in the Volkswagen commercial was originally composed for the commercial in 2005 as "Waiting in the Rain." The song was then remixed, renamed, and re-released as "Singing in the Rain" on the album *See You in the Morning*. The song was then released as a single on August 22, 2005. See "Faith and Hope Records: Mint Royale News," Faith and Hope Records, accessed July 17, 2008, http://www.faithandhope.co.uk/ 05artistis.asp?artistid=1.

81. Catherine Woolfe, Volkswagen's Communications Manager, presents this idea as the intended meaning of the ad. See Volkswagen, UK, "Gene Kelly".

82. For example, see Volkswagen UK, "Gene Kelly."

83. Genné and Clover offer alternative readings of the dancing in the film musical number. Their readings further complicate what the film brings to the ad, the meaning generated by the parody, and how one reads the commodity-sign generated by the ad. Beth Genné, "Dancin' in the Street: Street Dancing on Film and Video from Fred Astaire to Michael Jackson," in *Rethinking Dance History: A Reader*, ed. Alexander Carter (New York: Routledge, 2004), 132–142 and Carol J. Clover, "Dancin' in the Rain," in *Hollywood Musicals: The Film Reader*, ed. Steven Cohan (New York: Routledge, 2002), 157–174.

84. Gottschild, *Digging the Africanist*, 11–19; Thomas F. DeFrantz, "The Black Beat Made Visible: Hip Hop Dance and Body Power," in *Of the Presence of the Body: Essays on Dance and Performance Theory*, ed. André Lepecki (Middletown, CT: Wesleyan University Press, 2004), 64–81.

85. Richard Dyer, *Only Entertainment*, 2nd edition (New York: Routledge, 2002), 20–21; Rick Altman, *The American Film Musical* (Bloomington, IN: Indiana University Press, 1989), 60–70; Jane Feuer, *The Hollywood Musical* (Bloomington, IN: Indiana University press, 1982).

86. DeFrantz, "The Black Beat," 67–68.

87. Richard, *Only Entertainment*, 19–35; Altman, *The American Film Musical*, 59–89; Feuer, *The Hollywood Musical*, 67–85.

88. The concept of innovation also furthers the connection of hip hop and African-American movement principles: "The dancing body is itself considered the generative force of movement only through the act of stylization. In this process of personal invention, the dancer approaches a goal of purity, of expressing the self by manipulating basic movement utterances." DeFrantz, "The Black Beat," 73.

89. Stanley C. Pelkey and Antony Bushard, eds., *Anxiety Muted: American Film Music in a Suburban Age* (New York: Oxford University Press, 2015).

90. Here I refer to the larger cultural history of dance in the United States: the transfer of dances developed within African-American expressive culture to white bodies and the history of racial segregation within dance. While I do not know the exact racial background of all three of the dancers who perform in the ad, only one is identified as non-white online, and he is Latino, rather than African-American. Thus, my point is not that the dancers perform in "white face" so much as that the movement stands in for historical bodies.

CHAPTER 4

1. The Black Eyed Peas, "Boogie that Be," by Adams Will, Stephens John Roger, and Van Musser Thomas *Elephunk*, A&M Records, 2003, CD.

2. The song, "Orange Blossom Special," has been recorded by several artists, including Johnny Cash in 1965.

3. The ad was created by Goodby, Silverstein & Partners for Hewlett Packard to advertise the Apple iPod made for Hewlett Packard (HP) computers. HP, "Mash Up," directed by Paul Hunter, commercial aired 2004, 1 minute, accessed June 2, 2015, http://adland.tv/commercials/hp-hewlett-packard-apple-ipod-collide-mash-2004-060-usa. The campaign and product were part of a brief collaboration between HP and Apple, which ended a year later when they discontinued the product in 2005. It was not considered an Apple product and was, at that point, the only time that iPod and iTunes had been licensed to another company; see "HP and Apple Partner to Deliver Digital Music Player and iTunes to HP Customers," Apple Newsroom, January 8, 2004, accessed June 2, 2015, https://www.apple.com/pr/library/2004/01/08HP-and-Apple-Partner-to-Deliver-Digital-Music-Player-and-iTunes-to-HP-Customers.html. Details about the relationship and its discontinuance can be found at Nicola D'Agostino, "The Apple iPod by HP," Stories of Apple.net, accessed June 2, 2015, http://www.storiesofapple.net/the-apple-ipod-by-hp.html.

4. Ian Burkitt, "Subjectivity, Self and Everyday Life in Contemporary Capitalism," *Subjectivity* 23 (2008): 237.

5. The notion of dance as a performance of racial identity that is simultaneously essential and constructed has been addressed previously. For example, see Susan Manning, "Danced Spirituals," in *Of the Presence of the Body: Essays on Dance and Performance Theory*, ed. André Lepecki (Middletown, CT: Wesleyan University Press, 2004), 82–96.

6. Thorstein Veblen, *The Theory of the Leisure Class* (New York: Oxford University Press, 2007), accessed June 20, 2016, Proquest eBook Central.

7. Pallabi Chakravorty, "From Interculturalism to Historicism: Reflections on Classical Indian Dance," in *The Routledge Dance Studies Reader*, 2nd edition, ed. Alexandra Carter and Janet O'Shea (New York: Routledge, 2010), 275.

8. I am thinking of the effects of interculturalism on contemporary culture and theories of cultural hybridity. I argue globalization produces both intra and interculturalism as a fundamental part of culture and is a phenomenon that plays a substantial role in the lives of American people. For interculturalism as productive ambiguity, see Lorna Sander, "Akram Khan's *Ma*: An Essay in Hybridisation and Productive Ambiguity," in *Decentring Dancing Texts: The Challenge of Interpreting Dances*, ed. Janet Lansdale (New York: Palgrave Macmillan 2008), 55–72.

9. The punk dance scene seems to consist largely of something closer to pogoing. However, there are moments of what might be slam dancing; see Sherill Dodds, "Slamdancing with the Boundaries of Theory and Practice: The Legitimization of Popular Dance," in *The Routledge Dance Studies Reader*, 2nd edition, ed. Alexandra Carter and Janet O'Shea (New York: Routledge, 2010), 344–353.

10. Danielle Robinson, *Modern Moves: Dancing Race during the Ragtime and Jazz Eras* (New York: Oxford University Press, 2015), 62.

11. Several dance scholars have identified this characterization operating within dance history. For example, see Robinson, *Modern Moves*, 59–69 and 93–98; Manning, *Danced Spirituals*, 84; Nadine George-Grave, "'Just like Being at the Zoo': Primitivity and Ragtime Dance" in *Ballroom, Boogie, Shimmy Sham, Shake: A Social and Popular Dance Reader*, ed. Julie Malnig (Chicago, IL: University of Illinois Press, 2009), 63–67; David Garcia, "Embodying Music/Disciplining Dance: The Mambo Body in Havana and New York City," in *Ballroom, Boogie, Shimmy Sham, Shake: A Social and Popular Dance Reader*, ed. Julie Malnig (Chicago, IL: University of Illinois Press, 2009), 175; and Brenda Dixon Gottschild, *Digging the Africanist Presence in American Performance: Dance and Other Contexts* (Westport, CT: Praeger Publishers, 1998).

12. I refer to the control and moderation of country-western's "booty bumping" and the fabric-shrouded version of working and shaking it found in polka compared to the more exposed bodies of the house party and the freer, more articulate isolations of the house and b-boy dancers. For more on cultural discourses associating African-American dance practices with a more sexualized body, see Robinson, *Modern Moves* and Gottschild, *Digging the Africanist*.

13. See David Harvey, *A Brief History of Neoliberalism* (New York: Oxford University Press, 2005).

14. Anthropologists and post-colonial, dance, and cultural theorists have interrogated issues of cultural appropriation and its relationship to the concept of interculturalism; see Aijaz Ahmad *In Theory: Classes, Nations, Literature* (New York: Verso, 1994); Andrée Grau, "Intercultural Research in the Performing Arts," *Dance Research: The Journal of the Society for Dance Research* 10, no. 2 (Autumn 1992): 3–29; Andrée Grau and Stephanie Jordan, eds., *Europe Dancing: Perspectives on Theater Dance and Cultural Identity* (New York: Routledge, 2000); Patrice Pavis, ed., *The Intercultural Performance Reader* (New York: Routledge, 1996); and Roberto Una and Lucy Mae San Pablo Burns, eds., *The Color of Theater: Race, Culture and Contemporary Performance* (New York: Continuum, 2002).

15. Pallabi Chakravorty, "From Interculturalism to Historicism," 274.

16. Chakravorty, "From Interculturalism to Historicism," 275.
17. Harvey, *A Brief History*, 2.
18. Harvey, *A Brief History*, 3.
19. For mimicry, see Homi K. Bhabha, *The Location of Culture* (New York: Routledge, 1994).
20. Thomas F. DeFrantz, "The Black Beat Made Visible: Hip Hop Dance and Body Power," in *Of the Presence of the Body: Essays on Dance and Performance Theory*, ed. Andre Lepecki (Middletown, CT: Wesleyan University Press, 2004), 70.
21. See Thomas F. DeFrantz, "Unchecked Popularity: Neoliberal Circulation of Black Social Dance," in *Neoliberalism and Global Theatres: Performance Permutations*, eds. Lara D. Nielsen and Patricia Ybarra (New York: Palgrave Macmillan, 2012), 128–139.
22. Linda Hutcheon, *A Theory of Parody: The Teachings of Twentieth-century Art Forms* (Chicago, IL: University of Illinois Press, 2000), 32.
23. See DeFranzt's work on African American social dances and his analysis of how they function as "expressive body talking—as a productive means of group formation and social connectivity," see DeFrantz, "Unchecked Popularity," 128.
24. I refer to the characteristic commonalities identified by dance scholars Brenda Dixon Gottschild, *Digging the Africanist*, and Kariamu Welsh Asante, "Commonalities in African Dance," in *African Culture: The Rhythm of Unity*, eds. Molefi Kete Asante and Kariamu Welsh Asante (Westport, CT: Greenwood Press, 1968), 71–82 as well as art historian Robert Farris Thompson, "An Aesthetic of the Cool: West African Dance," in *The Theater of Black Americans: A Collection of Critical Essays*, ed. Errol Hill (Englewood Cliffs, NJ: Prentice Hall, 1987), 99–111.
25. I introduced nostalgia without memory in Chapter Three. Here I place it into conversation with post-colonial theories of mimicry and ambivalence to suggest that they contribute to this form of nostalgia. See Paul David Grainge, "Advertising the Archive: Nostalgia and the (Post)National Imaginary," *American Studies* 41, nos. 2–3 (Summer/Fall 2000): 137–157.
26. I do not have complete production data; see Red Rose Tea, "Savoy Ritz," commercial aired 1960, accessed December 8, 2016, https://youtu.be/-918OMwCx6w.
27. I know of at least one more recent example of this stereotype. In 1993 AT&T's internal company magazine included a cartoon depicting an AT&T African customer as a monkey. The image appeared on the "Fun N' Games" page of the *AT&T Focus Magazine*, which was distributed internationally to the company's 300,000 employees. The cartoon showed customers on several continents making phone calls; all of them were human with the exception of the African. An article in *Jet* discusses the ad and cites AT&T as having not noticed the cartoon during the production process, because the cartoon was drawn by an independent cartoonist and produced by an external design agency. They apologized and said they were embarrassed. The cartoonist said it was supposed to be humorous, not racist, and that he used gorillas in his work all the time. See "AT&T apologizes for its 'Racist' Cartoon Depicting African Caller as a Monkey," *Jet* 84, no. 23 (1993): 4–5.
28. Grainge, "Advertising the Archive," 137.
29. Grainge, "Advertising the Archive," 138.
30. Red Rose Tea is a product of the Brook Bonds Food brand. The company signed the Marquis Chimps to perform in a three-commercial campaign in which they starred in the following scenarios: a wild west shoot out, a golf match, and a jazz performance at the Savoy; see Ed Golick, "Swinging with the Red Rose

Tea Chimps," The Detroit Kids Show, accessed December 8, 2016, http://www.detroitkidshow.com/red_rose_tea.htm.

31. The name "Savoy Ritz" is a reference to actual places in both the United States and England. The name references the Savoy Theater built in 1881 by Richard D'Oyly Carte as a home for the Gilbert & Sullivan operettas; its original manager César Ritz later went on to open the luxury hotel, The Ritz. Well-known bands that played at the Savoy include Savoy Orpheans and Savoy Havana Band. It also references the Savoy Ballroom in New York City's Harlem. See John Rockwell, "The Home of Gilbert and Sullivan Reopens After a Fire. With a Ballet: Gilbert & Sullivan Home Reopens. With a Ballet," *New York Times*, July 22, 1993: C11; Clive Walker, "More than Simply a Bed for the Night," *Conference and Incentive Travel* (supplement Center Stage), December 2006: 19–20; and Andrew Gumbel, "Europe: Putting on the Ritz. The Founder of Paris's Most Famous Hotel was Not as his Image Portrays. Now the Ritz has Thrown Discretion to the Winds," *The Guardian*, Oct. 15, 1993.

32. The chimps are not actually talking, obviously; however, the voiceover is timed to the movement of their mouths to create this impression.

33. Online sources give conflicting information about the exact date and original intended target audience of the commercial. One claims the ad was originally made for the British market in 1957, while another says the chimps were signed in 1960 as part of a campaign for the American market. See Ed Golick, "Swinging with the Red" and Rich Kienzle, "'Red Rose Tea': TV Commercial to Local Hit Single," *Pittsburgh Post-Gazette*, Monday November 4, 2013, accessed July 14, 2016, http://communityvoices.post-gazette.com/arts-entertainment-living.

34. Homi K. Bhabha, "Of Mimicry and Man: The Ambivalence of Colonial Discourse," in *The Location of Culture* (New York: Routledge, 1994), 86, original emphasis.

35. The Marquis Chimps were a part of a British Music Hall act, Marquis and Family, that acrobat Gene Detroy created in the 1950s. Detroy taught the chimpanzees a variety of "tricks" that mimicked a wide range of human behavior. See Ed Golick, "Swinging with the Red".

36. Karen Hubbard and Terry Monaghan, "Negotiating Compromise on a Burnished Wood Floor: Social Dancing at the Savoy," in *Ballroom, Boogie, Shimmy Sham, Shake: A Social and Popular Dance Reader*, ed. Julie Malnig (Chicago, IL: University of Illinois Press, 2009), 126–145.

37. Hubbard and Monaghan, "Negotiating Compromise," 126–145.

38. This dynamic was the continuation of a history of exchange that crossed racial lines through dancing; see Danielle Robinson, "The Ugly Duckling: The Refinement of Ragtime Dancing and the Mass Production and Marketing of Modern Social Dancing," *Dance Research* 28, no. 2 (2010): 179–199, and Danielle Robinson, *Modern Moves: Dancing Race during the Ragtime and Jazz Eras* (New York: Oxford University Press, 2015).

39. Larry Billman, *Film Choreographers and Dance Directors: An Illustrated Biographical Encyclopedia with a History and Filmographies, 1893 through 1995* (Jefferson, NC: McFarland &Company, Inc., Publishers, 1997), 66.

40. Lawrence Grossberg, Ellen Wartella, and D. Charles Whitney, *Media Making: Mass Media in a Popular Culture* (Thousand Oaks, CA: Sage Publications, Inc., 1998), 222–223.

41. Coco Fusco, *English is Broken Here: Notes on Cultural Fusion in the Americas* (New York: The New Press, 1995). Historically, black slaves in the United States were compared to African primates and these images circulated within popular culture through literature, film, cartoons, and theater. For more on this history,

see Jake Spindle, "Victorian Juvenilia and the Image of the Black African," *Journal of Popular Culture* 9 (Feb. 1975): 51–65 and Wayne Martin Mellinger, "Postcards from the Edge of the Color Line: Images of African Americans in Popular Culture, 1893–1917," *Symbolic Interaction* 15, no. 4 (Winter 1992): 429–430. Richard Dyer also addresses this representation in relation to British depictions of the Irish; see Dyer, *White* (New York: Routledge, 1997), 52–57. In addition, *Bamboozled*, directed by Spike Lee (New Line Cinema, 2000), offers evidence of the prevalence of visual caricatures comparing blacks to primates throughout the history of minstrelsy in the United States.

42. See Robinson, "Ugly Ducklin" and *Modern Moves*; Nadine George-Graves, "Just Like Being"; and Richard Dyer, *Only Entertainment*, 2nd edition (New York: Routledge, 1992), 155.

43. Gottschild, *Digging the Africanist*.

44. Golick, "Swinging with the Red."

45. Kienzle, "'Red Rose Tea.'"

46. The song was referred to as "Rock and Roll Dance Party" when played by DJs Zeke Jackson and Frank "Crazy D" DiMino on a Pittsburgh radio station in 1968, and was then later licensed from the Red Rose parent company Brooke Bonds Foods and released by Jackson and DiMino on their Gink label as "Red Rose Tea" Gink #9612. See Youtube https://youtu.be/G0tQO1TjXLM, Wikipedia https://en.wikipedia.org/wiki/Red_Rose_Tea, and Detroitkidshow.com (accessed June 20, 2016)

47. Doug Krentzlin, "Classic Commercials: 'Red Rose Tea' with the Marquis Chimps," Classic TV Examiner, *Examiner.com*, March 23, 2010, accessed March 29, 2014, http://www.examiner.com/article/classic-commericals-red-rose-tea.

48. I am referring primarily to commentary left on Youtube postings of the ad; see https://youtu.be/prVRwXAWFeA and https://youtu.be/-918OMwCx6w, accessed December 11, 2016.

49. See Albert Bergesen, "Race Riots of 1967: An Analysis of Police Violence in Detroit and Newark," *Journal of Black Studies* 12, no. 3 (March 1982): 261–274; J. Shantz, "'They Think They're Fannies are as Good as Ours': The 1943 Detroit Riot," *Studies in the Literary Imagination* 40, no. 2 (Fall 2007): 75–92, and PBS, "Detroit Race Riots 1943," *American Experience: TVs Most-watched History Series*, accessed December 11, 2016, http://www.pbs.org/wgbh/americanexperience/features/general-article/eleanor-riots/.

50. In 1955 Martin Luther King Jr. rose to national prominence with the Montgomery Alabama bus boycott; the intensity of the movement peaked in 1960 with the Greensboro sit-ins, which were followed by the Freedom Rides in 1961, James Meredith's admission to the University of Mississippi in 1962, the March on Washington in 1963, and the Selma to Montgomery Voting Rights March in 1965. These actions on the part of citizens corresponded with the passing of the Civil Rights Act of 1964 and the Voting Rights Act of 1965. Gerald Webster, Toby Moore, Leah C. Aden, James U. Blacksher, Michael L. Clemens, and Jonathan I. Leib, "Interventions on the 50th Anniversaries of Events in the American Civil Rights Movement," *Political Geography* 48 (2015): 146–158.

51. Advertising's appropriation of African-American cultural products functions in its construction of Americanness similarly to that of the paradoxical employment of the indigenous Indian as a figure of Otherness and a symbol of national identity in the United States; see Jacqueline Shea Murphy, *The People Have Never Stopped Dancing: Native American Modern Dance Histories* (Minneapolis, MN: University of Minnesota Press, 2007).

52. Miranda Joseph, "The Performance of Production and Consumption," *Social Text* no. 54 (Spring 1998): 34

53. Joseph, "The Performance of Production," 35–37.

54. Joseph, "The Performance of Production," 36.

55. Anthea Kraut, *Choreographing Copyright: Race, Gender, and Intellectual Property Rights in American Dance* (New York: Oxford University Press, 2016), xiv.

56. Within the law, social dance, as well as steps in concert dance, are treated as words or ideas, as fundamental building blocks, and are thus required to remain part of the public domain. See Joi Michelle Lakes, "A Pas de Deux for Choreography and Copyright," *NYU Law Review* 80, no. 1829 (December 2005).

57. Kraut, "Choreographing Copyright," xiii.

58. Kraut, "Choreographing Copyright," xiii.

59. Kraut, "Choreographing Copyright," xiv.

60. Kraut, "Choreographing Copyright," xiv.

61. Brian Massumi, *Parables of the Virtual: Movement, Affect, Sensation* (Durham, NC: Duke University Press, 2002), 88.

62. For those that are unfamiliar with Gottschild's work, the five Africanist principles, or premises, she outlines are embracing the conflict, polycentrism/polyrhythm, high-affect juxtaposition, ephebism, and the aesthetic of cool. The aesthetic of the cool is a concept identified previously by Art historian Robert Farris Thompson. These principles overlap to a degree with the commonalities of African dance identified by dance scholar Kariamu Welsh Asante; see Gottschild, *Digging the Africanist*, 11–20.

63. Gottschild, *Digging the Africanist*, xiv.

64. This song in combination with the single "Night Fever" is credited with relaunching the Bee Gees' music career. Both singles are part of the film's (*Saturday Night Fever*) soundtrack. Larry Starr and Christopher Waterman, *American Popular Music: From Minstrelsy to MTV* (New York: Oxford University Press, 2003), 362.

65. Choreography by AC Ciulla. I was not able to obtain detailed production information for this commercial. See "Travis Wall: Portrait of the Young Man as an Artist," *Movement Magazine: Dance and Pop Culture Together as a Lifestyle*, June 20, 2006, accessed December 13, 2016, http://www.movmnt.com/travis-wall-portrait-of-the-youg-man-as-an-artist_0020.html.

66. Ephebism "encompasses attributes such as power, vitality, flexibility, drive, and attack"; see Gottschild, *Digging the Africanist*, 15.

67. I refer specifically to constructions of whiteness grounded in corporeality. For further information about the body's relationship to constructions of race at different moments in US history, see Julie Malnig, ed., *Ballroom, Boogie, Shimmy Sham, Shake: A Social and Popular Dance Reader* (Chicago, IL: University of Illinois Press, 2009); Robinson, *Modern Moves*; and Gottschild, *Digging the Africanist*.

68. In Dyer's words, "... capitalism as productive relations can just as well make a profit from something that is ideologically opposed to bourgeois society as something that supports it." See Richard Dyer, *Only Entertainment* (New York: Routledge, 1992), 153.

69. Starr and Waterman, *American Popular Music*, 358 and 362.

70. Dyer, *Only Entertainment*, 155.

71. Dyer, *Only Entertainment*, 155 and Starr and Waterman, *American Popular Music*, 361–364.

72. Starr and Watermn, *American Popular Music*, 361; Dyer, *Only Entertainment*; and Tim Lawrence, "Beyond the Hustle: 1970s Social Dancing, Discotheque Culture,

and the Emergence of the Contemporary Club Dancer," in *Ballroom, Boogie, Shimmy Sham, Shake: A Social and Popular Dance Reader*, ed. Julie Malnig (Chicago, IL: University of Illinois Press, 2009), 201.

73. Joseph articulates capitalism's creation of social possibilities: "The positive opportunities provided by the disintegrative effects of the development of capitalism have been noted by feminist and gay historians, who have shown how industrialization freed young women from parental authority and allowed gay people to congregate in urban centers outside the reach of the patriarchal and communal situations from which they had come." See Joseph, "The Performance of Production," 38.

74. Lawrence, "Beyond the Hustle," 201.

75. Lawrence, "Beyond the Hustle," 201–202.

76. Lawrence, "Beyond the Hustle."

77. Starr and Waterman, *American Popular Music*, 362.

78. Lawrence, *American Popular Music* and Cynthia J. Novack, "Looking at Movement as Culture: Contact Improvisation to Disco," in *The Routledge Dance Studies Reader*, 2nd edition, eds. Alexandra Carter and Janet O'Shea (New York: Routledge, 2010), 176.

79. Novack, "Looking at Movement," 176.

80. Joseph, "The Performance of Production," 36.

81. Massumi, *Parables of the Virtual*, 88.

82. The ramifications of capitalism's pervasive control of meaning-making have been addressed by a range of scholars. In relation to performance forms, see Lara D. Nielsen and Patricia Ybarra eds, *Neoliberalism and Global Theaters: Performance Permutations* (New York: Palgrave Macmillan, 2012).

83. Joseph, "The Performance of Production," 37.

84. Vernacular term for natural, bright, orange-red hair.

85. "Machiavelli" is a term used within vogue balls to name a move consisting of a "dramatic spin and dip that is executed on the beat of the music." It is part of the movement vocabulary involving "hard, fast, aggressive execution" seen at contemporary vogue balls. See Marlon W. Bailey, *Triangulations: Lesbian/Gay/Queer Theater/Drama/Performance: Butch Queens up in Pumps: Gender, Performance, and Ballroom Culture in Detroit* (Ann Arbor, MI: University of Michigan Press, 2013), 142–143.

86. Contemporary vogue culture, sometimes referred to as New Way vogue, refers to the continuation of ballroom culture in US inner cities after 1990 and continuing into the 2000s. Reference to New Way acknowledges developments in the movement vocabulary that have been further clarified by being grouped into categories, see Bailey, *Triangulations*; Thomas F. DeFrantz, "Bone-Breaking, Black Social Dance, and Queer Corporeal Orature," *The Black Scholar* 46, no. 1 (2016): 66–74; and Santiago Freeman, "Strike a Pose 2.0," *Dance Spirit* 12, no. 6 (July/Aug. 2008): 112–115.

87. Created by 72andSunny, Amsterdam. Axe for Men (Unilever USA, Inc.), "Find Your Magic," directed by François Rousselet, commercial aired 2016, 1 minute, accessed December 4, 2016, https://youtu.be/WzTSE6kcLwY.

88. Both Ritts and Mapplethorpe were homosexual men who photographed both men and women. To varying degrees, both photographers are known for their homoerotic photographs that emphasize artistic form as well as the male nude as erotic object. Ritts began his career in the early 1980s with a photo of then little-known actor Richard Gere; his first exhibit was a collective show at the G. Ray Hawkins

Gallery in 1985 and one of his earliest works, *Fred with Tires, Hollywood* (1984), appeared in the Italian magazines *Lei and Per Lui*. For more on Ritts, see Charles Isherwood, "Work in Progress," *Advocate* no. 720 (November 12, 1996): 50–58; Degen Pener, "Putting on the Ritts," *POZ* no. 90 (April 2003): 24–29; and Carol Vernallis, "The Aesthetics of Music Video: An Analysis of Madonna's Cherish," *Popular Music* 17, no. 2 (May 1998): 153–185. Mapplethorpe is broadly known due to the NEA/Congressional funding controversy surrounding the 1988 retrospective exhibition of his work (1960–1988), shortly before his AIDs-related death in March of 1989. The cancellation of his exhibit at the Corcoran Gallery of Art in Washington, DC, led to his work playing a pivotal role in congressional debates over arts funding that centered on questions of obscenity, censorship, and artistic freedom. For more on Mapplethorpe and this controversy, see Judith Tannenbaum, "Robert Mapplethorpe: The Philadelphia Story," *Art Journal* 50, no. 4 (Winter 1991): 71–76; Arthur Danto, *Playing with the Edge: The Photographic Achievement of Robert Mapplethorpe* (Berkeley, CA: University of California Press, 1996); and Richard Meyer, *Outlaw Representation: Censorship and Homosexuality in 20th Century American Art* (Boston, MA: Beacon Press, 2002). For more on the larger history of gay erotica see Thomas Waugh, *Gay Male Eroticism in Photography and Film from their Beginnings to Stonewall* (New York: Columbia University Press, 1996).

89. Mark Simpson, "Two Women is Chic; Two Men is a Threat," *The Independent*, London, UK, July 25, 1994 and "This Trend is not Dead, but Dead Common—Just Look at Gavin Henson," *The Times*, London, UK, April 7, 2006: 4.

90. For the German beginnings of this movement, see Karl Toepfer, *Empire of Ecstasy: Nudity and Movement in German Body Culture, 1910–1935* (Berkeley, CA: University of California Press, 1997). For its influence on American physical culture, see Gertrude Pfister, "The Role of German Turners in American Physical Education," *The International Journal of the History of Sport* 26, no. 13 (October 2009): 1893–1925; Thomas K. Hagood, *A History of Dance in American Higher Education: Dance and the American University* (Lewiston, NY: E. Mellen Press, 2000); and Linda Tomko, *Dancing Class: Gender, Ethnicity, and Social Divides in American Dance, 1890–1920* (Bloomington, IN: Indiana University Press, 1999).

91. Ramsay Burt, *The Male Dancer: Bodies, Spectacle, Sexualities* (New York: Routledge, 1995); Susan L. Foster, "Closets Full of Dances: Modern Dance's Performance of Masculinity and Sexuality," *Dancing Desires: Choreographing Sexualities on and off the Stage* (Madison, WI: University of Wisconsin Press, 2001), 147–207.

92. Shelly McKenzie, *Getting Physical: The Rise of Fitness Culture in America* (Lawrence, KS: University Press of Kansas, 2013).

93. Simpson, "This Trend is Not."

94. While her work is less current now, Radway offers relevant analyses and my familiarity with the genre attests to the continuation of this trend. However, in the 2000s the romance genre is greatly diversified as it includes mass market works for LBGQT, bondage, and poly audiences as well. See Janice A. Radway, *Reading the Romance: Women, Patriarchy, and Popular Literature* (Chapel Hill, NC: University of North Carolina Press, 1984).

95. Quinn Miller, "Queer Recalibration," *Cinema Journal* 53, no. 2 (Winter 2014): 140–144.

96. Madonna, "Vogue" (music video), directed by David Fincher (Burbank, CA: The Burbank Studios, 1990), accessed August 8, 2017, https://youtu.be/GuJQSAiODqI; *Paris Is Burning*, directed by Jennie Livingston (Burbank, CA:

Miramax Home Entertainment, distributed by Buena Vista Home Entertainment, 1990), DVD (2005); DeFrantz, "Bone-Breaking, Black Social Dance, and Queer Corporeal Orature," *The Black Scholar* 46, no. 1 (2016): 66–74; Freeman, "Strike a Pose"; Bailey, *Triangulations*, 174.

97. Livingston, *Paris Is Burning*.

98. Livingston, *Paris Is Burning*; Bailey, *Triangulations*.

99. For "throwing shade," see Livingston *Paris Is Burning* and Bailey, *Triangulations*. For "talking trash" and "signifyin,'" see Henry Louis Gates, Jr., *The Signifying Monkey: A Theory of Afro-American Literary Criticism* (New York: Oxford University Press, 1988).

100. Bailey, *Triangulations*; Ashley Clark, "Burning Down the House: Why the Debate over *Paris Is Burning* Rages on" *The Guardian* June 24, 2015, accessed February 8, 2016, https://www.theguardian.com/film/2015/jun/24/burning-down-the-house-debate-paris-is-burning.

101. Bailey, *Triangulations*, 143 and 174; DeFrantz, "Bone-Breaking," 68.

102. The Ukraninan synthpop boy band produces music on its own label. Heel choreography consists largely of a mixture of hyper-feminine gestures and postures, similar to what is seen in voguing, and the highly-stylized, heteronormative, sexualized feminine postures of contemporary burlesque, lap dancing, and music videos. See Kazaky, "Love" (music video), directed by Yevgeniy Timokhin, aired 2011, accessed January 4, 2017, https://youtu.be/BhN5yv8lvdc, and Yanis Marshall, "Yanis Marshall Heels Choreography '7/11' Beyoncé Millennium in Los Angeles Filmed by @timmilgram" (video of class), accessed February 2, 2015, https://youtu.be/OuXlo_xTmto.

103. Joseph, "The Performance of Production," 45.

104. David Savran, "Branding the Revolution: *Hair* Redux," in *Neoliberalism and Global Theatres: Performance and Permutations*, eds. Lara D. Nielsen and Patricia Ybarra (New York: Palgrave Macmillan, 2012), 70. He is quoting Douglas B. Holt, *How Brands Become Icons: The Principles of Cultural Branding* (Boston, MA: Harvard Business School Press, 2004), 58–59.

105. Savran, "Branding the Revolution," 71.

106. DeFrantz, "Unchecked Popularity," 128–129.

107. DeFrantz, "Unchecked Popularity," 128.

108. DeFrantz, "Unchecked Popularity," 130.

109. DeFrantz, "Unchecked Popularity," 130.

110. DeFrantz, "Unchecked Popularity," 130.

111. For a concise history, analysis, and case study of black social dance in television advertising, see Carla Stalling Huntington, *Black Social Dance in Television Advertising: An Analytical History* (Jefferson, NC: McFarland & Co., Inc., Publishers, 2011).

112. In the first shot, the camera captures the front of his body; the button-down shirt he wears is mostly open, revealing his chest, and the black briefs that he wears are form-fitting. While he could be a transsexual individual, it is impossible to positively identify his sexuality or gender simply from viewing the commercial.

113. Henry Jenkins, *Convergence Culture: Where Old and New Media Collide* (New York: New York University Press, 2006).

114. Alessandro D'Arma, "Content Aggregation in the Age of Online Video: An Analysis of the Impact of Internet Distribution on the Television Business," *Journal of Media Business Studies* 8, no. 3 (2011): 1–17; Tim Baysinger, "For Ad VOD Players, Success is a Blend of Linear, Digital Models" *Broadcasting and Cable*

(August 15, 2016):18; and Stan J. Liebowitz and Alejandro Zentner, "Clash of the Titans: Does Internet Use Reduce Television Viewing?" *The Review of Economics and Statistics* 94, no. 1 (February 2012): 234–245.

115. Rosemary J. Coombe, *The Cultural Life of Intellectual Properties: Authorship, Appropriations, and the Law* (Durham, NC: Duke University Press, 1998), 57.

116. Coombe, *The Cultural Life*, 57.

117. Dr. Pepper Snapple Group, Inc., "/1," directed by Chris Miller, featuring Misty Copeland, commercial aired 2013, 30 seconds, accessed June 25, 2017, http://youtu.be/pwGkG-pLARQ. Created by Deutsch, Los Angeles as part of a campaign consisting of spots featuring real people with "one of a kind" stories. Numbers in the ad are said to be "mathematically accurate"; see Shareen Pathak, "See the Spot: Dr. Pepper Highlights Individuals with Unique Stories," *Advertising Age*, December 28, 2012.

118. Created by Droga5, New York and Reset Films. Under Armour, "I Will What I Want," directed by Johnny Green, featuring choreography by Marcello Gomes performed by Misty Copeland, commercial aired 2014, accessed July 5, 2016, https://youtu.be/ZY0cdXr_1MA. *Advertising Age* reports the commercial quickly went viral, reaching more than 9 million views on Youtube; see Alexandra Jardine, "Creativity 50 2015: Misty Copeland: Dancer," *Advertising Age*, December 21, 2015, accessed January 5, 2017, http://adage.com/article/special-report-creativity-50-2015/creativity-50-2015-misty-copeland/301748/.

119. Meredith Turits, "Misty Copeland, American Ballet Theatre's First African-American Soloist in 20 Years, Talks Breaking Barriers with Aplomb," *Glamour Magazine* (April 23, 2012) http://www.glamour.com/story/misty-copeland-american-ballet (accessed January 5, 2017).

120. Diana Pearl, "Misty Copeland Remembers her Former Collaborator Prince: 'He Will Forever Live On,'" *People Magazine*, May 2, 2016, accessed January 5, 2017, http://people.com/celebrity/misty-copeland-remembers-prince/.

121. Judith Lynn Hanna, "Advertising with Dance: Body, Sex, and Gender," *Dance: Current Selected Research Vol. 2*, eds. Lynnette Y. Overby and James H. Humphrey (New York: AMS Press, Inc., 1990), 117–138.

122. Nancy Reynolds, *Remembering Lincoln* (New York: Ballet Society, 2007); Nancy Reynolds, "In His Image: Diaghilev and Lincoln Kirstein," in *Moving History/Dancing Cultures: A Dance History Reader*, eds. Ann Cooper Albright and Ann Dils (Middletown, CT: Wesleyan University Press, 2001), 323–331.

123. Hanna, "Advertising with Dance," 131–133. I extend her reading of the images in my description, drawing on the work of dance scholars such as Susan Foster; see Susan Leigh Foster, "The Ballerina's Phallic Pointe," in *Corporealities: Dancing, Knowledge, Culture, and Power*, ed. Susan Leigh Foster (New York: Routledge, 1996), 1–26 and *Choreography and Narrative: Ballet's Staging of Story and Desire* (Bloomington, IN: Indiana University Press, 1996).

124. There are too many interviews and biographies to list all, but I offer these examples: *Misty Copeland with Charisse Jones Life in Motion: An Unlikely Ballerina* (New York: Touchstone, Simon & Schuster, Inc., 2014); Nelson George, dir. *A Ballerina's Tale* (Urban Romances, Inc., Sundance Selects, 2015) DVD; Rivka Galchen, "An Unlikely Ballerina," *New Yorker* 90, no. 28 (September 22, 2014): 54; Emanuell Grinberg, "Misty Copeland is First Black Principal Dancer at American Ballet Theatre," CNN, July 1, 2015, accessed June 2, 2016, http://www.cnn.com/2015/06/30/living/feat-misty-copeland-dancer-abt/index.html; Julia Griffin, "Grit and Limbs Propelled Misty Copeland's Improbably

Rise through Ballet's Ranks," PBS Newshour, August 8, 2014, accessed June 2, 2016, http://www.pbs.org/newshour/art/misty-copelands-grand-rise-ballets-pinnacle/; Roslyn Sulcas, "A Singular Ballerina's Multiple Paths: Misty Copeland Recounts her Life as a Black Dancer in a Largely White Milieu," *Paris* (February 2014): 12.

125. Galchen, "An Unlikely Ballerina."

126. According to Gottschild, Balanchine maintained a "basically segregated ensemble . . . with less than a handful of exceptions over a period of four decades." Gottschild, *Digging the Africanist*, 64–65.

127. Gottschild, *Digging the Africanist*, 67.

128. Gottschild, *Digging the Africanist*; Brenda Dixon Gottschild, *Joan Meyers Brown and the Audacious Hope of the Black Ballerina: A Biohistory of American Performance* (New York: Palgrave Macmillan, 2012); Gay Morris, *A Game for Dancers: Performing Modernism in the Postwar years (1945–1960)* (Middletown, CT: Wesleyan University Press, 2006).

129. A recent CNBC news story states that Copeland is "one of the few dancers who is business savvy enough to have become a brand of her own." Valerie Block, "Misty Copeland's Grand Leap to Ballet Megabrand," *CNBC Online*, July 29, 2016, accessed January 5, 2017 http://www.cnbc.com/2016/07/29/misty-copelands-grand-leap-from-homelessness-to-ballet-megabrand.html.

130. Ben Popken, "Jock Brand Under Armour Sells Itself to the Ladies in Ad," *USA Today*, July 31, 2014, accessed July 5, 2016, http://www.today.com/money/ballerina-misty-copeland-new-under-armour-ad-women-1D80001926.

131. Laura Mulvey, "Visual Pleasure and Narrative Cinema," *Screen* 16, no. 3 (Autumn 1975): 6–18.

132. In the context of the numerous publicity images and photos of Copeland available online, this reading of her sexuality is reinforced, as she often appears in a variety of poses and attire that echo those of swimsuit models and *Maxim* cover girls, while highlighting her athleticism and dance training. My point is that woman-as-sex remains a dominant cultural concept despite social changes, such as the focus on women as powerful athletes. Numerous photographs are available via a simple Google search as well as in a coffee-table book collection of art photography; see Gregg Delman, *Misty Copeland* (New York: Rizzoli International Publications, Inc., 2016).

133. Foster, "Phallic Pointe."

134. Gottschild, *Digging the Africanist*, 37–38.

135. While I do not have space to delve into the topic here, the twentieth-century promotion of female empowerment through sexuality and its emphasis on the *choice* to assume an eroticized identity seems tied not only to shifting gender roles and fashion, but also the history of burlesque in American culture.

136. Created by Wieden + Kennedy, Amsterdam. Nike Women's, "Keep Up," directed by Johan Redick, featuring choreography by Jamie King performed by Sofia Boutella, commercial aired 2005, 1 minute, accessed July 3, 2017, https://youtu.be/HHO6oL-1KIA. Boutella also appears in a second ad: Nike Women's, "Sofia," directed by Dawn Shadforth, featuring Sofia Boutella and choreography by Luther Brown, commercial aired 2006, 1 minute, accessed July 5, 2017, https://youtu.be/-CEQMv3vfYE. Created by Wieden + Kennedy, Amsterdam and Black Dog, London.

137. DeFrantz, "The Black Beat"; Joseph G. Schloss, *Foundation: B-boys, B-girls, and Hip-hop Culture in New York* (New York: Oxford University Press, 2009).

138. One example of this shift is her role in *Street Dance 2*, directed by Max Giwa and Dania Pasquini (Alliance Studios, 2012) DVD.

139. Created by Droga5 and Reset Films. "Under Armour," directed by Wally Pfister, featuring Misty Copeland, commercial aired 2015, 1 minute, accessed July 5, 2017, https://youtu.be/mmUCu8VWsWg.

140. Created by Young & Rubicam, New York. Oikos Greek Yogurt, "Unstoppably You," directed by Matt Bieler, commercial aired 2016, 30 seconds, accessed August 10, 2017, https://youtu.be/3xAfwm4pjhk.

141. Galchen, "An Unlikely Ballerina."

142. Diana Pearl, "Misty Copeland Remembers her Former Collaborator Prince: 'He will forever live on,'" *People Magazine*, May 2, 2016, accessed January 5, 2017, http://people.com/celebrity/misty-copeland-remembers-prince/.

143. See Nicolas Bourriaud, *Relational Aesthetics* (France: Les Presses du Réel, 2002); Brian Massumi, *Parables of the Virtual*, and Erin Manning, *Relationscapes: Movement, Art, Philosophy* (Cambridge, MA: The MIT Press, 2009).

CHAPTER 5

1. I use quotation marks around nationalities to indicate their potentially contentious nature given that my labeling derives from my reading of the commercial's intended meaning.

2. I refer to the white man as "American" based on two things: one, the commercial was aired in the United States for a US market, and two, he fits a common stereotype in which Americans are identifiable when on holiday by the fact that they always wear sneakers.

3. Created by BBDO New York. Diageo Plc./Red Stripe, "White Man Dancing," directed by Marcos Siega, commercial aired 2002, 30 seconds, accessed May 25, 2016, https://youtu.be/cSRr7-w_Kwk.

4. Red Stripe beer has a complex relationship to nationality in terms of production and marketing. The label claims it is a "Jamaican-style beer." Originally brewed in the United States, production was supposedly moved to Jamaica; however, in August 2015 consumers filed suit against the company for misleading marketing, because the version of the beer sold in the United States was actually brewed in Pennsylvania. Following the suit, the company indicated it would brew in Jamaica; see "Red Stripe Sued Over Misleading 'Jamaican' Beer Claims," Fox News Food & Drink, published August 4, 2015, accessed July 5, 2017, http://www.foxnews.com/food-drink/2015/08/04/red-stripe-sued-over-misleading-jamaican-beer-claims.html and "Dear Red Stripe: Welcome Home," Heineken, published September 8, 2016, accessed August 5, 2017, http://heinekenusa.com/2016/09/dear-red-stripe-welcome-home/.

5. Don Slater briefly describes the Protestant work ethic in relationship to consumer culture; see Don Slater, *Consumer Culture and Modernity* (Malden, MA: Polity Press, 1997), 97. For more on differences between Europeanist and Africanist movement values and dance in the American context, see Brenda Dixon Gottschild, *Digging the Africanist Presence in American Performance: Dance and Other Contexts* (Westport, CT: Praeger, 1996).

6. Gottschild, *Digging the Africanist*.

7. I use "subjectivity" to refer to identity grounded in self-knowledge and the state of being subject to discursive structures and power. I use the term "self" to refer to one's sense of oneself as a social and physical being. While I do not adopt his distinctions, Ian Burkitt offers a detailed discussion of these terms and their

relationship to critical theory and social psychology in his work; see Burkitt, "Subjectivity, Self and Everyday Life in Contemporary Capitalism," *Subjectivity* 23 (2008): 236–245.

8. Vera Maletic, *Body, Space, Expression: The Development of Rudolf Laban's Movement and Dance Concepts* (New York: Mouton de Gruyter, 1987); Peggy Hackney, *Making Connections: Total Body Integration through Bartenieff Fundamentals* (New York: Gordon Breach Science Publishers, 1998); and Irmgard Bartenieff, *Body Movement: Coping with the Environment* (New York: Gordon and Breach Science Publishers, 1980).

9. Slater, *Consumer Culture*.

10. Slater, *Consumer Culture*, 63–99.

11. David Savran, "Branding the Revolution: *Hair* Redux," in *Neoliberalism and Global Theatres: Performance and Permutations*, eds. Lara D. Nielsen and Patricia Ybarra (New York: Palgrave Macmillan, 2012), 69.

12. Pierre Bourdieu, *Distinction: A Social Critique of the Judgement of Taste* (Cambridge, MA: Harvard University Press, 1984); Don Slater, *Consumer Culture and Modernity* (Malden, MA: Polity Press, 1997); Carrie Noland and Sally Ann Ness, *Migrations of Gesture* (Minneapolis, MN: University of Minnesota Press, 2008).

13. Paul Bains, *A Shock to Thought: Expression after Deleuze and Guattari*, ed. Brian Massumi (New York: Routledge, 2001), 101–107; Burkitt, "Subjectivity, Self."

14. Slater, *Consumer Culture*; Gilles Deleuze and Felix Guattari, *A Thousand Plateaus: Capitalism and Schizophrenia* (Minneapolis, MN: University of Minnesota Press, 1987).

15. I draw on Brian Massumi's theory of subjectivity and its grounding in relations and belonging, which he discusses through the analogy of a soccer game: "From one point of view (the rulemakers' and referees') variation is a departure from identity. From another point of view identity is a moment (a productive lapse) in the continuation of variation," Massumi, *Parables of the Virtual*, 79.

16. Slater, *Consumer Culture*, 83–88 and Jean Baudrillard, *The Consumer Society: Myths and Structures* (Los Angeles, CA: Sage Publications, Inc., 2009).

17. Currently, I do not have production details; however, the commercial aired in the late 1990s and was the work of ad agency Oglivy and Mather, which Cotton Inc. worked with for thirty years before moving their advertising to DDB. Oglivy and Mather are responsible for creating the original "Fabric of Our Lives" campaign, to which the commercial I discuss here belongs. Cotton Inc. was created in 1970 to help save the declining cotton industry by uniting the various stages of cotton production and promoting cotton fabrics through marketing; see Cotton Inc., accessed July 15, 2017, http://youtu.be/0yGxwsPPDSQ.

18. Leo Braudy, "Acting: Stage vs. Screen," from *The World in a Frame*, in *Film Theory and Criticism: Introductory Readings*, 4th edition, eds. Gerald Mast, Marshall Cohen, and Leo Braudy (New York: Oxford University Press, 1992), 387–394.

19. Debby Thompson, "'Is Race a Trope': Anna Deavere Smith and the Question of Racial Performativity," *African American Review* 37, no. 1 (2003), 128. Discussions of this concept of subjectivity arise in several works. In relation to acting in live theater, see Liz Tomlin, *Acts and Apparitions: Discourses on the Real in Performance Practice and Theory, 1990–2010* (New York: Manchester University Press, 2013), 14 and 100–101. Discussion of the concept in relation to consumer

culture can be found in Don Slater, *Consumer Culture*. Descartes'concept of subjectivity is also addressed and radically revised in Brian Massumi, *Parables of the Virtual*.

20. Philip Auslander, *From Acting to Performance: Essays in Modernism and Postmodernism*, (New York: Routledge, 1997), 30.
21. Thompson, "Is 'Race' a Trope," 128–129.
22. Thomas Elsaesser and Malte Hagener, *Film Theory: An Introduction through the Senses* (New York: Routledge, 2010).
23. Theater scholar Liz Tomlin refers to this concept as the naturalization of an essential or authentic self, drawing on postmodernism's dismantling of Descartes' theory of the "transcendental self"; see Tomlin, *Acts and Apparitions*, 14 and 100–101.
24. Judith Butler, *Gender Trouble: Feminism and the Subversion of Identity* (New York: Routledge, 1990), 142.
25. Nancy Lee Chalfa Ruyter, "The Delsarte Heritage," *Dance Research: The Journal of the Society for Dance Research* 14, no. 1 (Summer 1996): 62–63.
26. Ruyter, "The Delsarte Heritage," 69.
27. Carrie J. Preston, *Modernism's Mythic Pose: Gender, Genre, Solo Performance* (New York: Oxford University Press, 2011), 64.
28. Preston, *Modernism's Mythic*, 64. Preston also notes this idea formed the basis of James-Lange's theory of emotion in the 1880s.
29. Maletic, *Body, Space, Expression*; Hackney, *Making Connections*; Bartenieff, *Body Movement*; and Isa Partsch-Bergson, *The Makers of Modern Dance in Germany: Rudolph Laban, Mary Wigman, and Kurt Jooss* (Hightstown, NJ: Princeton Book Co., 2003).
30. Preston, *Modernism's Mythic*, 60 and 82–99.
31. Eve Kosofsky Sedgwick, *Touching Feeling: Affect, Pedagogy, Performativity* (Durham, NC: Duke University Press, 2003), 93–122.
32. Somatic-based modern dance techniques emphasize moving from within and understanding the body as a thinking-feeling body rather than a mere tool for the expression of an interior "I," which corresponds with Massumi's contemporary theories of affect, the body, subjectivity, and cognition, see Massumi, *Parables of the Virtual*.
33. The term "mudra" refers to the hand positions used both abstractly and for symbolic and expressive meaning; arm movements and positions coordinate with hand positions and footwork. See Anne-Marie Gaston, *Bharata Natyam: From Temple to Theatre* (New Delhi, India: 1996), 257–262.
34. The dance form is grounded in the temple dances of the Devadasi, but in its rebirth it was fashioned as a part of the cultural heritage of the Brahmin. In the Indian diaspora it became a part of upper and middle-class society through the institution of the arangetram, a debut recital. Gaston, *Bharata Natyam*, 222–228. See also Pallabi Chakravorty, "From Interculturalism to Historicism: Reflections on Classical Indian Dance," in *The Routledge Dance Studies Reader*, 2nd edition, eds. Alexandra Carter and Janet O'Shea (New York: Routledge, 2010), 273–284; Janet O'Shea, "Dancing through History and Ethnography: Indian Classical Dance and the Performance of the Past," in *Dancing from Past to Present: Nation, Culture, Identities*, ed. Theresa Jill Buckland (Madison, WI: University of Wisconsin Press, 2006).
35. O'Shea, "Dancing through History."

36. This sense of the individual subject and her interior world as a source of authenticity corresponds to Romanticism's approach to the subject and expression, Slater, *Consumer Culture*, 95–97.

37. Auslander, *From Acting to Performance*, 28–29; Jacques Derrida, *Writing and Difference*, trans. Alan Bass (Chicago, IL: University of Chicago Press, 1978), 278–294; Luc Ferry and Alain Renaut, *French Philosophy of the Sixties: An Essay on Antihumanism*, trans. Mary Schnackenberg Cattani (Amherst, MA: University of Massachusetts Press, 1985).

38. Butler, *Gender Trouble*, 140.

39. Butler, *Gender Trouble*, 141.

40. Susan Leigh Foster, "Choreographies of Gender," *Signs: Journal of Women in Culture and Society* 24, no. 1 (1998), 3–5.

41. Foster, "Choreographies," 5.

42. Created by Team One, LA. Boost Mobile, "Party," directed by Tom Kuntz and Mike Maguire, commercial aired 2002, 30 seconds, accessed July 15, 2017, http://youtu.be/R4Ru2M24avo.

43. Gottschild, *Digging the Africanist*, 8 and 14, and Robert Farris Thompson, "Hip Hop 101," in *Droppin' Science: Critical Essays on Rap Music and Hip Hop Culture*, ed. William Eric Perkins (Philadelphia, PA: Temple University Press, 1996), 217.

44. Luke, "Raise the Roof," featuring No Good but so Good (Island Records, 1997).

45. The ad also reproduces heterosexual, patriarchal gender roles through costuming: women in skirts or dresses, men in slacks and shirts.

46. One example of this trend is the popular and commercially successful dissemination of "poppin' the cootchie" that began socially in the South and eventually made its way to MTV as part of 2Live Crew's music videos, see Anna Beatrice Scott, "Dance," in *Culture Works: The Political Economy of Culture*, ed. Richard Maxwell (Minneapolis, MN: University of Minnesota Press, 2001), 107–130; Theresa Renee White, "Missy Misdemeanor Elliott and Nicki Minaj: Fashionistin' Black Female Sexuality in Hip-hop culture—Girl Power or Overpowered?" *Journal of Black Studies* 44, no. 6 (September 2013): 607–626.

47. Anna Beatrice Scott, "Dance," 107–130 and Julie Malnig, "Apaches, Tangos, and other Indecencies: Women, Dance and New York Nightlife of the 1910s," in *Ballroom, Boogie, Shimmy Sham, Shake: A Social and Popular Dance Reader*, ed. Julie Malnig (Chicago, IL: University of Illinois Press, 2009), 72–90.

48. What constitutes a successful performance is defined by socially constructed conventions and movement values, which signal "authenticity" through acceptable repetition and variation, see Foster, "Choreographies," 1–33.

49. Fabolous, "Young'n (Holla Back), *Ghetto Fabolous* (Elektra, 2001). I understand the ad to be gesturing toward dance styles arising within African-American, particularly hip hop's, expressive culture. My understanding comes from various sources, but I offer the following two here: Gottschild, *Digging the Africanist*; Thomas F. DeFrantz, "The Black Beat Made Visible: Hip Hop Dance and Body Power," in *Of the Presence of the Body: Essays on Dance and Performance Theory*, ed. André Lepecki (Middletown, CT: Wesleyan University Press, 2004), 64–81.

50. Luke, "Raise the Roof," featuring No Good but so Good (Island Records, Inc., 1997),

51. James R. Curtis, "Barrio Space and Place in Southeast Los Angeles, California," in *Hispanic Spaces, Latino Places: Community and Cultural Diversity in Contemporary America*, ed. Daniel D. Arreola (Austin, TX: University of Texas Press, 2004),

125–141; Susan A. Phillips, "Physical Graffiti West: African American Gang Walk and Semiotic Practice," in *Migrations of Gesture*, eds. Carrie Noland and Sally Ann Ness (Minneapolis, MN: University of Minnesota Press, 2008); Gregory Christopher Brown, James Diego Vigil and Eric Robert Taylor, "The Ghettoization of Blacks in Los Angeles: The Emergence of Street Gangs," *Journal of African-American Studies* 16 (2012): 209–225; and Samantha Chang, *Social Spaces of Los Angeles River Graffiti at the Meeting of Styles: LA (2007)*, PhD diss., UC Santa Barbara, Ann Arbor, MI, 2013: ProQuest Database.

52. Denise M. Sandoval, "The Politics of Low and Slow/Bajito y Suarecito: Black and Chicano Lowriders in Los Angeles, from the 1960s through the 1970s," in *Black and Brown in Los Angeles: Beyond Conflict and Coalition*, eds. Josh Kun and Laura Pulido (Los Angeles, CA: University California Press, 2014), 176–201.

53. *The Fast and Furious*, directed by Robert Cohen (Universal Pictures, 2001).

54. Slater, *Consumer Culture*, 94–95.

55. Thorstein Veblen, *The Theory of the Leisure Class* (New York: Oxford University Press, 2009).

56. Slater, *Consumer Culture*, 91–92.

57. Slater, *Consumer Culture*, 88–95.

58. Slater, *Consumer Culture*, 91.

59. Slater, *Consumer Culture*, 91–92.

60. Slater, *Consumer Culture*, 95.

61. Savran, "Branding the Revolution," 69.

62. Savran, "Branding the Revolution," 71.

63. Earlier theories of consumer culture make similar claims, see Slater, *Consumer Culture*, 88.

64. Colleen Dunagan, "Performing the Commodity-Sign: Dancing in the Gap," *Dance Research Journal* 39, no. 2 (Winter 2007): 3–22.

65. This period is also significant because it corresponds to a shift in dance's visibility. The revival of Lindy hop and the rise of salsa during this period mark a return to partnered social dance as a widespread recreational activity. This moment was also a turning point for dance in mass media as it would lead to the revival of the popularity of television programs focused on dance (*SYTYCD* and *DWTS*) and Hollywood dance films and musicals (*Dance with Me, Centerstage, Bring It On, Chicago* . . .).

66. The commercials were produced by Gap's in-house creative team under the under the creative direction of Lisa Prisco: "Khaki Country," directed by McG, choreography by Jerry Grans, commercial aired 1999, 30 seconds, set to Dwight Yoakam's cover of "Crazy Little Thing Called Love," accessed July 15, 2017, https://youtu.be/MF93iwcWCZE; (1999); "Khaki-a-go-go," directed by Mike Mills, choreography by Marguerite Derricks, commercial aired 1999, 30 seconds, set to James Clark's "Wild Elephants," accessed July 15, 2017, https://youtu.be/z4kfS4rQi3M?list=PL382A3D15A9A6FE44; "Khaki Soul," directed by Hype Williams, choreography by Fatima Robinson and dancers, commercial aired 1999, 30 seconds, set to Bill Withers' "Lovely Day," accessed July 15, 2017, https://youtu.be/BpSazW3_cZg; "Khakis Swing," directed by Matthew Rolston, choreography by Travis Page, commercial aired 1998, 30 seconds, set to Brian Setzer's cover of "Jump, Jive, & Wail," accessed July 15, 2017, https://youtu.be/knW1hGwmEXQ?list=PL382A3D15A9A6FE44; "Khakis Groove," directed by Roman Coppola, choreography by Tony Basil, commercial aired 1999, 30 seconds, set to music by Bill Mason, accessed July 15, 2017, https://youtu.be/7v2-Qzqdkws; and "Khakis Rock," directed by

Jonas and Josh Pate, choreography by Keith Young, commercial aired 1998, 30 seconds, set to Crystal Method's "Busy Child". Gap Inc., accessed July 15, 2017, https://youtu.be/ux0h4nU-Xig?list=PL382A3D15A9A6FE44. "The Beat Goes on with New Gap Khakis Campaign; Three New Spots to Debut on Academy Awards," March 16, 1999, accessed January 9, 2017, http://www.prnewswire.com/news-releases/the-beat-goes-on-with-new-gap-khaksi-campaign.

67. "Upstage" refers to the sense of space produced by both the camera and the choreography. The dancers tend to face away from the sign and fence, and the camera films from the opposite side of the space, assuming the audience's perspective.

68. Dwight Yoakam, "Crazy Little Thing Called Love," *The Game* (EMI Elektra, 1999). The song is a cover of Queen's 1979 single "Crazy Little Thing Called Love". The commercial resembles his music video in its basic concept; however, the ad appears to use professional dancers, while the video's dancers appear to be amateur line dancers. There are variations in set, staging, and choreography—including the physical absence of Yoakam in the ad.

69. Foster, "Choreographies," 7.

70. Gottschile, *Digging the Africanist.*

71. Foster, "Choreographies," 5.

72. Colleen Dunagan, "Dance and Theater: Looking at Television's Deployment of Theatricality through Dance," in *The Oxford Handbook of Dance and Theater*, ed. Nadine George-Graves (New York: Oxford University Press, 2015), 169–195.

73. Janelle Reinelt, "The Politics of Discourse: Performativity Meets Theatricality," *Substance* 31, nos. 2–3 (2002): 207–208.

74. Reinelt, "The Politics of Discourse," 208.

75. Reinelt, "The Politics of Discourse," 208.

76. Overall, the ads seek inclusivity via a nod to diversity while casting predominately white dancers. Unison is a key element with the exception of "Khakis Swing," "Khakis Groove," and "Khaki Soul".

77. Perspex is transparent acrylic or acrylic glass that is strong enough to allow the dancers to perform on it but clear enough to allow the camera to film through it. The technique of filming from below a Perspex floor was being used in music videos in the late 1990s, making it a recognizable trope.

78. Gottschild, *Digging the Africanist*, 17–18 and 139.

79. This substitution performs a variation on Busby Berkeley's tendency to use bird's eye, overhead shots and in-camera editing to equate women and objects.

80. Created by TBWA\Chiat\Day, Los Angeles. Nissan North America, Inc., "Interpretive Dancers," directed by Malcom Venville, choreography by Fatima Robinson, featuring Emily Williams and Robert Prescott Lee, commercial aired 2013, 30 seconds, accessed May 15, 2016, https://youtu.be/vikTTWg-qNw.

81. Both dancers are white, conservatively dressed, with nondescript, brown hair, and the only people visible in the ad are the couple and the boy on the skateboard.

82. Robert Goldman, *Reading Ads Socially* (New York: Routledge, 1992); Judith Williamson, *Decoding Advertisements: Ideology and Meaning in Advertising* (London: Boyars, 1978).

83. Celia Lury, "Style and the Perfection of Things," in *High Pop: Making Culture into Popular Entertainment*, ed. Jim Collins (Malden, MA: Blackwell Publishers, Ltd., 2002), 209.

84. Savran, "Branding the Revolution," 69–71; Naomi Klein, *No Logo: Taking Aim at the Brand Bullies*, (New York: Picador, 2000); Douglas B. Holt, *How Brands Become Icons: The Principles of Cultural Branding* (Boston, MA: Harvard Business School Press, 2004), 5 and 13–38.

85. Henry Jenkins, *Convergence Culture: Where Old and New Media Collide* (New York: New York University Press, 2006).

86. Jean Baudrillard, *The Consumer Society: Myths and Structures* (London: Sage, 1998) and *For a Critique of the Political Economy of the Sign* (St. Louis, MO: Telos Press, 1981); Jacques Derrida, *Writing and Difference* (Chicago, IL: University of Chicago Press, 1978).

87. Robert Cooper, "Interpreting Mass: Collection/Dispersion," *The Sociological Review* 42, no. S2 (2001): 24.

88. Cooper, "Interpreting Mass," 16.

89. Cooper, "Interpreting Mass," 26.

90. Slater, *Consumer Culture*, 94.

91. Robert Goldman, *Reading Ads Socially* (New York: Routledge, 1992).

92. Deleuze and Guattari, *A Thousand Plateaus*, 149–166.

93. Created by Y&R New York and HIS Productions. Campbell Soup Company, "Classroom," directed by Paul Hunter, featuring Savion Glover, commercial 2004, 30 seconds, accessed January 12, 2017, http://www.tvspots.tv.

94. DeFrantz, "The Black Beat," and "Unchecked Popularity: Neoliberal Circulation of Black Social Dance," in *Neoliberalism and Global Theatres: Performance Permutations*, eds. Lara D. Nielsen and Patricia Ybarra (New York: Palgrave Macmillan, 2012), 128–139.

95. Massumi, *Parables of the Virtual*, 13.

96. Massumi, *Parables of the Virtual*, 14.

97. Massumi, *Parables of the Virtual*, 14.

98. Massumi, *Parables of the Virtual*, 32–33.

99. Massumi, *Parables of the Virtual*, 48–49.

100. Massumi, *Parables of the Virtual*, 89.

101. Ian Burkitt, "Subjectivity, Self and Everyday," 242.

CONCLUSION

1. Julie Van Camp views the identity of artworks through the lens of copyright law; Rosemary Coombe's work places questions of copyright into dialogue with appropriation and cultural meaning-making; and Anthea Kraut offers a detailed analysis of race, gender, dance, and choreographic copyright; see Rosemary J. Coombe, *The Cultural Life of Intellectual Properties: Authorship, Appropriation, and the Law* (Durham, NC: Duke University Press, 1998), Anthea Kraut, *Choreographing Copyright: Race, Gender, and Intellectual Property Rights in American Dance* (New York: Oxford University Press, 2016), and Julie Van Camp, "A Pragmatic Approach to the Identity of Works of Art," *The Journal of Speculative Philosophy* 20, no. 1 (2006): 42–55.

2. Kraut, *Choreographing Copyright*, xiii.

3. My information on advertising contracts with performers and choreographers derives from a phone interview; see Caroline Hanley, interview by author, Long Beach (CA), August 8, 2017.

4. Tim Nudd, "Silhouette says iPod too Pricey," *Ad Week*, August 16, 2005, accessed January 9, 2017, http://www.adweek.com/adfreak/silhouette-says-ipod-too-pricey-20337.

5. As Coombe states: "Celebrity images I would contend, always maintain their aura because they bind subjects in affective and historically mediated relationships that preclude their appropriation as pure objects." Coombe, *The Cultural Life*, 103.

6. Choreography is set to "Mutant Brain" by Sam Spiegel and Ape Drums, and the ad agency is Framework. Kenzo World, "My Mutant Brain," directed by Spike Jonze, choreography by Ryan Heffington, featuring Margaret Qualley, commercial aired 2016, 3 minutes 48 seconds, accessed August 29, 2017, https://youtu.be/ABz2m0olmPg.

7. For example, see Richard Vine, "Spike Jonze Gets Freaky for Kenzo: Where Film Meets Beauty," *The Guardian*, August 31, 2016, accessed August 29, 2017, https://www.theguardian.com/fashion/2016/aug/31/spike-jonze-gets-freaky-for-kenzo-where-film-meets-beauty.

8. I noticed the similarities on my initial viewing of the work, being familiar with Spike Jonze's music videos. However, the relationship is also called out in a *Dance Magazine* article. Madeline Schrock, "Spike Jonze + Ryan Heffington + Former Ballet Dancer = Absolute Magic," *Dance Magazine*, September 1, 2016, accessed January 17, 2017, http://dancemagazine.com/views/spike-jonze-ryan-heffington-former-ballet-dancer-absolute-magic/.

9. I take liberties with Brian Massumi's use of the term *transducer*. Massumi borrows the scientific terminology to describe what I understand as essentially a medium of transmission that transforms and extends what passes through it. At one point, he describes it as "a local organization of forces . . . responding to and transformatively prolonging another force. . . ." Brian Massumi, *Parables of the Virtual: Movement, Affect, Sensation* (Durham, NC: Duke University Press, 2002), 104.

10. Diesel, "The A to Z of Dance," directed by Jacob Sutton, commercial aired 2014, 3 minutes 30 seconds, accessed January 12, 2017, https://youtu.be/UFZxK8edZWA.

11. Coombe, *The Cultural Life*.

12. Film and music videos, while held to be "guilty" of commercialism by way of their association with mass and popular culture, have garnered more attention than advertising, which has more consistently received attention from business, sociology, and communications studies. There are, of course, notable exceptions arising out of philosophy and cultural studies (e.g., Jean Baudrillard, Roland Barthes, Susan Bordo, and/or Raymond Williams).

13. The ad was produced by RSA Films and released in Sweden and online. H&M, "School is Back—Dance-off," directed by Christian Larson, choreography by Tricia Miranda, commercial aired 2016, 1 minute 43 seconds, accessed August 29, 2017, https://youtu.be/LjDUyXhl80I.

14. Anthea Kraut, *Choreographing Copyright*, xiii.

15. These awards first began as the LA Dance Awards (1994–1995), then evolved into the Bob Fosse Awards and the Fosses (1996–1997), before becoming the American Choreography Awards (1998–2004).

SELECTED BIBLIOGRAPHY

Ahmed, Sara. "Happy Objects." In *The Affect Theory Reader*, edited by Melissa Gregg and Gregory J. Seigworth, loc. 390–726. Durham, NC: Duke University Press, 2010. Kindle.

Alexmanolski, Margarita. "Music as First Order and Second Order Conditioning in TV Commercials." *Music and the Moving Image* 3 (Summer 2010): 39–50.

Althusser, Louis. *Essays on Ideology*. London: Verso Editions, 1984.

Altman, Rick. *The American Film Musical*. Bloomington: Indiana University Press, 1989.

Armstrong, Charles K. "The Cultural Cold War in Korea 1945–1950." *The Journal of Asian Studies* 62, no. 1 (Feb. 2003): 71–99.

Auslander, Philip. *Liveness: Performance in a Mediatized Culture*. New York: Routledge, 1999.

Bailey, Marlon W. *Triangulations: Lesbian/Gay/Queer Theater/Drama/Performance: Butch Queens up in Pumps: Gender, Performance, and Ballroom Culture in Detroit*. Ann Arbor: University of Michigan Press, 2013.

Barthes, Roland. *Image Music Text*. New York: The Noonday Press, 1977.

Batson, Glenna with Margaret Wilson. *Body and Mind in Motion: Dance and Neuroscience in Conversation*. Chicago: Intellect, University of Chicago Press, 2014.

Baudrillard, Jean. *For a Critique of the Political Economy of the Sign*. Translated by Charles Levin. Candor, NY: Telos Press Ltd., 1981.

Baudrillard, Jean. *Consumer Society: Myths and Structures*. Los Angeles, CA: Sage Publications, Ltd., 1998.

Baudrillard, Jean. *Simulacra and Simulation*. Translated by Sheila Faria Glaser. Ann Arbor: University of Michigan Press, 1999.

Berger, Jonah. *Contagious: Why Things Catch On*. New York: Simon & Schuster, Inc., 2013.

Bhabha, Homi K. *The Location of Culture*. New York: Routledge, 1994.

Billman, Larry. *Film Choreographers and Dance Directors: An Illustrated Biographical Encyclopedia with a History and Filmographies 1893 through 1995*. Jefferson, NC: McFarland & Co., 1997.

Bolens, Guillemette. "Kinesthetic Empathy in Charlie Chaplin's Silent Films." In *Kinesthetic Empathy in Creative and Cultural Practices*, edited by Matthew Reason and Dee Reynolds, 143–156. Chicago: Intellect Ltd., 2012.

Bourdieu, Pierre. *Distinction: A Social Critique of the Judgement of Taste*. Cambridge, MA: Harvard University Press, 1984.

Bourriaud, Nicolas. *Relational Aesthetics*. France: Les Presses du Réel, 2002.

Brandstetter, Gabriele. "'Listening': Kinesthetic Awareness in Contemporary Dance." In *Touched and Being Touched: Kinesthesia and Empathy in Dance and Movement*, edited by Gabriele Brandstetter, Gerko Egert, and Sabine Zubarik, 163–180. Berlin, Germany: Walter de Gruyter Gmbh, 2013.

Brannigan, Erin. *Dancefilm: Choreography and the Moving Image*. New York: Oxford University Press, 2011.

Brejzek, Thea. "From Social Network to Urban Intervention: On the Scenographies of Flash Mobs and Urban Swarms." *International Journal of Performance Arts and Digital Media* 6, no. 1 (2010): 109–122, DOI 10.1386.

Browning, Barbara. *Infectious Rhythms: Metaphors of Contagion and the Spread of African Culture*. New York: Routledge, 1998.

Burkitt, Ian. "Subjectivity, Self and Everyday Life in Contemporary Capitalism." *Subjectivity* 23 (2008): 237.

Burns, Elizabeth. *Theatricality: A Study of Convention in Theater and in Social Life*. London: Longman Group, 1972.

Burt, Ramsay. *The Male Dancer: Bodies, Spectacle, Sexualities*. New York: Routledge, 1995.

Burton, Justin D. "Dancing Silhouettes: The Mobile Freedom of iPod Commercials." In *The Oxford Handbook of Mobile Music Studies*, edited by Sumanth Gopinath and Jason Stanyek, 311–338. New York: Oxford University Press, 2014.

Butler, Judith. *Gender Trouble: Feminism and the Subversion of Identity*. New York: Routledge, 1990.

Caldwell, Thorton. *Televisuality: Style, Crisis, and Authority in American Television*. New Brunswick, NJ: Rutgers University Press, 1995.

Chakravorty, Pallabi. "From Interculturalism to Historicism: Reflections on Classical Indian Dance." In *The Routledge Dance Studies Reader, 2nd ed.*, edited by Alexandra Carter and Janet O'Shea, 273–284. New York: Routledge, 2010.

Cohan, Steve, ed. *Hollywood Musicals: The Film Reader*. New York: Routledge, 2002.

Cook, Guy. *The Discourse of Advertising*. New York: Routledge, 1992.

Coombe, Rosemary J. *The Cultural Life of Intellectual Properties: Authorship, Appropriations, and the Law*. Durham, NC: Duke University Press, 1998.

Cooper, Robert. "Interpreting Mass: Collection/Dispersion." *The Sociological Review* 49, no. S2 (2001): 16–43.

Debord, Guy. *La Société du Spectacle*. Paris: Gallimard, 1992.

de Certeau, Michel. *The Practice of Everyday Life*. Berkeley: University of California Press, 1984.

DeFrantz, Thomas F. "The Black Beat Made Visible: Hip Hop Dance and Body Power." In *Of the Presence of the Body: Essays on Dance and Performance Theory*, edited by Andre Lepecki, 64–81. Middletown, CT: Wesleyan University Press, 2004.

DeFrantz, Thomas F. "Unchecked Popularity: Neoliberal Circulations of Black Social Dance." In *Neoliberalism and Global Theaters: Performance Permutations*, edited by Patricia Ybarra, 128–139. New York: Palgrave Macmillan, 2012.

DeFrantz, Thomas F. "Bone-Breaking, Black Social Dance, and Queer Corporeal Orature." *The Black Scholar* 46, no. 1 (2016): 66–74.

Deleuze, Gilles and Felix Guattari. *Anti-Oedipus: Capitalism and Schizophrenia*. Minneapolis: University of Minnesota, 1983.

Deleuze, Gilles and Felix Guattari. *A Thousand Plateaus: Capitalism and Schizophrenia*. Minneapolis: University of Minnesota Press, 1987.

Derrida, Jacques. *Writing and Difference*. Translated by Alan Bass. Chicago: University of Chicago Press, 1978.

Diamant, Lincoln. *Television's Classic Commercials: The Golden Years 1948–1958*. New York: Hastings House Publishers, 1971.

Dixon, Robert. *The Baumgarten Corruption: From Sense to Nonsense in Art and Philosophy*. East Haven, CT: Pluto Press, 1995.

Dodds, Sherril. *Dance on Screen: Genres and Media from Hollywood to Experimental Art*. London: Palgrave Macmillan, 2004.

Dodds, Sherril. "Slamdancing with the Boundaries of Theory and Practice: The Legitimization of Popular Dance." In *The Routledge Dance Studies Reader*, *2nd ed.*, edited by Alexandra Carter and Janet O'Shea, 344–353. New York: Routledge, 2010.

Dunagan, Colleen. "Performing the Commodity-Sign: Dancing in the Gap." *Dance Research Journal* 39, no. 2 (Winter 2007): 3–22.

Dunagan, Colleen. "Consuming Dance: A Brief History of the Dance Commercial." In *Proceedings of the Thirty-first Annual Conference, Society of Dance History Scholars*, Skidmore College, June 12–15. Riverside: Dance History Scholars, 2008.

Dunagan, Colleen. "Theatrical Conventions and the Performance of the Real: Dance on Television and the Construction of the Identity." In *The Oxford Handbook of Dance and Theater*, edited by Nadine Georges-Grave, 169–195. New York: Oxford University Press, 2015.

Dyer, Richard. *Only Entertainment, 2nd ed*. New York: Routledge, 1992.

Dyer, Richard. *White*. New York: Routledge, 1997.

Edgerton, Gary R. and Peter C. Rollins, eds. *Television Histories: Shaping Collective Memory in the Media Age*. Lexington: University Press of Kentucky, 2001.

Elsaesser, Thomas and Malte Hagener. *Film Theory: An Introduction Through the Senses*. New York: Routledge, 2010.

Felton-Dansky, Miriam. "Artistic Epidemiology." *PAJ: A Journal of Performance and Art* 33, no. 2 (May 2011): 115–119.

Felton-Dansky, Miriam. "Viral Performance: Contagious Hoaxes in the Digital Public Sphere." *Theater* 42, no. 2 (2012): 118–137.

Feuer, Jane. "The Concept of Live Television: Ontology as Ideology." In *Regarding Television: Critical Approaches—An Anthology*, edited by Ann Kaplan, 12–22. Frederick, MD: University Publications of America, 1983.

Feuer, Jane. *The Hollywood Musical, 2nd ed*. Bloomington: Indiana University Press, 1993.

Fife Donaldson, Lucy. "Effort and Empathy: Engaging with Film Performance." In *Kinesthetic Empathy in Creative and Cultural Practices*, edited by Matthew Reason and Dee Reynolds, 157–174. Chicago: Intellect Ltd., 2012.

Foster, Susan L. "Closets Full of Dances: Modern Dance's Performance of Masculinity and Sexuality." In *Dancing Desires: Choreographing Sexualities on and off the Stage*, edited by Jane Desmond, 147–207. Madison, WI: University of Wisconsin Press, 2001.

Foster, Susan Leigh. *Reading Dancing: Bodies and Subjects in Contemporary Performance*. Berkeley, CA: University of California Press, 1986.

Foster, Susan Leigh. *Choreographing Empathy: Kinesthesia in Performance*. New York: Routledge, 2010.

Foster, Susan Leigh. "Why not Improv Everywhere?" In *The Oxford Handbook of Dance and Theater*, edited by Nadine Georges-Graves, 196–210. New York: Oxford University Press, 2015.

Franko, Mark. *Dancing Modernism/Performing Politics*. Bloomington: Indiana University Press, 1995.

Fusco, Coco. *English is Broken Here: Notes on Cultural Fusion in the Americas*. New York: The New Press, 1995.

Gallagher, Shaun. *How the Body Shapes the Mind*. Oxford, UK: Clarendon Press, 2005.

Gardner, E. and J. Martin. "Coding of Sensory Information." *Principles of Neural Science* 4 (2000): 411–429.

Gates, Jr., Henry Louis. *The Signifying Monkey: A Theory of Afro-American Literary Criticism*. New York: Oxford University Press, 1988.

Gaudreault, André and Tom Gunning. "Introduction: American Cinema Emerges (1890–1909)." In *American Cinema, 1890–1909: Themes and Variations*, edited by André Gaudreault, 1–21. New Brunswick, NJ: Rutgers University Press, 2009.

Georges-Graves, Nadine, ed. *The Oxford Handbook of Dance and Theater*. New York: Oxford University Press, 2015.

Goldman, Robert. *Reading Ads Socially*. New York: Routledge, 1992.

Goodwin, Andrew. *Dancing in the Distraction Factory: Music Television and Popular Culture*. Minneapolis, MN: University of Minnesota Press, 1992.

Gore, Georgiana. "Flash Mob Dance and the Territorialisation of Urban Movement." *Anthropological Notebooks* 16, no. 3 (2010): 125–131.

Gottschild, Brenda Dixon. *Digging the Africanist Presence in American Performance: Dance and Other Contexts*. Westport, CT: Praeger Publishers, 1998.

Gottschild, Brenda Dixon. *Joan Meyers Brown and the Audacious Hope of the Black Ballerina: A Biohistory of American Performance*. New York: Palgrave Macmillan, 2012.

Grainge, Paul David. "Reclaiming Heritage: Colourization, Culture Wars, and the Politics of Nostalgia." *Cultural Studies* 13, no. 4 (Oct. 1999): 621–638.

Grainge, Paul David. "Advertising the Archive: Nostalgia and the (Post)National Imaginary." *American Studies* 41, nos. 2–3 (Summer/Fall 2000): 137–157.

Grau, Andrée. "Intercultural Research in the Performing Arts." *Dance Research: The Journal of the Society for Dance Research* 10, no. 2 (Autumn 1992): 3–29.

Grossberg, Lawrence. *We Gotta Get Out of this Place: Popular Conservatism and Postmodern Culture*. New York: Routledge, 1992.

Grossberg, Lawrence. *Dancing in Spite of Myself: Essays on Popular Culture*. Durham, NC: Duke University Press, 1997.

Grossberg, Lawrence, Ellen Wartella, and D. Charles Whitney. *Media Making: Mass Media in a Popular Culture*. Thousand Oaks, CA: Sage Publications, Inc., 1998.

Hanna, Judith Lynn. "Advertising with Dance: Body, Sex, and Gender." *Dance: Current Relected Research, vol. 2*, edited by Lynnette Y. Overby and James H. Humphrey, 117–138. New York: AMS Press, Inc., 1990.

Harvey, David. *A Brief History of Neoliberalism*. New York: Oxford University Press, 2005.

Heath, Stephen and Gillian Skirrow. "Television: A World in Action." *Screen* 18, no. 2 (1977): 7–59.

Huntington, Carla Stalling. *Black Social Dance in Television Advertising: An Analytical History*. Jefferson, NC: McFarland & Co., Inc., 2011.

Hutcheon, Linda. *A Theory of Parody: The Teachings of Twentieth-Century Art Forms*. Chicago, IL: University of Illinois Press, 2000.

Jacque, Jason T., Mark Perry, and Per Ola Kristtensson. "Differentiation of Online Text-based Advertising and the Effect on Users' Click Behavior." *Computers in Human Behavior* 50 (2015): 535–543.

Jenkins, Henry. *Convergence Culture: Where Old and New Media Collide*. New York: New York University Press, 2006.

Johnson, Mark and George Lakoff. *Metaphors We Live By*. Chicago, IL: University of Chicago Press, 1980.

Johnson, Mark and George Lakoff. *Women, Fire, and Dangerous Things: What Categories Reveal About the Mind*. Chicago, IL: University of Chicago Press, 1987.

Johnson, Mark and George Lakoff. *Philosophy in the Flesh: The Embodied Mind and its Challenge to Western Thought*. New York: Basic Books, 1999.

Kavka, Misha. *Reality Television, Affect and Intimacy: Reality Matters*. New York: Palgrave Macmillan, 2008.

Kavka, Misha. *Reality TV*. Edinburgh: Edinburgh University Press, 2012.

Kavka, Misha and Amy West. "Temporalities of the Real: Conceptualising Time in Reality TV." In *Understanding Reality Television*, edited by Su Holmes and Deborah Jermyn, 136–153. New York: Routledge, 2004.

Kloetzel, Melanie and Caroline Pavlov, eds. *Site Dance: Choreographers and the Lure of Alternative Spaces*. Gainseville: University of Florida Press, 2009.

Kraut, Anthea. *Choreographing Copyright: Race, Gender, and Intellectual Property Rights in American Dance*. New York: Oxford University Press, 2016.

Langer, Susanne. *Feeling and Form: A Theory of Art Developed from Philosophy in a New Key*. New York: Charles Scribner's Sons, 1953.

Lohr, Lenox R. *Television Broadcasting: Product, Economics, Technique*. New York: McGraw-Hill, 1940.

Lury, Celia. "Style and the Perfection of Things." In *High Pop: Making Culture into Popular Entertainment*, edited by Jim Collins, 201–224. Malden, MA: Blackwell Publishers, Ltd., 2002.

Maletic, Vera. *Body, Space, Expression: The Development of Rudolf Laban's Movement and Dance Concepts*. New York: Mouton de Gruyter, 1987.

Malnig, Julie, ed. *Ballroom, Boogie, Shimmy Sham, Shake: A Social and Popular Dance Reader*. Chicago, IL: University of Illinois Press, 2009.

Manning, Erin and Brian Massumi. "Just Like That: William Forsythe—Between Movement and Language." In *Touched and Being Touched: Kinesthesia and Empathy in Dance and Movement*, edited by Gabriele Brandstetter, Gerko Egert, and Sabine Zubarik, 35–62. Berlin, Germany: Walter de Gruyter Gmbh, 2013.

Manning, Susan. "Danced Spirituals." In *Of the Presence of the Body: Essays on Dance and Performance Theory*, edited by André Lepecki, 82–96. Middletown, CT: Wesleyan University Press, 2004.

Marchbank, Thomas. "Intense Flows: Flashmobbing, Rush Capital, and the Swarming of Space." *Philament: An Online Journal of the Arts and Culture* 4 (2004), accessed May 5, 2009, http://www.philamentjournal.com/issue4/marchbank-intense/

Marx, Karl, Edward B. Aveling, Friedrich Engels, and Samuel Moore. *Capital, Vol. I, Book One, The Process of Production of Capital: A Critique of Political Economy*. London: Electric Book Co., 2001.

Massumi, Brian. *A Shock to Thought: Expression after Deleuze and Guattari*. New York: Routledge, 2001.

Massumi, Brian. *Parables of the Virtual: Movement, Affect, Sensation*. Durham, NC: Duke University Press, 2002.

Miller, Gretchen and Sara Rubidge, eds. *Choreographic Dwellings: Practicing Place*. London: Palgrave Macmillan, 2014.

Mitoma, Judy, ed. *Envisioning Dance on Film and Video*. New York: Routledge, 2002.

Mittell, Jason. *Television and American Culture*. New York: Oxford University Press, 2010.

Moore, Barbara, Marvin R. Bensman, and Jim Van Dyke. *Prime-time Television: A Concise History*. Westport, CT: Praeger, 2006.

Mulvey, Laura. "Visual Pleasure and Narrative Cinema." *Screen* 16, no. 3 (Autumn 1975): 6–18.

Muse, John H. "Flash Mobs and the Diffusion of Audience." *Theater* 40, no. 3 (2010): 8–23.

Ness, Sally Ann and Carrie Noland, eds. *Migrations of Gesture*. Minneapolis, MN: University of Minnesota Press, 2008.

Noland, Carrie. *Agency and Embodiment: Performing Gestures/Producing Culture*. Cambridge, MA: Harvard University Press, 2009.

Novack, Cynthia J. "Looking at Movement as Culture: Contact Improvisation to Disco." In *Routledge Dance Studies Reader, 2nd ed.*, edited by Alexandra Carter and Janet O'Shea, 168–180. New York: Routledge, 2010.

Paterson, Mark. "On 'Inner Touch' and the Moving Body: Aesthesis, Kinaesthesis, and Aesthetics." In *Touched and Being Touched: Kinesthesia and Empathy in Dance and Movement*, edited by Gabriele Brandstetter, Gerko Egert, and Sabine Zubarik, 115–131. Berlin, Germany: Walter de Gruyter Gmbh, 2013.

Phelan, Peggy. *Unmarked: The Politics of Performance*. New York: Routledge, 1993.

Preston, Carrie J. *Modernism's Mythic Pose: Gender, Genre, Solo Performance*. New York: Oxford University Press, 2011.

Proske, U. "Kinesthesia: The Role of Muscle Receptors." *Muscle Nerve* 34, no. 5 (2006): 545–558.

Radway, Janice A. *Reading the Romance: Women, Patriarchy, and Popular Literature*. Chapel Hill, NC: University of North Carolina Press, 1984.

Reed, Ishmael. *Mumbo Jumbo*. New York: Atheneum, 1989.

Reinelt, Janelle. "The Politics of Discourse: Performativity Meets Theatricality." *Substance* 31, nos. 2–3 (2002): 201–215.

Reynolds, Dee. "Kinesthetic Empathy and the Dance's Body: From Emotion to Affect." In *Kinesthetic Empathy in Creative and Cultural Practices*, edited by Matthew Reason and Dee Reynolds, 121–138. Chicago: Intellect, University of Chicago Press, 2012.

Reynolds, Dee. "Empathy, Contagion and Affect: The Role of Kinesthesia in Watching Dance." In *Touched and Being Touched: Kinesthesia and Empathy in Dance and Movement*, edited by Gabriele Brandstetter, Gerko Egert, and Sabine Zubarik, 212–231. Berlin, Germany: Walter de Gruyter Gmbh, 2013.

Reynolds, Dee and Matthew Reason. *Kinesthetic Empathy in Creative and Cultural Contexts*. Chicago, IL: University of Chicago Press, 2012.

Robinson, Danielle. "The Ugly Duckling: The Refinement of Ragtime Dancing and the Mass Production and Marketing of Modern Social Dancing." *Dance Research* 28, no. 2 (2010): 179–199.

Robinson, Danielle. *Modern Moves: Dancing Race During the Ragtime and Jazz Eras*. New York: Oxford University Press, 2015.

Rosenberg, Douglas. *Screendance: Inscribing the Ephemeral Image*. New York: Oxford University Press, 2012.

Rubin, Martin. *Showstoppers: Busby Berkeley and the Tradition of Spectacle*. New York: Columbia University Press, 1993.

Ruyter, Nancy Lee Chalfa. "The Delsarte Heritage." *Dance Research: The Journal of the Society for Dance Research* 14, no. 1 (Summer 1996): 62–74.

Sander, Lorna. "Akram Khan's *Ma*: An Essay in Hybridisation and Productive Ambiguity." In *Decentring Dancing Texts: The Challenge of Interpreting Dances*, edited by Janet Lansdale, 55–72. New York: Palgrave Macmillan, 2008.

Savran, David. "Branding the Revolution: *Hair* Redux." In *Neoliberalism and Global Theatres: Performance and Permutations*, edited by Lara D. Nielsen and Patricia Ybarra, 65–77. New York: Palgrave Macmillan, 2012.

Sedgwick, Eve Kosofsky. *Touching Feeling: Affect, Pedagogy, Performativity*. Durham, NC: Duke University Press, 2004.

Sheets-Johnstone, Maxine. *The Corporeal Turn: An Interdisciplinary Reader*. Charlottesville, VA: Imprint Academic, 2009.

Sheets-Johnstone, Maxine. *The Primacy of Movement, expanded 2nd ed.* Philadelphia, PA: John Benjamin's Publishing Company, 2011.

Slater, Don. *Consumer Culture and Modernity*. Malden, MA: Polity Press, 1997.

Starr, Larry and Christopher Waterman. *American Popular Music: From Minstrelsy to MTV.* New York: Oxford University Press, 2003.

Stillman, B. "Making Sense of Proprioception: The Meaning of Proprioception Kinesthesia and Related Terms." *Physiotherapy* 88, no. 11 (2002): 667–676.

Thompson, Debby. "'Is Race a Trope': Anna Deavere Smith and the Question of Racial Performativity." *African American Review* 37, no. 1 (2003): 127–138.

Toepfer, Karl. *Empire of Ecstasy: Nudity and Movement in German Body Culture, 1910–1935*. Berkeley, CA: University of California Press, 1997.

Tomkins, Silvan S. "What and Where are the Primary Affects?: Some Evidence for a Theory." *Perceptual and Motor Skills* 18 (1964): 119–158.

Tomko, Linda. *Dancing Class: Gender, Ethnicity, and Social Divides in American Dance, 1890–1920*. Bloomington, IN: Indiana University Press, 1999.

Van Zile, Judy. *Perspectives on Korean Dance*. Middletown, CT: Wesleyan University Press, 2001.

Varela, Francisco J., Evan Thompson, and Eleanor Rosch. *The Embodied Mind: Cognitive Science and Human Experience*. Cambridge, MA: MIT Press, 1991.

Veblen, Thorstein. *The Theory of the Leisure Class*. New York: Oxford University Press, 2007. Ebook.

Vernallis, Carol. "The Aesthetics of Music Video: An Analysis of Madonna's Cherish." *Popular Music* 17, no. 2 (May 1998): 153–185.

Waugh, Thomas. *Gay Male Eroticism in Photography and Film from their Beginnings to Stonewall*. New York: Columbia University Press, 1996.

Wernick, Andrew. *Promotional Culture: Advertising, Ideology, and Symbolic Expression*. London: Sage Publications, 1991.

Wernick, Andrew. "Resort to Nostalgia: Mountains, Memories and Myths of Time." In *Buy this Book: Studies in Advertising and Consumption*, edited by Mica Nava, 207–223. London: Routledge, 1997.

Whybrow, Nicolas. *Art and the City*. New York: Palgrave Macmillan, 2011.

Williams, Raymond. *The Long Revolution*. New York: Harper & Row, 1966.

Williamson, Judith. *Decoding Advertisements: Ideology and Meaning in Advertising*. New York: Marion Boyars Publishers, Ltd., 1978.

INDEX

CPSIA information can be obtained
at www.ICGtesting.com
Printed in the USA
BVHW041320120519
548059BV00001B/1/P